I0141176

FAITH IN THE PSALMS

Faith in the Psalms

The Hymnal of the Old Testament

Norman Shields
Additional material by: Rev. Dr. Dwight Singer

AFRICA CHRISTIAN TEXTBOOKS

2016

Faith in the Psalms

© 2015 Faith in the Psalms text by Norman Shields., Footnotes, study guide and bibliography by Dwight Singer.

Africa Christian Textbooks (ACTS)

ACTS Bookshop, International HQ, TCNN,
PMB 2020, Bukuru, Plateau State, 930008, Nigeria
GSM: +234 (0) 803-589-5328; E-mail: info@acts-ng.com
Website: http://www.acts-ng.com

ISBN: 978-978-905-281-3 Print
ISBN: 978-978-905-282-0 ePub
ISBN: 978-978-905-283-7 Mobi

All rights reserved.

No part of this publication may be reproduced, stored in a retrieval system or transmitted, in any form by any means electronic, mechanical, photocopying, recording or otherwise, without prior permission in writing from the author and the publisher except for brief quotations embodied in articles and reviews.

Unless otherwise indicated, Scripture quotations are from the Holy Bible, *New International Version* Copyright 1973, 1978, 1984 by International Bible Society.

First Printing: 2016

CONTENTS

PREFACE

Speak to one another with psalms, hymns and spiritual songs.

—Ephesians 5:19

In this verse Paul uses three words to show how believers in Christ could joyfully express their belief and their trust in the Lord. They could use psalms (Greek, *psalmoi*), hymns (Greek, *humnoi*) and songs (Greek, *ōdais*).

In Greek, which was, of course, the language in which Paul wrote:

- *A psalm (psalmos)* was a song sung to the accompaniment of music played on a harp.
- *A hymn (humnos)* was a song of celebration and praise, which in the Septuagint (Greek translation of the OT) and its two New Testament occurrences (Eph. 5:19; Col. 3:16) was always addressed to God. The associated verb, *humneō*, meant "to sing to the praise of God" (Matt. 26:30; Mark 14:26; Acts 16:25; Heb 2:12).
- *A song (ōdē)* was a musical ode, which in Scripture is always a song in praise either of God or of Christ. In Ephesians 5:19 there is a qualifying adjective, "spiritual" (Greek, *pneumatikais*), to show that the songs in the apostle's mind were those that gave expression to the spiritual relationship between the believer and God. The word is also used in the Book of Revelation to refer to the songs in praise of God and of the Lamb sung by the hosts in heaven (Rev. 5:9; 14:3 (twice) and 15:3).

Our main purpose in this study is to examine the varying categories of psalm, hymn and song that occur in the Old Testament Book of the Psalms. The intention is not to provide a commentary or a detailed exposition of the psalms or even of some of them. It is rather to highlight the various types of psalm and to summarise briefly the emphasis and meaning of one or two examples of each type.

Hopefully, those who love the psalms will not be too disappointed, if some favourites receive no more than a passing mention to indicate the group or groups into which they most appropriately fit. Hopefully, too, our studies will also lead to a discovery of the relevance of the psalms to us as Christians and to our worship of the Lord today.

In Part 2 a number of more specialised studies have been included. These deal with topics that arise from a study of the psalms and should be of interest to the serious-minded student of Scripture.

The psalms teach us a great deal about the nature of the God Israel worshipped and whom we also worship. They also teach us much about our own nature – our sinfulness and our need of God's gracious forgiveness. They show us that we must approach him in faith – believing that he really exists and that he listens to the cries of his creatures. They tell us much about what he required of his ancient people, and, indeed, of what he demands from all mankind, in terms of worship, devotion and behaviour.

The psalms have always had a prominent place in Christian thinking and Christian worship. Because they figured frequently in the thinking and the teaching of our Lord and the apostles, the psalms have, down the centuries, been regarded as providing models we can use to give expression to our prayers and to our devotion to the Lord.

It will be obvious to many that some of our most popular hymns often echo the thoughts and the very words of the psalmists. There are, maybe, as many as two hundred such echoes in more traditional hymn books and lots more in modern collections. For example Martin Nystrom's 1983 song – "As the deer pants for the water, so my soul longs after you," picks up the yearnings of the Sons of Korah for a relationship with God that would dispel depression and despair (cf. Ps. 42:1).

Most, if not all, English speaking Christians, are familiar with the metrical version of Psalm 23 – "The Lord's my Shepherd..." and with the hymn, "The King of love my Shepherd is," which paraphrases the message of the psalm and adds to it elements from Jesus' teaching about the Good Shepherd searching for his single "lost sheep" (Luke 15:1-7; cf. John 10:1-18).

Similarly Psalm 100 has given rise to the paraphrase, "All people that on earth do dwell" and to the hymn, "Before Jehovah's awful throne, ye nations bow with sacred joy..."

Isaac Watts based the hymn, "O (Our) God our help in ages past," on Psalm 90 and, "Give to our God immortal praise," on Psalm 136. John Milton's, "Let us with a gladsome mind…" also displays links to the emphasis on divine providence in that psalm.

The Book of Psalms is, then, a most important body of devotional literature. It has been used widely in Christian worship and, when read devotionally, has the capacity of actually stimulating our worship. Who could, for example, carefully read and absorb Psalm 8 or Psalm 19 without realising something of the wonders of creation and of the one who created the universe. When we consider God's heavens, the moon and the stars that he has set in place, we realise our own puny insignificance and ask, "What is man that you, O Lord, even deigned to think of him?" And, because he did think of man and make him just a little lower than the angels, we too bow in awe and wonder and say:

> O LORD, our Lord
> how majestic is your name in all the earth.

It is the author's sincere prayer that these studies will be used by the Holy Spirit to stimulate that kind of response in those who may happen to read them. May one of these psalms or one of the hymns derived from them become what has been called a "firm song" (Latin, *cantus firmus*) to those called upon to endure adversities or sufferings. How many sincere believers have found comfort and solace in Psalm 23—"The Lord's my shepherd…"?

It is important that I record here my sincere thanks to my wife, Joan, who has acted as my primary proof-reader. I must also thank my friend, Dr. James Davison, for his careful reading of the text and for the many suggestions that have, I am sure, greatly improved the finished work.

Norman Shields

> *Speak to one another with psalms,*
> *hymns and spiritual songs.*
>
> —Ephesians 5:1

CHAPTER 1

POETRY IN SCRIPTURE

Poetry is found all through the Bible but especially in the Poetic, Wisdom and Prophetic books of the Old Testament. Sadly its special forms were not recognised by the translators of the English Authorised and Revised Versions, who presented it, as if it were narrative prose. Modern versions try to show it by the way they lay it out in print. While they also identify some possible poetic passages in the New Testament, they often fail to do so.

Hebrew poetry differs greatly from classical Greek and Latin and traditional English poetry. In our hymns, for example, meter or measure is very important – the number of vowels and thus of "feet" in each line and in the same line of succeeding verses must be right. Rhyming of sounds from line to line and assonance within the line is also important. Take, for example, the hymn, "Like a river glorious", in which, as an eight liner, the meter is 6.5.6.5.6.5.6.5. At the same time the last words of alternate lines rhyme with each other:

Like a river *glorious*

is God's perfect <u>peace</u>

Over all *victorious*

in its bright <u>increase</u>

Perfect yet it *floweth*

fuller every <u>day</u>

Perfect yet it groweth

deeper all the <u>way</u>

Hebrew poetry exhibits several distinctive characteristics, of which parallelism is probably the most important.

1. Parallelism

Parallelism is the most distinctive feature of Hebrew poetry. It is rhythm of thought or sense rather than of sound. The thought in a line relates to and parallels that of preceding or succeeding line(s). Parallelisms can be simple two line affairs or much more complex structures involving a group of lines or even paragraphs.

We should be able to catch the basic idea by highlighting parallel thoughts in two examples. In the first the second line repeats the thought of the first but uses different words to do so. In the second the third line also does so:

> Give *your eyes* **no sleep**
> and your *eyelids* **no slumber**.
>
> —Prov. 6:14

> Let <u>love and faithfulness</u> **never leave you**
> ***Bind*** <u>them</u> **around your neck**
> ***Write*** <u>them</u> **on the tablet of your heart**.
>
> —Prov. 3:3, a three line parallelism

There are four main types of parallelism, synonymous, antithetic, constructive (or stair-like) and chiastic. We will briefly examine and illustrate them in that order:

1) Synonymous parallelism

In this the second or subsequent lines exactly repeat a thought or thoughts from the first. Proverbs 6:14 highlighted in the previous paragraph is an excellent illustration of such parallelism.

However even these simple parallelisms are often woven into more complex patterns. Take for example the well known words of Isaiah, where there are two distinct couplets each displaying simple parallelisms:

> *The ox* **knows his master**
>   and *the donkey [knows]* **his master's manger**.
> But *Israel* **does not know**,
>   *my people* **do not understand**.
>
> —Isaiah 1:3

But these two couplets belong together and, when doubled up, form a more complex parallelism:

> *The ox* **knows his master** and *the donkey* **[knows] his master's manger.**
> But *Israel* **does not know [its Master]**, *my people* **do not understand** *[the source of their sustenance].*

Often a word or a phrase is omitted in the second or subsequent line(s). The sense is clear and the reader or listener automatically supplies the missing idea. In the following examples such missing words or thoughts are supplied in brackets:

> **Hear this** <u>all you peoples</u>
> **Listen** *[to this]* <u>all who live in this world,</u>
>
> —Psalms 49:1

> <u>The ungodly</u> ***shall not stand in the day of judgment***
> **nor** [shall] <u>sinners</u> [stand] ***in the congregation of the righteous***
>
> —Psalms 1:5

The Book of Proverbs sometimes uses vivid similes in its basic parallelisms. This is especially the case in chapters 25-27, in which many proverbs begin with either "like" or "as." Good examples are:

> Free yourself, ***like*** a gazelle from the hand of the hunter.
> ***Like*** a bird from the snare of the fowler.
>
> —Psalms 6:5

> ***Like clouds and wind without rain.***
> is a man who boasts of gifts he does not give.
>
> —Psalms 25:14

Well-known words of Jesus in the Sermon on the Mount (Matt. 7:7-8) fall into two sets of triplets which interrelate to give a six line parallelism. Unfortunately even recent versions fail to set it out as poetic parallelism:

> <u>Ask</u> and ***it will be given you***
> <u>Seek</u> and ***you will find***

Knock and **the door will be opened to you**
   For everyone who asks **receives**
   He who seeks **finds**
   And to him who knocks **the door will be opened.**

2) Antithetic Parallelism

In this form the second line emphasises the thought of the first by being set in antithesis or opposition to it. It states a contrast introduced by words like, "but" or "yet." It is common in the Book of Proverbs. For example:

For the Lord detests **a perverse man**
   But takes **the upright** into his confidence

                       —Proverbs 3:32

The wise woman **builds her house**
   But with her own hands *the foolish one* **tears hers down.**

                       —Proverbs 14:1

3) Synthetic parallelism

This form is also called "constructive" or "stair-like" parallelism. The reason is that two or more ideas are placed side by side in sequence so that the thoughts are put together (synthesised) and built up or constructed into a unit. The second and, if applicable, the subsequent lines build on what precedes in order to complete the construction of the thought.

Just as, when climbing stairs each step takes us forwards as well as upwards, so in constructive parallelism the thought is carried forward.

In the following examples, the words in italics represent the additional element of thought added to the first line.

Keep *your heart* with all vigilance
   for *from it* flow the springs of life.

                       —Proverbs 4:23

Do not envy a violent man
or choose any of his ways
   For *the Lord detests a perverse man*

But takes the upright into his confidence.

—Proverbs 3:31-32

In the latter example the first two lines are in synonymous parallelism while lines three and four are in antithetic parallelism with each other. At the same time lines 3 and 4 build on lines 1 and 2 and so form a synthetic (constructive or stair-like) parallelism with them.

In the New Testament our Lord's words recorded in Matthew 11:28-30 provide an important example, which, again, is not set out as poetry in most versions. The phrases in bold italics indicate a third level of construction:

Come to me, *all you who are weary and burdened*
    and I will give *you* rest.
Take my yoke *upon you* and learn from me
    for I am gentle and humble in heart
and *you will find rest for your souls*
    for my yoke is easy and my burden is light.

4) Chiastic Parallelism

In this form at least four lines – often six or eight or even more – are involved in something of a crossover arrangement. The name is based on the Greek letter Chi (χ), from which we have derived the English word, "chicane." The pattern is usually shown by labelling the lines, A, B, C etc. and by indentations like those in the following illustration:

A) Have mercy on me, O God
    B) *according to your unfailing love*
    B) *according to your great compassion*
A) blot out my transgressions

—Psalms 51:1

In this the first and fourth lines (labelled A) are parallel and more or less synonymous. The same is true of Lines 2 and 3 (labelled B).

In his great allegory of the shepherd and his flock (John 10:1-18) Jesus depicted himself as the Good Shepherd – "I am the Good shepherd" – and made important affirmations about his role as the Good Shepherd (vv. 14-15).

A) **I am the good shepherd;**
   B) *I know* *my sheep*
      C) *and my sheep know me*
      C) *just as the Father knows me*
   B) and *I know* the Father
A) **and I lay down my life for the sheep.**

In this case the parallels are very clear.

The two A lines focus on our Lord as the shepherd, whose goodness towards his sheep extends to giving up his life for them.

The two B lines focus on and parallel his knowledge of the sheep with the Father's knowledge of him—he knows and the Father knows.

The two C lines turn this knowledge into the passive voice – he is known by the sheep and by the Father!

Another way of viewing this is to think of the thought as running around in a circle and coming back virtually to the point at which it started. In the example just cited the first and last lines emphasise the thought that Jesus is essential and ultimate goodness – the Good Shepherd who lays down his life for the benefit of his sheep.

Circularity of thought was a prominent, perhaps even the most prominent, element in the expression of Hebrew thought. It is still prominent in many cultures around the world. The worthies of the Old Testament, as well as Jesus and his apostles, thought in that circular way rather than in the Graeco-Roman and modern western linear pattern. Where westerners lay down premises and proceed to deduce conclusions, they made a statement and then wove information they judged relevant around it, before hammering home the original statement by repeating it in similar words.

Jesus' eight beatitudes follow this circular pattern. They begin and end with the assertion, "theirs is the kingdom of heaven" (Matt. 5:3-10).

A) Blessed are the poor in spirit
 for theirs is the kingdom of heaven
   B) Blessed are those who mourn
      for they will be comforted
      C) Blessed are the meek
         for they will inherit the earth
         D) Blessed are those who hunger and thirst ...
            for they will be filled
         D) Blessed are the merciful
            for they will be shown mercy
      C) Blessed are the pure in heart
         for *they will see God*
   B) Blessed are the peacemakers
    for they will be called sons of God
A) Blessed are those who are persecuted ...
 for theirs is the kingdom of heaven.

Paul's great poem in honour of Christ (Phil. 2: 6:11) follows the same pattern. It starts with his deity, "being in very nature God" and ends on the same note, "Jesus Christ is Lord," which means, "he is God."

Sometimes larger portions of Scripture – paragraphs, chapters and even whole books - are arranged in chiastic parallelism. Take, for example Psalm 12, in which a suppliant pleads with God (vv. 1-2), a servant (possibly a prophet) speaks to God for the suppliant (vv. 3-4) and then the Lord himself responds after which the servant affirms the reliability of God's word and then the suppliant again speaks to God, but now with new confidence (vv.7-8).

5) Interpreting Parallelism

Parallelism profoundly affects the meaning of biblical poetry and must be taken into account by those who try to interpret its message. Different words in the various lines do not require us to understand, as some "wooden literalists" have thought, that the meaning is different.

Parallelism shows us that the Holy Spirit often inspired the writers to use different words to emphasise or to expand their thoughts. The interpreter must try to make the thought connections between lines that parallel each other.

2. Word play

This is somewhat like the witticism we know as a pun, in which two or more meanings of a word or two words of similar sound are played off against each other usually with a humorous intent.

In our English versions of Scripture word plays are mostly obscured by translation but Jeremiah 1:11-12 in the Jerusalem Bible will show something of what it is:

> The word of Yahweh was addressed to me asking, Jeremiah, what do you see? I see a branch of a *watchful* tree, I answered. Then Yahweh said, Well seen! I too *watch* over my word.

James Moffatt also managed to indicate the word play by translating the words of the Lord and of Jeremiah as,

> **I said, "the shoot of a *wake*-tree..."**
> You have seen right
> for I am *wake*ful over my word to carry it out.

The NIV, like the AV, failed to get the point by rendering the Hebrew noun, as "almond tree", which is, of course the tree that first produces flowers each year – it is the waker tree!

> I see the branch of the almond tree
> I am watching to see that my word is fulfilled.

The almond is, indeed, an early flowering plant, the appearance of whose flowers signals the waking of new life in the spring. It is variously known as "the waker" and "the watchful tree." While the translation, almond, is valid, it totally obscures the word play and the poetic imagery that gives the meaning of the passage.

Those, who read German, will appreciate Luther's renderings:

> Ich sehe einen er*wachen*der Zweig
> > Ich will *wachen* über mein Wort.

3. Acrostic

A number of Old Testament poems are acrostic in form and use the 22 letters of the Hebrew alphabet to achieve that goal. These are Psalms. 25; 34; 37; 111; 112; 119; 145 and Lamentations 1; 2; 3 and 4. Lamentations 5 also has 22 verses, but for some unknown reason does not have an acrostic arrangement of its verses.

Psalm 119 has 22 paragraphs of eight verses, each of which begins with the same letter of the Hebrew alphabet. Verses 1 to 8 begin with the first letter, *Aleph*, verses 9 to 16 with *Beth* and so on.

Psalms 25 and 34 have 22 verses beginning with the letters of the Hebrew alphabet in order, *Aleph, Beth, Gimmel* etc... Psalms 111 and 112 each have 11 verses of 2 lines, making 22 lines in all. Each line begins with a letter of the alphabet in order, *Aleph, Beth* etc. Psalm 37 has a complicated acrostic based on the 22 letter alphabet but dividing the 88 lines in a unique pattern—16 x 4 lines, 3 x 3 lines and 3 x 5 lines.

In the Book of Lamentations Chapters 1 and 2 have 22 verses each of 3 lines. Each verse begins with a letter of the alphabet in order. Chapter 3 has 66 verses of one line, arranged in 22 sets of three that begin with the same letter. Verses 1, 2 & 3 begin with *Aleph*, verses 4 to 6 with *Beth* and so on. Chapter 5 has 22 verses but no acrostic.

Like word play, acrostic is a poetic skill that is lost in translation. It is of little significance for interpretation, except, perhaps, in Psalm 145, where each verse begins with a letter of the alphabet but, for some reason, one letter, *"nun"* (equivalent to our "n"), together with an accompanying two-line verse, is missing in the Hebrew Bible and in earlier English versions. However, when, before our Lord's time, the Hebrew of the Psalm was put into the Greek in the version known as the Septuagint, two lines that seemed to represent that missing verse were included—"The Lord is faithful in his words and righteous (or lovingly kind) towards all he has made."

A scroll of the Psalms, found at Qumran in the late 1940s and originating before 70 AD, i.e., more than a thousand years earlier than any then extant manuscript also included the same verse beginning with the letter "nun." That discovery convinced scholars that it was part of the psalm and had somehow been lost from the usual Hebrew text. It is, therefore included in recent English translations – the RSV, NIV, JB, NLT etc. – as two extra lines in verse 13:

> The LORD is faithful to all his promises
> and loving towards all he has made (NIV).

Whatever the origin of these two lines, they clearly add to the overall impact of the psalm. They affirm the ever-valid truth that the Lord is faithful and kind and they lead into the couplet that follows—"The Lord upholds all those who fall and lifts up all who are bowed down" (v. 14).

CHAPTER 2

THE SONGS OF SCRIPTURE

1. Hebrew songs

Some Hebrew poetry was clearly meant for singing. The songs can be analysed into a number of types.

1) Hymns of thanksgiving

These were sung to express gratitude to God for a whole variety of blessings. For example:

Thanks for victory – Miriam sang:

> Sing to the LORD,
>> for he is highly exalted.
> The horse and his rider
>> he has hurled into the sea.
>>>> —Ex. 15:21; cf. Moses song 15:1-18

Thanks for recovered health – Hezekiah sang:

> The living, the living—they praise you
>> as I am doing today...
>>>> —Isa. 38:10-20

Thanks for the gift of a child – Hannah sang:

> My heart rejoices in the LORD...
>>>> —1 Sam. 2:1-10

Thanks for deliverance from God's anger – Looking forward to the work of God's Messiah, the Branch from Jesse, a Davidic king, ultimately Jesus, God's redeemed people sing:

> I will praise you O LORD.
>> Although you were angry with me,
>>> your anger is turned away
>>> and you have comforted me

—Isa. 12:1

Thanks for God's presence in Zion:

> God is our refuge and strength,
>> an ever present help in trouble ...

—Ps. 46:1; cf. Pss. 48; 76; 86

Thanks for the reign of God as King:

> Sing praises to God, sing praises;
>> Sing praises to our King, sing praises

—Ps 47:6; cf. Pss. 93 & 96-99

2) Dirge or lament songs

In this type of song a disaster was mourned and appropriate prayer for deliverance was offered. There are two types:

(1) Personal laments

When faced with his son Absalom's revolt, David sang:

> O LORD, how many are *my* foes!
>> How many rise up against me!
> Many are saying of me,
>> God will not deliver him.

—Ps. 3:1, cf. Pss. 6; 7; 51 etc.

(2) Communal laments

In Psalms. 12; 74; 79; 137 and in Lamentations 1-5 God's people unite to bemoan some plight. In most cases the songs move on to positive affirmations of trust in the Lord and to prayer for his delivering power to act on their behalf:

> Why have you rejected **us** for ever, O LORD?
>> Why does your anger smoulder against the sheep of your pasture?
>>> —Ps. 74:1

> Rise up O God, and defend your cause.
>> —Ps. 74:22

3) Love Songs

These express the joys and disappointments of human love. Their presence shows that God is interested in such love.

The Song of Solomon is basically a rustic love song or a collection of such songs. Jews and Christians have often used it to illustrate God's love for his people.

Isaiah 5:1-7 is similar and, in context, is used symbolically to refer to God's relationship to his people:

> The vineyard of the LORD Almighty
>> is the house of Israel
> and the men of Judah
>> are the garden of his delight
>>> —Isaiah 5:7

4) Songs of Pilgrimage

These were probably sung by pilgrims making their way to celebrate one of the Old Testament worship festivals at the Temple in Jerusalem. Psalms 120-134, headed, "Songs of Ascent," meaning songs of going up to Jerusalem some 3000 feet above sea level, are examples. So also is Psalm 84:

> How lovely is your dwelling place
>> O LORD Almighty! ...
> Better is one day in your courts
>> than a thousand elsewhere;
> I would rather be a door-keeper in the house of my God
>> than dwell in the tents of the wicked.
>>> —vv. 1 and 10

5) Taunt songs

In these songs ridicule is poured either on an individual or a community. For example, Jeremiah pours scorn on the (false) prophets of Judah and Samaria (23:9-24). Habakkuk does so against Babylon (2:6-19) and Isaiah parodies the profligacy of Tyre and pictures that city as totally forgotten:

It will happen to Tyre as in the song of the prostitute:

> Take up a harp, walk through the city,
>   O prostitute forgotten;
> Play the harp well, sing many a song,
>   so that you will be remembered
>
> —Isaiah 24:15-16

Arguably the greatest taunt-song in all of Scripture is that found in Isaiah 14:4-21. It mocks the oppressive ways of Babylon and pictures its proud ruler dying and being brought down and taunted by the spineless shadows, the spirits of the departed that inhabit *Sheol*, the grave below. A few lines from this poem will surely whet the appetite and encourage us to read it fully and carefully:

> The grave below is all astir
>   to meet you at your coming;
> it rouses the spirits of the departed to greet you—
>   all those who were leaders in the world...
>   they will say to you,
> You also have become weak, as we are;
>   you have become like us.

6) Wisdom songs

These were sung to teach truth in an easily remembered form. Examples are Psalms 1; 37; 73; 78; 112 and 119.

> Blessed is the man who fears the LORD,
>   Who finds great delight in his commands...
> His heart is secure, he will have no fear...
>
> —Ps. 112:1, 8

7) Liturgical songs

These are songs that seem to have been designed for use in worship. In some cases they appear to present several voices participating antiphonally. Examples are Psalms 12; 15; 24; 60; 75 (cf. Isaiah 40).

Psalm 12 is a worship dialogue possibly involving three speakers, [1] whose contributions are arranged in the form of a chiastic parallelism. It begins with David pleading with God about the moral deterioration of his people (vv. 1, 2 or 1-4). Its centrepiece is a divine proclamation (v. 5), which is then followed by someone else, the servant-mediator, who endorses the proclamation. This leads into David's acceptance of the assurance promised by the Lord (vv. 7, 8). He is a changed person, no longer moaning, but rather expressing faith and trust:

> O LORD you will keep us safe
>> and protect us from such people for ever.
> The wicked freely strut about
>> when what is vile is honoured among men.

2. Possible New Testament Songs

1) Canticles in Luke 1 and 2

The narratives recounting the birth of our Lord have several songs, which echo some of those of the Old Testament. Mary's Magnificat (Luke 1:46-55) is so named because *"magnificat"* is its first word in the Latin New Testament (*Magnificat anima mea Dominum* – "My soul glorifies or magnifies the Lord." It echoes and uses the very words of the Song of Hannah (1 Sam. 2:1-10). The Benedictus, as Zechariah's song (Luke 1:68-79) is known, begins in the Latin, *"Benedictus Dominus Deus Israhel"* – "Praise be to the Lord, the God of Israel." It echoes and quotes a number of Old Testament passages, as does Simeon's song,

---

[1] Many scholars envisage only two speakers – the suppliant (vv. 1-4 and vv. 7, 8) and the Lord (vv. 5, 6).

the *Nunc Dimmittis*, which in the Latin begins, *"Nunc dimittis servum tuum ... in pace"* – "Lord, now let your servant depart in peace" (Luke 2:29, KJV).

2) Doxologies or ascriptions of glory to God

The song of the heavenly choir to mark the birth of Jesus (Luke 2:14) is both a song and a doxology:

> Glory to God in the highest,
>> and on earth peace to men on whom his favour rests.

Paul concludes his epistles and in some cases sections within them with ascriptions of praise and glory to God, i.e., with doxologies. Some of them are familiar to Christians, because they are widely used in our services of worship, for example, "to the only wise God be glory through Jesus Christ! Amen!" (Rom. 11:36) and, "Now to the King eternal, immortal, invisible, the only God, be honour and glory for ever and ever, Amen." (1Tim. 1:17). Other doxologies, like those in Romans 16:25-27; Galatians 6:18; 1 Timothy 6:15, 16 and Jude 24, 25 are well known but do not seem to have been written as poetry or intended to be used as songs.

The heavenly or angelic pronouncements of Revelation 4:8, 11; 5:9, 10, 12, 13; 7:12; 11:17-18; 12:10-12; 15:3-4; 16:5-6 and 19:1-3, 6-8 are lyrical and may well have come to John in a poetic or musical form. Two of these will serve as examples:

> You are worthy, our LORD and God,
>> to receive glory and honour and power,
> for you created all things,
>> and by your will they were created
>> and have their being

> —Rev. 4:11

> Great and marvellous are your deeds,
>> LORD God Almighty.
> Just and true are your ways, King of the ages.
> Who will not fear you, O LORD
>> and bring glory to your name?

For you alone are holy.
All nations will come
    and worship before you,
for your righteous acts have been revealed

—Rev. 15:3-4

3) Expressions of Awe and Wonder

There are a number of passages in the New Testament that express awe and wonder before God. In some cases they move on into a doxology that might well imply not just a poetic spirit but an intention that they be sung.

The use of the Greek language may, however, to some degree obscure underlying Hebrew or Aramaic thought patterns that dominated the minds of the early apostles. Paul, who regarded himself as a Hebrew – indeed, "a Hebrew of Hebrews" (Phil. 3:5) – used Greek to call on his readers in Ephesus (a mixture of Jews and Gentiles) to sing and make music in their hearts (Eph. 5:19). He may well have been something of a lyricist himself and, as occasion suited, may have expressed himself in poetry and song.

Several passages in Paul's epistles are regarded as having an underlying lyrical structure suitable for singing. Because this not provable they are not always set out as poetry in modern versions of the New Testament. They include:

- *Romans 8:31-39*, where Paul exults in confident assurance of the riches of God's provision in Christ.
- *1 Corinthians 13*, which is often called Paul's hymn about love. It is a passage of unsurpassed poetic beauty.
- *1 Corinthians 15:55-57*, where Paul, having expounded the nature of resurrection, throws out a challenge to death and affirms the victory of Christ:

    Where, O death, is your victory?
    Where, O death, is your sting?
    The sting of death is sin, and the power of sin is the law. But thanks
    be to God! He gives us the victory through our Lord Jesus Christ.

- *Ephesians 3:14-21,* where the apostle bursts into praise of God and his grace.
- *Philippians 2:5-11* is clearly lyrical. In it the apostle begins with an assertion of our Lord's deity and comes back full circle to an assertion of his lordship.

> Who, being in very nature God,
>   did not consider equality with God
>   something to be grasped,
> But made himself nothing,
>   taking the very nature of a servant,
>   being made in human likeness.
> And being found in appearance as a man,
>   he humbled himself
>   and became obedient to death –
>   even death on a cross!
> Therefore God exalted him to the highest place
>   and gave him a name that is above every name,
> that at the name of Jesus every knee should bow,
>   in heaven and on earth and under the earth,
> and every tongue confess that Jesus Christ is Lord,
>   to the glory of God the Father.

Clearly the Lord's people – those who really knew him, whether under the old covenant or the new – were always ready to express their faith in song.

CHAPTER 3

THE BOOK OF PSALMS

There are 150 psalms in the Old Testament Book of Psalms. They vary in length from the 5 lines of Psalm 117 to the 352 lines, (176 verses, 22 stanzas) of Psalm 119. They also vary widely in their content and emphasis.

1. Five Books of Psalms

The Hebrew Psalter is subdivided into five books, which are thought to have been constructed so as to parallel, at least numerically, the five books of Moses, i.e., the Pentateuch (Genesis, Exodus, Leviticus, Numbers and Deuteronomy). Actual parallels between the contents of the five books of Psalms and that of the Books of Moses are hard, or indeed, impossible, to find.

This five-book arrangement first appeared in the Greek translation known as the Septuagint dating from before 150 and, in some sections. Possibly, even from before 200 BC. It would seem, however, to have existed before that translation was made. Interestingly, each book of the five books ends with a doxology, an ascription of praise to the Lord. In the case of Book 5 the whole of Psalm 150 and possibly all of Psalms 146-150 is to be understood as its doxology.

Book 1	Psalms 1-41	Doxologies 41:13
Book 2	42-72	72:18-19
Book 3	73-89	89:52
Book 4	90-106	106:48
Book 5	107-150	150:1-6

2. Ten groups of Psalms

There are ten other groupings in the Psalter, which have fairly obviously been brought together by a compiler or group of compilers on the basis of some common factor, like a shared author or a shared theme. Somewhat strangely these groupings do not coincide with the five books mentioned above. The ten groups are:

1) Psalms of David

Collection A – Psalms 3-41

With the exception of Psalms 4; 10; 18; 33 the headings of these psalms attribute them to David. Their distinctive feature is a preference for the title "The LORD" (Hebrew, *Yahweh* or *Jehovah*), which occurs on 272 occasions, over the designation God (Hebrew, *Elohim*), which has a mere 15 occurrences.

2) Psalms of the Sons of Korah

Psalms 42-49

The Sons of Korah are thought to have been a group of Levites who took some responsibility for the arrangements for worship at the sanctuary – the tabernacle and/or the temple or both.

3) Psalms of David

Collection B – Psalms 51-72

Here we find the reverse of the characteristic of Collection A (Pss.3-41). There are 208 occurrences of God (*Elohim*) and only 48 of "the LORD" (*Yahweh/Jehovah*). Psalm 72 is headed, "of Solomon" but it is followed by a footnote saying that it marks the end of the prayers of David, son of Jesse.

4) Psalms of Asaph

Psalms 73-83

Asaph was a Levite songwriter, whom some scholars think may also have served as a choir leader in the temple.

5) *Psalms sung as Sabbath anthems*

Psalms 90-99
Psalm 92 is headed, "A song for the Sabbath Day." Psalms 93; 97 and 99 begin with the words, "the LORD reigns." Psalm 90 is attributed to Moses. Some scholars think that these psalms were prepared for use in the restored temple after the return of Jews from exile in Babylon.

6) *Thanksgiving Psalms*

Psalms 105-107
Strangely two of these three longish psalms (105 & 106) are in Book 4 and the third (107) is in Book 5. Psalm 107 celebrates and, therefore, originated after the return of Jewish exiles to Jerusalem, when they had been released from captivity in Babylon by Cyrus in 539 BC. It could even post-date the restoration of the temple in 516 BC.

7) *Festival Hallel Psalms*

Psalms 113-118
The words, "Praise the LORD" (Hebrew, *Halleluyah* or, NIV footnote, *Hallelu Yah*) recur in these psalms (113:1, 9; 115:18; 116:19; 117:2). Because of the mention of Egypt in Psalm 114:1, they are often called Égyptian Hallel Psalms.

8) *Songs of Ascents*

Psalms 120-134
These psalms seem to have been written for and used by pilgrims as they ascended to Jerusalem for the great Israelite festivals. Four psalms, 122; 124; 131 & 133, are attributed to David and one (Ps. 127) to Solomon.

9) *Psalms of David*

Collection C Pss. 108-110; 122; 131; 133; 138-145
These psalms, scattered through Book 5, are thought to have been preserved separately from the Davidic Collections A and B, which make up the main

bulk of Books 1 and 2. Some scholars think they are not really by David but were attributed to him at some stage in their transmission by those who added headings to many of the psalms. The reference to the prayers of David being concluded (Ps. 72:20) might well support that view.

10) Hallelujah Psalms

Psalms 146-150

Each begins with the phrase, "Praise the LORD" (Hebrew, *Halleluyah* or *Hallelu Yah*). Together they form a large doxology or benediction to the whole Psalter. They may have been prepared for and used at the great festivals.

3. Acrostic psalms

As was noticed in section 3 of our previous chapter, some Psalms have an acrostic structure based on the 22 letters of the Hebrew Alphabet. Most English versions only indicate this in the headings to the stanzas of Psalm 119. The Jerusalem Bible indicates the acrostic structure of Psalms 25; 34; 37; 111; 112 and 145 in a wide left hand margin.

It appears that Psalms 9 and 10 together were intended to be one psalm that took the form of an alphabetical acrostic. However, two letters (*daleth*, ד, pronounced as "d" and *yodh*, pronounced as "y"), and the four lines that would go with them are missing. In addition four other letters are missing but the material that seems to belong to them is present and the Jerusalem Bible has, therefore, supplied in brackets the four missing letters of the acrostic. These are *mem*, מ, (m), *nun*, נ, (n), *samekh*, ס (s) and *tsadhe*, צ (ts). These absences indicate that translators did not have an exact acrostic on their hands. It is possible that, as in the case of Lamentations 5, the poet or a subsequent editor was unable to complete the work of casting this poem into an acrostic form.

In Psalm 145 the acrostic is incomplete in most Hebrew manuscripts. One verse – 13b in modern English versions – is missing. This absence leaves a gap in the acrostic structure of the psalm – there is no verse beginning with the letter *nun* (n). In the Septuagint (the early Greek translation) a verse that harmonises well with the context does appear. In the NIV it is rendered:

The LORD is faithful to all his promises
and loving towards all he has made.

4. Psalm types

In the early twentieth century a German scholar, Herman Gunkel, pioneered the study of what came to be known as "the life-settings" (in German, *Der Sitz im Leben*) of the psalms. Even though at some points he speculated beyond any Scriptural warrant, his analysis of the psalms into different types is helpful to our understanding of their meaning and message. His primary distinction was between individual and communal or national songs. He thought that those in the first category were designed for use in the home and those on the second for corporate worship in the temple. He recognised, however, that neither category could be defined as having but one use. Some could, as we shall see presently, have been used in both the home and the temple and, indeed, in other situations.

As we examine a selection of psalms, we will try to show examples of the various types. As we do so the distinction between individual/personal and communal worship will emerge from time to time.

We will examine a number of psalms along the lines set out in the table that follows. It must always be remembered that in many cases a psalm displays more than one characteristic and serves more than one purpose. In the chapters that follow we will examine specimens of the various psalm types in the following order.

1.   *Hymns in praise of the Lord*

       Simple praise
       Thanksgivings
         Individual
         National/community
       Professions of trust
       Songs exulting in Zion
       Songs in praise of God as king

2.   *Laments*

       Individual laments
       National/community laments

3. ***Wisdom psalms***
4. ***Royal psalms***
5. ***Liturgical psalms***

We will then add a number of chapters on the theology and significance of the psalmists and their psalms.

PART I

PSALMS EXAMINED BY TYPE

CHAPTER 4

~⁊⊱⊰⊱~

PSALMS IN PRAISE OF GOD

More psalms can be categorised as psalms of praise than can be placed in any other group. They offer – directly or indirectly – praise to the LORD. Some, as we noticed earlier, are expressions of personal piety, while others have a communal or national reference and express the praise of God's people.

The psalms that fall into this category call on worshippers to give praise to God and to articulate such praise in words. They often back up the call to worship with a recitation of God's deeds that demand man's praise. Such direct praise of God is found in many psalms, of which the following are especially notable – Psalms 8; 19; 24; 29; 33; 65; 68; 100; 103-5; 111; 113-117.[1] 134-6; 139; 146-150.[2]

In this chapter we concern ourselves with two psalms that express praise to the Lord in a general manner that fits both individual persons and communities. We will begin with Psalm 8 and then examine, in outline only, Psalm 111.

Psalm 8

This is a psalm of David, but there is no indication of the occasion that gave rise to its writing. The phrase, "according to *gittith,*" in the heading is of uncertain

---

[1]Psalms 113-117 in the Festival Hallel Group, may have been sung in sequence at the temple festivals in Jerusalem (cf. also page 23).

[2]Psalms 146-150 form a little group, sometimes regarded as the doxology to the whole psalm collection. Each begins and ends with an exultant, "Hallelu Yah" – "Praise Yah – Praise the Lord!" They became part of the daily morning worship of the Jews (cf. also page 23).

meaning but is widely regarded as "a musical term" (e.g., NIV footnote). Some commentators think it indicates a song used by those who had the job of treading grapes in a winepress.

The psalm has three main sections:

1) Initial ascription of praise to the Lord (vv. 1, 2)

David begins his praise with the words:

> O LORD, our Lord,
>> how majestic is your name in all the earth!

This sentence has been described as one of the simplest and most profound praise-prayers in the Psalter. Praise explodes from a heart that loves and adores the Lord. David addresses God, as LORD (Hebrew, *Yahweh/Jehovah*[3]) and as "our Lord." Yahweh, the LORD, was his own and his people's Lord or Master (Hebrew, *Adonai*). In his 1535 English translation Miles Coverdale rendered these opening words as, "O Lorde, our governoure."

David recognised that Israel was in a covenant relationship with the Lord, in which he was Master or Governor and his people were vassals and servants. That being the case, David's approach was marked by real reverence – he was coming before his Sovereign Lord, whose name was majestic, transcendent or magnificent. His glory was such that his name had that significance "in all the earth."

At the same time David's approach to the Lord was marked by real warmth. He was talking to one he knew as his own Master, the One who had disclosed himself to his people by his name, Yahweh, meaning the eternal ever-living Lord, the "I am," who is always "I am" and who is ever present with his own people. There is surely a parallel with our Lord's presentation of God as Father and with his instruction that when we, his followers, pray, we should address him as "Our Father ..."

---

[3]*Yahweh* is the English transliteration of the probable Hebrew spelling of the name. The pronunciation *Jehovah* derives from the the combination of the consonants of the name Yahweh and the vowels of the Hebrew word "lord" (*'ădōnay*), yet modified by a German transliteration.

For Israel, the Lord's name was virtually synonymous with his person and his presence (Note Deut. 12:5; 14:23; Jer. 7:11). The Hebrew word, *shem*, not only means a name, but the reputation and character of the one who bears it and, in the case of the Lord, his presence with those who knew it. David knew this presence in his own life and could quite naturally address the Lord as his and his people's master – "our Lord, our master."

Some recent English versions (RSV, NRSV and NIV) insert a space that separates the second part of verse 1 from the first, but the validity of this is somewhat doubtful. The words, "You have set your glory above the heavens" build on and expand the opening thought. The two lines seem to belong together and to provide an example of constructive or stair-like parallelism – The majesty of the Lord's name fills the earth and his glory is higher than the heavens (NLT).

Verse 2 also builds on what has gone before:

> You have taught children and nursing infants
>   to give you praise.
>
> —NLT

So great, so majestic is the Lord that small children and even infants have been taught to sing his praise. This may be a way of saying that by comparison with the glories of praise above the heavens, the praise of David and his fellow Israelites is like the babbling songs of small children – they don't really know how to praise him as they ought!

The result of such praise, imperfect as it may be, is that the Lord's enemies are held at bay. The foe and the avenger are silenced – "they silence your enemies who were seeking revenge" (NLT). David's point would seem to be that praise of the Lord, voiced on earth and joined with that of the heavenly realms, plays a vital role in the conflicts both of earth and of heaven, the conflicts between good and evil, between righteousness and unrighteousness.

Praise is an aspect of worship that is vital to God's scheme for the defence of his people and of his own cause. It is a ministry to which every child of God is called. The writer to the Hebrews says, "Through Jesus, therefore, let us continually offer to God a sacrifice of praise—the fruit of lips that confess his

name" (Heb. 13:15; cf. Jas. 5:13). In the visions of the Revelation John heard
the host of heaven singing:

> To him who sits on the throne and to the Lamb
> be praise and honour and glory and power,
> for ever and ever!
>
> —Rev. 5:13; cf. 7:12

That is the kind of praise that burst forth from the heart of David in Psalm 8.
It is the kind of praise we Christians are called to emulate here on earth.

2) David's reasons for praising the Lord (vv. 3-8)

(1) The relative insignificance of mankind (vv. 3, 4)

The Psalmist reflects on what he sees, or has previously seen, a bright starry
night sky – "the moon and the stars," that the Lord has made and set in
their places. As he does so, he realises that man is relatively insignificant in
comparison to the immense majesty of the heavens.

This realisation forced him to ask the Lord a double-barrelled question:

> What is man (Hebrew, 'enosh, mortal man) that you think of him, the
> son of man (Hebrew, ben-adam) that you care for him?

He was clearly amazed that the God, who could create such magnificence as
is displayed in the night-sky, could be bothered with puny man – man that is
mortal and that is a weakling creature made from the dust of the earth.

(2) The amazing privileges of mankind (vv. 5-8)

In the first instance David's praise is based on the privileged status the Lord has
given to mankind – "You have made him a little lower than God" (v. 5a, NRSV,
NLT) The Hebrew, Elohim, means "God, the Almighty One" but is rendered as
"angels" in the AV and "heavenly beings" in the NIV, apparently to avoid giving
the impression that man has a status near to that of God. But that is, in fact
what David said – man was created just a little lower than, a little diminished
from what God is!

Man, made "in the image of God," was endowed with many of the qualities
that belong to God – he was made a person with power to think, to feel and to

will and with responsibility to make moral choices. He was "crowned with glory and honour" (v. 5b) and, though he seems insignificant against the backdrop of the stellar universe, and though his position was damaged by the intrusion of sin, he remains and is the crowning glory of God's creation.

(3) The awesome responsibilities of mankind (vv. 6-8)

Every privilege brings an accompanying responsibility! Privileged to bear the image of God, man, as God's agent on earth, was made responsible to rule over every part of the material and the animate world in which he was placed (vv. 6-8):

> You made him ruler over the works of your hands;
> you put everything under his feet ...
>
> —v.6

David next (vv. 7, 8) concentrates on the outworking of this responsibility in relation to animate life – flocks, herds, birds and fish. Man is ruler of these living creatures and as such is responsible for their well-being and, indeed, their survival. In the instructions given to Noah after the flood man was authorised to kill such creatures and to use them for his own food (Gen. 9:2-4). This was not, of course, a divine authorisation of cruelty to animals or of the greedy exploitation that results in the extinction of species. It was, rather, a delegated role that made man responsible to manage his relationship to animals, birds, fish and insects in a way that best accords with God's purposes for those orders of creation. The responsibility this places on mankind is surely awesome!

But there is more, for the material earth also comes into the picture. The psalm surely implies that the works of God's hands, the works over which he has made man ruler, embrace the material structures of earth as well as its living inhabitants. They too come within his sovereign rule and are included in man's responsibilities as his agent on earth. As Sovereign Lord, he rules over everything he has made, over human, animal, vegetable and mineral existences.

As more and more of the wonders of creation are unraveled, we, like David surveying the heavens, can only marvel at the works of God. In making scientific discoveries in a responsible way, humanity is indeed exercising its role of ruling over the works of God's hands. At the same time we must, as

David calls on us to do, give wholehearted praise to God the Creator and say, "O LORD, our Lord, how majestic is your name in all the earth" (vv. 1 & 9).

Men must always remember that they are stewards, who act on God's behalf, rather than masters, who act in their own interests. Their responsibility is to care for and manage the resources of the world in which he has placed them for his own benefit. They have authority to rule over and to use those resources but not to abuse them. A responsible attitude to the entire environment, animate and inanimate, is the solemn duty of all God's people. In an age of profligate exploitation and wasteful destruction of earth's resources Christians should be in the forefront of the battle for environmental and ecological conservation.

The sad fact is that, since the Fall, sin has made man a selfish exploiter, who happily destroys what nature provides in the interests of his own profit. He is not the responsible steward that God intended him to be. Sadly, too, there is very little emphasis in church circles on environmental protection and improvement. When, dare it be asked, did you last hear a sermon on this aspect of Christian duty?

As God's agent man is immensely privileged, but, as "ruler over the works of God's hands," he also bears a huge responsibility for the rest of creation – responsibility for animate and inanimate created life and for the physical and material environment that he and the rest of the living creation are privileged to inhabit. These responsibilities are, of course, additional to those Scripture imposes in relation to his own behaviour and to the care of his fellow human beings.

3) Final ascription of praise to the Lord (v. 9)

The final verse of the psalm repeats the praise affirmation of the first verse:

> O LORD, our Lord,
> how majestic is your name in all the earth.

Thus the psalm ends on the note with which it began. The glory of God that is above and exceeds that of the heavens demands that we, like David, bring our praise to the Lord. The second line of verse 2 tells us that God had ordained praise as an element in the spiritual battle he conducts with his enemies, a battle between God and Satan in which we, his people, are inevitably involved (Eph. 6:10-18). In this battle between good and evil, we should then follow the psalmist's strategy and be constant in praise:

> O LORD, our Lord,
>> how majestic is your name in all the earth.

Psalm 111

In this psalm, God is praised for his works in words that often parallel those of Psalm 8. There are, however, additional grounds for praise as well as an interest in the fostering of true wisdom: "the fear of the LORD is the beginning of wisdom …" (v. 10).

The psalm, which is not attributed to any particular author, has a simple ascription of praise as its heading: "Praise the LORD" (Hebrew, *Halleluyah*). It has an acrostic structure, its 22 lines beginning with the letters of the Hebrew alphabet in order (*Aleph, Beth, Gimmel, Daledh* etc.) As noted earlier. this acrostic pattern can be seen in the margin of the New English Bible.

1) The author's determination to praise the Lord (v. 1)

He practices what he preaches by voicing his own wholehearted devotion to the LORD, his God:

> I will extol the LORD with all my heart in the council of the upright and in the assembly.

2) The author's reasons for praising the Lord (vv. 2-9)

- His glorious and majestic deeds (vv. 2-4a)

> Great are the works of the LORD;
>> they are pondered by all who delight in them

> Glorious and majestic are all his deeds
> > and his righteousness endures for ever. ...

- His grace and compassion (v. 4b)

> The LORD is gracious and compassionate.

- His keeping of his promises to his people (v. 5)

> He provides food for those who fear him:
> > he remembers his covenant for ever...

- His provision of land for his people (v. 6)

> He has shown his people the power of his works, giving them the lands of other nations.

- His maintenance of moral integrity (vv. 7, 8)

> The works of his hands are faithful and just;
> > all his precepts are trustworthy.
> They are steadfast for ever,
> > done in faithfulness and uprightness.

- His acts of redemption (v. 9a, b)

> He provided redemption for his people;
> > he ordained his covenant[4] for ever ...

- His name that is holy and awesome (v. 9c)

> Holy and awesome is his name.

This points to the Lord's holiness, his "otherness," his utter purity and his absolute separateness from all that is evil or second-rate. It calls for real reverence on the part of men – His name (that is, he himself) is to be reverenced and appropriately worshipped – "Holy and awesome (to be revered) is his name" (v. 9c).

---

[4]In Chapter 21, below, there is a fuller treatment of how the psalmists handled God's covenant relationship with his people.

3) The author's teaching (v. 10)

In the final verse the author shows his hand. He is, in fact, a wisdom teacher, one who has meditated on the realities of life and who has turned his thoughts into an easily remembered maxim:

> The fear of the LORD is the beginning of wisdom;
>> all who follow his precepts have good understanding,
>> to him belongs eternal praise.

The psalmist insists that wisdom begins with the fear of the LORD, that is, with reverential trust in him. Revering his name (v. 9c) means resting one's trust in him, the one who bears that name. Doing so indicates and expresses a true understanding of God's sovereign rule and merciful love and of man's appropriate response to him.

He is the one "to whom belongs eternal praise." As was the case with David and his people, we Christians also have good reasons to give God our praise. As the writer to the Hebrews put it:

> Through Jesus, therefore, let us continually offer to God a sacrifice of praise—the fruit of lips that confess his name.
>
> —Heb. 13:15

CHAPTER 5

INDIVIDUALS THANKING GOD

Psalms of Thanksgiving are of two types, those that express the thanks of individuals and those that voice or appeal for the thanks of a whole community. Some, like Psalm 32, move from individual thanksgiving to a call for communal or national thanksgiving—"Sing all you who are upright in heart" (32:11).

Individual thanksgivings are marked by the use of the first person pronouns, "I," "my" and "mine." They include Psalms 32; 34 (vv. 1-10); 41; 66; classified as community psalm (by consensus); 92; 116; 118; classified as community psalm (by consensus) and 138. In this study of "individual thanksgivings" we will examine Psalms 30 and 32.

Psalm 30

The theme of this psalm is thanksgiving for deliverance from the fear of death. Possibly David had been seriously ill and was rejoicing in the blessing of recovery, but the mention of his enemies (v. 1c) could suggest that his life had been in danger in a time of war.

The heading – "for the dedication of the temple" – may indicate that the psalm was sung at some great act of temple dedication, like that under Zerubbabel after the return of the Jews from exile in Babylon in 516 BC, or like, as the Talmud (c. 500 AD) says, that in 165 or 164 BC commemorating its restoration by Judas Maccabaeus after the desecrations of Antiochus

Epiphanes.[1] At some point later it became part of the liturgy used annually at
the Jewish Feast of Dedication or Lights.

The psalm, which some scholars think was sung antiphonally, divides into
five stanzas:

1) David gives thanks to God (vv. 1-3)

He gives praise to the Lord because the Lord had answered his call for help
—"O Lord my God, I called to you for help and you healed me." He had been
lifted from the depths (of despair) and had been healed. He had been spared
the gloatings of his enemies and, more significantly, descent into the grave –
he had escaped from death.

2) David calls his people to thanksgiving (vv. 4, 5)

The psalmist challenged "the saints" to join him in singing God's praise (v. 4). He
then gives his reason for this in two couplets, which express his conviction that
the adversities he has experienced and that his fellows were then experiencing
were essentially fleeting:

> For his anger lasts only a moment,
>> but his favour lasts a lifetime;[2]
> Weeping may remain for a night,
>> but rejoicing comes in the morning.

—v. 5

The emphasis of these two antithetic parallelisms is on how God's favour over-
rides and outlives his anger and causes weeping to be replaced by rejoicing.
This aspect of God's character and providence towards David was a ground for
both his own personal thanksgiving and for a call to his fellow saints to join
him in celebratory praise.

---

[1]The record is in the Apocrypha – 1 Maccabees 4:47-59 (cf. Jn 10:22)
[2]These words remind us of the addendum to the second commandment: "I, the Lord your God, am
a jealous God, punishing the children for the sin of the fathers to the third and fourth generations
of those who hate me, but showing love to a thousand generations of those who love me and keep
my commandments."

3) David explains how terror had struck him (vv. 6, 7)

Enjoying God's favour, the psalmist had become self-confident saying to himself, "I shall never be shaken" (v. 6). He had basked in prosperity and had felt as secure as a mountain![3] He was trusting in what God had given him rather than in God, the Giver. Then suddenly God's favour seemed to have been withdrawn and the bottom had fallen out of his world – "You hid your face" (v.7b). His health had gone and he felt as good as dead, as on the way down to Sheol.[4] He was terrified and said, "when you hid your face, I was dismayed" (cf. vv. 1-3).

4) David records his prayer of desperation (vv. 8-10)

He tells the Lord how in his great need he had cried out to him—"To you, O LORD (Hebrew, *Yahweh*), I called; to the Lord (Hebrew, *Adonai*, Master) I cried[5] (for mercy)." The NIV has added the words "for mercy" apparently because verse 10 indicates that mercy was what he wanted from God:

> Hear, O LORD, and be merciful to me;
>> O LORD, be my help.

What he wanted was that the Lord in mercy would intervene and prevent him from dying.

In verse 9 he asked the LORD rhetorical questions that again remind us of Job. He wanted to know what God would gain by destroying him. He asked whether, if he were to go to the grave, he, as a dead man, as dust, indeed, would be able to praise the Lord or proclaim his faithfulness. The implication was that he could not have done these things and that there would have been no profit and no positive testimony to the Lord:

> Will the dust praise you?

---

[3]There are similarities here with the rich man of Luke 12:16-21.
[4]David's experience here has parallels with that of Job.
[5]Compare Psalm 8:1 and 9 (Chapter 4 above).

Will it proclaim your faithfulness?

—v. 9b

5) David witnesses to God's deliverance (vv. 11, 12)

In these verses David's mood is one of celebratory gratitude:

> You turned my wailing into dancing;
> You removed my sackcloth and clothed me with joy.

David had been delivered from impending death and now he was doing what God intended would be the result of his saving work. He was lifting his heart to sing to the Lord. He could not remain silent and had no alternative other than to thank and keep on thanking the Lord:

> O LORD my God, I will give you thanks for ever.

In these final words David was committing himself to a lifestyle dominated by thanksgiving. For the rest of his life he would express his gratitude in words of thanksgiving to God. This was a lifestyle that all God's people should embrace. The writer to the Hebrews puts this in a way that is particularly pertinent to Christians—"let us be thankful, and so worship God acceptably with reverence and awe" (Heb. 12:28). Worship that is acceptable to God is worship that involves genuine and continuous thanksgiving.

Psalm 32

In this psalm David sings thanksgiving for the blessing of God's forgiveness. The occasion of his receiving this forgiveness is not specified, but, as is the case with Psalm 51, his sins of adultery with Bathsheba and his subsequent murdering of her husband, Uriah, are the likely candidates.

In verses 1-2 and 8-10 the psalmist again dons the mantle of an ancient wisdom teacher:

> Blessed is he whose transgressions are forgiven …
> I will instruct you and teach you in the way you should go.

It is thought by some scholars that this psalm was used in temple worship after David's time and that it may have been sung antiphonally in that context.

It divides into six sections or stanzas as follows:

1)The blessedness of forgiveness (vv. 1, 2)

These verses are wisdom-type beatitudes, not unlike those in Psalm 1. They affirm the blessings of forgiveness for:

- **Transgression** (Hebrew, *pesha'*). This is a wilful breaching of God's laws. Forgiveness releases the transgressor from the debt created by his offences.
- **Sin**, (Hebrew, *chattah*). This means missing a target and refers to any failure to meet God's requirements. In forgiveness the offence is cancelled by virtue of atonement (a covering) having been made for it.
- **Iniquity** (Hebrew *'awon*). This refers to the perversity of heart and character that results from the Fall. Strangely the NIV and NLT render it as "sin," while the JB has "guilt" and the RSV and NRSV translate more satisfactorily by "iniquity." When God forgives, iniquity is no longer counted against the sinner. Rather, he is justified, accepted as and declared to be righteous.

These three terms, **transgression, sin** and **iniquity**, sum up the biblical understanding of the defects that separate man from God and make him liable to God's wrath both in this life and in the life to come. Taking them in reverse order we can say that, because man is perverted in heart, he sins or falls short of God's requirements and he is a rebel who deliberately crosses over the boundaries set by God, thus making himself a transgressor. But the one, who experiences God's forgiveness at all three levels is truly blessed. He is then guided along the right path he should take. As a result he is blessed, truly happy (Hebrew, *'ashre*, meaning "guided aright").

The final line of verse 2 is a vital part of the experience of forgiveness. The man, who is blessed with forgiveness, is the one "in whose spirit there is no deceit." David is teaching that forgiveness, the blessing on which he focuses, demands sincere honesty and frank confession before God. The lesson for us, as for David's immediate readers, is that, if in our inner spirits we are not honest with the Lord, if we prevaricate and pretend, we **are not** among the forgiven.

2) David's pre-forgiveness guilt (vv. 3, 4)

David honestly tells the Lord about the sense of guilt that had overwhelmed him. This is not mentioned in 2 Samuel 12 and 13 and only emerges here as David personally testified to it. He had, in fact, like many people down the ages and still today, kept his sin to himself. But the guilt of it had plagued his mind by day and by night. He felt that God's hand was heavy upon him and, like Jonah in the scorching heat of Assyria, felt that the very sap of life had dried up within him:

> Day and night your hand was heavy upon me;
> my strength was sapped as in the heat of summer.

—v. 4

This is a wonderful picture of the effect of sin. David had been refusing to face up to the reality of his offences. He had deceived himself that he could get away with what he had done, but deep down he knew only too well that his sin would find him out. He had been bottling up an awful sense of guilt before God.

3) David's experience of forgiveness (v. 5)

Continuing his story, David says:

> Then I acknowledged my sin to you
> and did not cover up my iniquity.

Honesty before God had taken over – he had become one of those "in whose spirit there was no deceit" (v. 2c). He had, as we might say, "come clean before God." He had removed the mask of hypocrisy he had been wearing up to the point at which Nathan had confronted him with the immortal words, "You are the man" (2 Sam. 12:7). Then, as Nathan developed the incongruity of his sin, David came to a point at which he acknowledged it—"I have sinned against the LORD" (2 Sam 12:13). It was then that Nathan was privileged to bring him

God's good news and declare his sin forgiven[6]—"The LORD has taken away your sin. You are not going to die" (2 Sam. 12:13b).

David had found God's forgiveness immediately available to him when, in repentance, he confessed his sin. He had said, "I will confess my transgressions to the LORD" and the Lord had responded instantly. He forgave the guilt of his sin (v. 5b, c). David could now rejoice in the grace of the Lord and could call on others to rejoice in the Lord with him (v. 11).

David's experience finds a parallel in that of Paul after his Damascus Road encounter with the Risen Lord. For three days he was so troubled that he could not eat food. Then, as Ananias ministered God's word to him, the burden of his guilt lifted, he arose and was baptised – i.e., he openly professed his faith in Christ and, taking food again, he was strengthened.

Guilt before God is a serious thing. It points forward to divine wrath and eternal punishment. It calls for honest confession and real penitence such as David displayed. As Paul told the philosophers of Athens, God "commands all people everywhere to repent" (Acts 17:30). Why is it, we must ask, that so very few people today, even those with knowledge of Biblical ethics, seem able to acknowledge their sinfulness before God? Why is it that we rarely hear or read testimonies that tell of repentance from sin and the assurance of forgiveness. Surely the heart of the Christian Gospel relates to our Lord paying the price due to us for our sins and calling on us to confess our sins in repentance as we turn around and commit ourselves to him in faith and dependent trust (Note: 1 John 1:8-10 etc).

4) David's confident assurance (vv. 6, 7)

On the basis of what had happened to him – forgiveness following frank confession – David asserts the need for everyone who belongs to and believes in God to do what he had done – pray to the Lord for forgiveness, while he could be found.

Therefore let everyone who is godly pray to you

---

[6]Nathan was doing what Jesus authorised his disciples to do (John 20:23), i.e, to declare the sins of penitents forgiven (not, of course, to actually forgive the sins!)

> while you may be found;
> surely when the mighty waters rise,
> they will not reach him.[7]

—v. 6

The enjoyment of forgiveness was such that David could do nothing other than commend it to others by calling on them to follow his example and seek it from the Lord, while there was opportunity and before great danger – the rush of mighty waters – should engulf and destroy them.

David himself was now able to address the Lord in complete confidence. He had called on the Lord; he was forgiven and was filled with the joy of a right relationship to the Lord. He knew that the Lord would protect him from trouble – including the troubles that assail the guilt-ridden sinner – and would fill his life with song:

> You are my hiding place;
> you will protect me from trouble
> and surround me with songs of deliverance.

—v. 7

Such was David's testimony. Such is the testimony of all who genuinely make an honest confession of their sins to the Lord and who ask for his forgiving mercy. Trusting him in genuine faith, they receive his forgiveness. It can be your testimony if you come to him in this way. It was Jesus who said, "whoever comes to me I will never drive away" (John 6;37).

5) David's wise counsel for all (vv. 8, 9, 10).

In these verses David[8] again acts as a teacher of wisdom. On the basis of his experience he counsels his subjects, his fellow-worshippers and others in the

---

[7]We get an echo of these words in Isaiah 55:6 – "Seek the LORD while he may be found; call upon him while he is near."

[8]Some scholars think that the speaker of these "wisdom-type" verses was not David, but God speaking, possibly, through some unidentified prophet. On the other hand it might be that David himself became God's spokesman or prophet and was simply giving expression to truth that had been revealed to him.

way they should live—"I will instruct you and teach you in the way you should go" (v. 8). He wants them to follow a right path and to avoid the folly that had given him a conscience troubled by terrible guilt. He said, "When I kept silent, my bones wasted away through my groaning all day long" (v. 3).

At the same time he recognised that those to whom he was speaking were not immune to temptation. They were not enclosed in glass cases and beyond the reach of the devil and his wiles. To avoid sin they must abandon their headstrong self-will and trust in the Lord and his unfailing love. They must not be like a horse or a stubborn mule, which don't have man's powers of reasoning or his ability to choose between right and wrong and which can only be enticed to obedience by the imposition on them of a bit and a bridle. The implication is that, as morally responsible persons, human beings must voluntarily take steps to seek the Lord and to come to him confessing their sin and asking for mercy and forgiveness.

> Do not be like the horse or the mule,
>   which have no understanding
> But must be controlled by bit and bridle
>   or they will not come to you.
>
> —v. 9

These words seem to carry the implication that those, who do not draw near to God for forgiveness, lower themselves to the level of a stubborn brute beast and must expect to be treated accordingly and be disciplined by God's judgment. As David adds with the voice of experience, "many are the woes of the wicked" (v. 10a). He had known those woes and was now very glad to be relieved of them!

It is surely, then, better to keep short accounts with God and to receive humbly whatever guidance and correction he sees fit to give. Knowing that to be the case, David can again affirm his faith—"the LORD's unfailing love" surrounds the man who trusts in him (v. 10b, c).

6) David's concluding call to rejoicing (v. 11)

Finally, David calls on the righteous, that is, those whose sins have been forgiven and against whom the Lord is no longer counting iniquity, to express their rejoicing in song. Because of the Lord's unfailing love, such must rejoice and sing in appreciation and thanksgiving:

> Rejoice in the LORD and be glad, you righteous;
> sing, all you who are upright in heart!

—v. 11

Conclusion

This psalm thus calls each and every individual to open his own heart to God, to acknowledge and confess his sin and to receive from the hands of a loving God forgiveness and restoration to the enjoyment of fellowship with him.

It then calls on those who have experienced God's forgiveness to express in song and thanksgiving the incomparable joys of sins forgiven and of peace with God.

CHAPTER 6

❧

COMMUNITY THANKSGIVINGS

Community or communal Thanksgiving Psalms have characteristics similar to those in which individuals expressed their thanksgivings. In them it is the community that has experienced some deliverance at the hand of the Lord and that voices its thanksgiving to him. Psalms 67; 75; 105; 106; 107; 124; 129 and 136 are examples. We look at Psalms. 107 and 124.

Psalm 107

This psalm has no heading. Its main feature is a series of four illustrative stanzas (vv. 4-32) each of which depicts the experience of people, who, in great distress, called on the LORD and were delivered – redeemed – by him.

1. Its possible life situation

None of the four stanzas identifies the time or the reasons why those it pictures were in serious distress. There is, however, a clue in verses 2 and 3, which refer to people whom the Lord had redeemed and gathered from the east and the west, the north and the south. The background is most likely to be the conquest of Judah by the Babylonians in 587/6 BC. These events resulted in a dispersion of God's people as exiles to Babylon. Facing that fate, many fled as fugitives to Arabia, Libya, Cyprus, Asia Minor and Egypt. Descendents of these people became known as the Diaspora or Dispersion. Their plight provides a picture of almost any trouble or suffering that can in any age beset the people of God.

There were then members of God's chosen people dispersed to the east, west, north and south of their own homeland. Isaiah, addressing Jews, who would be alive in the days of the Exile (Isa. 43), conveyed the Lord's promise:

> Fear not, for I have redeemed you;
>> I have summoned you by name; you are mine.
>
>> —Isaiah 43:1b

> Do not be afraid, for I am with you;
>> I will bring your children from the east
>> and gather you from the west.
> I will say to the north, Give them up!
>> and to the south, 'Do not hold them back,
> Bring my sons from afar
>> and my daughters from the ends of the earth—
> everyone who is called by my name,
>> whom I created for my glory,
>> whom I formed and made.
>
>> —Isaiah 43:5-7

Psalm 107 presents a possible fulfilment of this very promise given through Isaiah. Exiles from Babylon and some, at least, of the fugitives from other places had returned to the Land. When, under Zerubbabel and his high-priestly colleague, Jeshua, the returned exiles restored the foundations of the temple, they sang praise and thanksgiving to the Lord. In doing so they used words that are repeatedly echoed in our psalm—"He is good, for his love to Israel endures for ever" (Ezr. 3:11). In redeeming his people he had delivered them from bondage and fear.

The psalmist therefore called on the redeemed – whether returned exiles or those redeemed from other situations – to give thanks to the Lord and to declare the reality of his redeeming works.

> O give thanks to the LORD, for he is good;
>> for his steadfast love endures for ever
> Let the redeemed of the LORD say so,
>> those he redeemed from trouble
> and gathered in from the lands,

from the east and the west,
from the north and the south.

—vv. 1-3, NRSV

2. Its calls to thanksgiving

1) In the opening paragraph (vv. 1-3)

The psalm begins by calling on those who had been redeemed to give thanks to the Lord (vv. 1-3). That theme, with appropriate adaptations, becomes a refrain at the end of each of the four main stanzas (vv. 8, 15, 21, 31). The thrust of the whole psalm is to challenge the community of worshipping people to be truly thankful to the Lord for what he had done in redeeming them.

Thanks was/is also due to the Lord because of his character – "because he is good." The Hebrew word translated "good" is *tubh*,[1] meaning the essence of goodness. He is good as none other being is or could be. As Jesus said, "No-one is good—except God alone" (Luke 18:19). As an explanation of that unequalled goodness, the psalmist could add, "his love[2] endures for ever." The Lord is forever loyal to those he has been pleased to bring into a covenant relationship with himself – he keeps his word and his promises to them and can be relied upon to do so. He is the "faithful God."

2) In a cycle of four illustrations (vv. 4-32)

The psalmist provides four pictures of misery to illustrate what those who were now redeemed had suffered. His figures of speech that add colour to his historical allusions. While the events that befell the Jews at the hands of the Babylonians may be the primary focus, the language is surely appropriate to God's people in every age.

(1) Their pattern of thought

These four illustrative stanzas follow a common pattern of thought:

---

[1] An alternative transliteration of the Hebrew for "good" could be *ṭôb*.

[2] The Hebrew word, *chesedh*, means loyal and steadfast love, rather than mercy as the AV rendered it.

- A description of plight and suffering (vv. 4-5, 10-12, 17-18, 23-27).
- A record of the fact of prayer for deliverance being offered and using the same words (vv. 6, 13, 19, 28).
- A declaration that God had answered the prayer (vv. 7, 14, 20, 29).
- A refrain repeating and reinforcing the call to thanksgiving in verse 1 (vv. 8, 15, 21, 31).

In three cases a reason for thanksgiving is added (vv. 9, 16, 22). In the fourth the call is for collective or community thanksgiving:

> Let them exalt him in the assembly of the people
> and praise him in the council of the elders.
>
> —v. 32

(2) Their pictures of misery

1. Lostness (vv. 4, 5)

Exile in Babylon or asylum-seeking in some far corner of the world produced a strong sense of lostness. Far from home and temple, they yearned for their own land. Hunger and thirst had plagued them and left them on near to death (v. 5). Psalm 137 surely highlights the feelings of those in exile—"By the rivers of Babylon we sat down and wept, when we remembered Zion."

But now God had satisfied their longings – he had saved them from their distress and set them free. They were back home and must, therefore, voice their thanks to the Lord who breaks down the gates and bars that kept them separated from that home (vv. 15, 16).

It takes no great stretch of imagination to see the abiding spiritual implications of this picture. We Christians were once also lost – separated from God and our true spiritual home. We wandered aimlessly in a wilderness of selfishness and sin till we finally cried to the Lord for mercy and by his grace found in Christ a city, a habitation for our souls (v. 7). We too must thank the Lord, who satisfies the thirsty and fills the hungry with good things (cf. John 4:10; 6:41, 48; 7:37-39, where Jesus cast himself in the roles of living water and the bread of life).

2. Bondage (vv. 10-16)

Those who were carried off captive by the Assyrians and the Babylonians were slaves in bondage. They went as prisoners because they had rebelled against the Lord. In the labour camps of their captors they became convinced that the way of transgressors is hard and as a result cried to the Lord, who answered their prayer. He saved them, delivering them by setting them free from their gloom.

Again the only appropriate response was thanksgiving— "let them give thanks to the LORD. ..." (vv. 16, 17). And the same is true of all who, having been in bondage to sinful habits, have been saved through faith in Christ. They too must give thanks to the Lord.

3. Foolishness (vv. 17-22)

The first word in the opening sentence (Hebrew, *ewil*,[3] meaning a fool, an impious or a perverse person) is key to the meaning of this section. Those in view were suffering loss of appetite and consequent emaciation – they had become ill and had seemed to be dying.[4] But this was as a result of their iniquitous and rebellious ways (v.17). They were fools in the sense that they rejected the ways of the Lord and the wisdom that comes from a proper reverence for him. As the proverbial saying has it, "the fear of the LORD is the beginning of wisdom" (Ps. 111:10). These people didn't have that reverential fear that would have compelled them to obey his commands – they were fools!

Because their sins had found them out, they eventually turned around and cried to the Lord. Then they too were saved from their distress. The Lord healed them – they did not die, because he had heard their cries of penitence.

Again it is not difficult to see an application to our own lives. We may well have reaped something of the wild oats we sowed in earlier years. But, and it's a big big but, God heard our cry of despair and intervened to bring us healing of soul and possibly also of body or mind – he delivered us from our crazy path of self-destruction and gave us new life in Christ. Let such, all Christians, indeed,

---

[3] An alternative transliteration for the Hebrew "fool" could be *ĕwîl*. No further comment concerning transliterations given in this book is provided. Note only that different conventions exist.

[4] Hence the RSV and NRSV renderings. "some were sick."

heed the call to thank the Lord for his unfailing love and as a thank-offering
present our whole selves to him as living sacrifices, holy and pleasing to him.
Offering ourselves to him and to his service is true spiritual worship (Rom.
12:1, 2).

4. Business activity (vv. 23-32)

Here we have a picture of people, who carry on their normal business, who ply
their trade using boats either in the Mediterranean or on lakes like the Sea of
Galilee. Seafearers always encounter the mighty works of the Lord as storms
arise and they are tossed up and down by the waves. They find themselves in
peril, staggering like drunks, terrified, lacking in courage and at their wits end.
Confronting the uncontrollable forces of nature, man's puny insignificance and
weakness becomes all too evident. The Psalmist pictures such men crying to
the Lord, who in response made them glad by guiding them through calmer
waters to their desired destination.

There is little evidence of Israelites trading across the Mediterranean, but
their neighbours, the Phoenicians, were famous for doing so. It was probably
a Phoenician ship that Jonah boarded at Joppa (Jon. 1:3). In the Gospels we
have abundant evidence of fishing on Galilee and of fearsome storms arising to
frighten the fishermen and jeopardise their safety (Matt. 4:18-22; 8:23-27 and
parallels in the other Gospels, John 21:1-14). The Psalmist may, however, have
been using the figure of storms at sea to illustrate the misfortunes of Israel and
Judah. In any event his picture fits life in every age. Men go about the business
of life – they are full of busyness – till suddenly storm clouds break and they
find themselves in some kind of distress and feel that they are being destroyed.

Such, perhaps, were you when your situation caused you to cry to the Lord
in despair. He brought you to faith in Christ and brought his peace and calm
into your life. Like those the psalmist addressed, your duty is to give him your
thanks, not just in private, but in places of public concourse:

> Let them give thanks to the LORD for his unfailing love
>   and his wonderful deeds for men.
> Let them exalt him in the assembly of his people
>   and praise him in the council of the elders.

3. Its wise conclusions (vv. 33-43)

This section summarises the implications of the earlier stanzas and in the manner of the wise teachers of Israel calls on listeners/readers to learn the lessons. The Psalmist gives us his considered view of the relationship between God and his creatures on earth – his philosophy was that:

- The Lord is not bound by the laws, his own laws, of nature – he turns them upside down! (vv. 33-35).
- The Lord reacts to the wickedness of people by changing – degrading – their environments (vv. 33 34). As a result population decreases as the wicked endure oppression, calamity and sorrow (vv. 39, 40).
- On the other hand the Lord blesses those who cry to him and trust him, by enhancing the natural world in their environment (vv. 35-38, 41). He "lifts the needy out of their affliction and increases their families like flocks."
- Upright people, those who plough a straight furrow through life, see and understand how God operates – righting the wrongs of life – and as a result they rejoice (v. 42a).
- The wicked are silenced – their mouths are shut – they have nothing to say and they can only accept God's sovereign handling of their lives.

Finally, the Psalmist appeals to everyone – whoever is wise should and, indeed, must take heed to his message and focus on the great love, the steadfast loyal love of the Lord for his people (v. 42). Despite all their waywardness and sin, he had not given them up (cf. Hos. 11:8). He had, on the contrary, redeemed them from many a disastrous situation and especially from exile in Babylon. If they heeded the message, their hearts would constantly bubble up in thanksgiving to the Lord, their Redeemer.

What of us who read the Psalm today? Surely its message is that we too must give thanks to the Lord, who in Christ has redeemed us from the power of, the guilt of and the ultimate punishment due to sin. Those who know themselves to be redeemed and forgiven must give thanks:

> Give thanks to the LORD, for he is good
> his love endures for ever

Let the redeemed of the LORD say this—
  those he redeemed from the hand of the foe.

—vv. 1, 2

Let them give thanks to the Lord for his unfailing love
  and his wonderful deeds for men

—vv. 8, 15, 21, 31

Paul puts our Christian duty clearly—"whatever you do … do it all in the name of the Lord Jesus, *giving thanks to God the Father* through him" (Col. 3:17).

Psalm 124

This is one of the group of Psalms headed, "A song of ascents," which are thought to have been sung by pilgrims making the ascent to Jerusalem for the great festivals held at the Temple. That does not, however, mean that they were written specifically for those occasions.

The psalm is headed, "Of David" (Hebrew, *Ledavidh*). The Hebrew preposition, *le*, is imprecise and could mean "to," "towards," "for," or, "with respect to." It does not, then, assert that David was the author. Some scholars think that two words in the psalm that appear to show an Aramaic influence suggest that it originated in later times than those of David and indeed after the return of the Jewish exiles from Babylon.

The words, "Let Israel say" (v. 1b), seem to be an instruction to the Temple congregation or to a choral group and may indicate that the Psalm was intended for liturgical use. It may have been sung antiphonally, with one group in the choir or congregation emphasising a point and another responding to it (cf. Pss 118:2; 129:1).

The psalm clearly celebrates some great act of God in delivering his people, Israel, from destruction. There are a variety of views as to its "setting in life" (what German theologians call its "*sitz im leben*"):

• The deliverance of Israel under Moses from the slavery of Egypt (Ex. 12ff.). This was the essential element in the annual celebration of Passover and of other "Feasts" and would have been prominent in the minds of the psalmists throughout the Old Testament era.

- Some deliverance in David's time – possibly the defeat of the Philistines (2 Sam. 5:17-25) or of the Ammonites and the Arameans or Syrians (2 Sam. 10).
- The deliverance of Judah from the Assyrians in the time of Hezekiah (701 BC). It will be remembered that King Hezekiah under the influence of Isaiah prayed to God and in the night the Angel of the LORD struck the Assyrian camp, leaving most of the soldiers dead (2 Kgs. 18; 2 Chr. 32; Isa. 36, 37).
- The deliverance of the Jews from exile in Babylon in 539 BC (Ezr. 1ff.).
- The deliverance of the Jews from the machinations of Sanballat and his allies in Nehemiah's time (Neh. 4-6).
- Some unspecified danger, which never actually materialised because of a divine act of deliverance – The Lord had been on the side of Israel and had enabled them to escape. This may be the most likely theory.

The Psalm is divided into two stanzas:

1. An affirmation of God's deliverance (vv. 1-5)

The first lines of verses 1 and 2 are rhetorical affirmations designed to conjure up in the minds of singers, and readers, the fact that, if it had not been that the Lord was on the side of his people, disaster would have struck.

The occasion of such a potential disaster would have been an attack by an enemy (v. 2b). The Psalmist then says that, if the Lord had not been on the side of his people, their enemies would, in their blazing anger, have swallowed them ("us") alive. As some awesome monster might have swallowed a man or a small animal so the enemy, whoever it was, would have devoured and ended the life of Israel.

Another picture follows in verses 4 and 5. It is of a raging torrent, like some we see periodically on our television screens, carrying all before them and leaving scenes of utter devastation – houses collapsed (cf. Matt 7:26, 27), cars and chattels swept away, and often the lives of men and animals lost. If the Lord had not been on their side, an invading army would have engulfed and swept them away.

Such was the situation envisaged in our psalm – one of absolute hopelessness. But that had not happened because the Lord was on the side of his people and delivered them from the impending disaster. Because of his care for them, they were able to praise and thank him for that deliverance.

2. An expression of fervent gratitude (vv. 6-8)

This stanza begins with a call to worship, praise and thank the Lord – "Praise be to the LORD." The Hebrew verb (*barak*) translated "praise" means to kneel in worship and so to acknowledge the immense worth of God, the God who had spared them from annihilation by an enemy.

Praise and thanks were then due to the Lord who didn't allow them to be torn by the teeth of an enemy. They had escaped from his clutches as a bird might escape from a snare that had become broken. In the case of the events portrayed in the psalm it was the Lord who had broken the snare and secured his people's freedom. If the Psalm celebrates the deliverance of the Jews from exile there is an obvious parallel with Ps. 107:10-16, which pictures prisoners being released from chains and bars of iron.

For the psalmist the deliverance of his people is wonderful, too wonderful almost for words. He can only cry out in adoring praise, "Our help is in the name of the LORD, the Maker of heaven and earth" (v. 8).

That the psalm calls the Lord "the Maker of heaven and earth" testifies to his absolute and ultimate power. If he made all that exists, he can act in the interests of what he has made and especially of those he has brought into a covenant relationship with himself. As such Israel, was his special, his chosen, people and their help in times of need was to be found in him. His name – again a synonym for himself and for his presence – was their refuge and their source of help and salvation.

The call here is to the people of Israel inviting them corporately to worship the Lord in real thankfulness. While individual Christians can use its words in a personal way, it is essentially a call to worship that in terms that are also appropriate to the church as the body of Christ. It is a body of people rescued from a world-culture, which is destined to perish, but which in the meantime would try to swallow up and destroy God's people.

Guaranteed an eternal inheritance in heaven, God's new people in Christ must also burst out continually in heartfelt and thankful worship of the Lord:

Let us be thankful and so worship God acceptably with reverence and awe ...

—Heb. 12:28

CHAPTER 7

PROFESSIONS OF TRUST IN GOD

In these psalms praise is expressed through an expression – a profession – of trust in God. Some, like Psalms 11; 23; 62; 91 and 131 are simple expressions of such trust. Others, like Psalms 3; 4; 16 and 27 begin with prayer for God's blessing and proceed to a climax involving a strong profession of faith. David concludes Psalm 4 with such a profession—"I will lie down and sleep in peace, for you alone, O LORD, make me dwell in safety" (v. 8).

For the purpose of this study we will concentrate on Psalms 4 and 23.

Psalm 4

This psalm has eight verses, seven of which have two lines and one, verse 1, has three lines. Traditionally it has been closely linked with Psalm 3, which also has eight verses and seventeen lines (three in verse 7). The heading to Psalm 3 associates it with David's flight from Jerusalem on the occasion of his son Absalom's revolt (2 Sam. 15). The heading to Psalm 4 is a musical direction that gives no indication of an original life-setting. That lack may, in fact, make the psalm more readily applicable to believers in every age. However, the close association with Psalm 3 and the fact that the Psalmist not only calls on God for help but complains about men, who were trying to shame him, points to a situation of some distress brought about by some group that did not accept his status as the Lord's anointed king or that was mocking his trust in God.

It is generally agreed that these two psalms, both of which are headed, "a psalm of David," have been placed side by side for purposes of worship. Psalm 3 is sometimes recognised as a morning psalm and Psalm 4 as an evening one.

The two are the first of some fifty psalms that feature the word, "Selah," the exact force of which is not clearly understood today. It is sometimes regarded as making an emphasis through an instruction like, "Think of that," or as a musical directive meaning something like "Lift up the voices" or "strengthen the musical sound," more or less as the word, forte, does on musical scores today.

1. A plea for God's help (v. 1)

This verse is an urgent call for help:

> Answer me when I call to you, O my righteous God.
> Give me relief from my distress;
>   be merciful to me and hear my prayer.

But it is also a profession of trust in the Lord. David addresses him as "my righteous God" or as the AV has it, "God of my right." The implication was that he saw the Lord as One whom he had proved in the past and on whom he could and would now depend for vindication. He also knew that God could and would hear his prayer and relieve his distress by extending grace and mercy to him.

The NRSV renders the second line as a statement rather than as a request —"You gave me room when I was in distress." This seems closer to the sense of the Hebrew verb, *rachab*, which means "to make wide, enlarge, liberate etc." It seems that David was backing up his request for help by reminding the Lord that he had previously and possibly repeatedly enjoyed such help – he had been liberated from previous trouble. This was, then, a prayer spoken in faith and grounded in David's experience of the Lord's faithfulness.

2. Remonstrance with opponents (vv. 2-5)

In these verses David seems to challenge a group of men who have set themselves up in opposition to him. By slanderous accusations or innuendos they were undermining his authority and destroying his good name – turning his honour, his glory, into shame! Whoever David was addressing, he knew that their slanders were the product of their way of life – the result of vanities and lies. "How long" he asked them, "will you love delusions and seek false gods?" (RSV and NRSV, "How long will you love vain words and seek after lies?") In both translations one implication is clear; David had had enough of their misrepresentations! Why were they continuing with them?

These villains must learn that David, the godly or faithful one, had been set apart by the Lord for himself. He was the Lord's chosen and anointed king, set apart or consecrated to serve the Lord by leading and overseeing his people. David knew this and was, therefore, assured that the Lord would hear his prayer (v. 3). At this point his faith, his trust in his Lord is again clearly evident – "the LORD will hear me when I call to him."

There is some uncertainty about who was being addressed in verses 4 and 5—"in your anger do not sin ..." They may have been a second group, possibly friends of David, who were less antagonistic than those addressed in verses 2 and 3. They might have been angry[1] against or even in support of David, but either way they must avoid sin. They must not, as they lay in bed, devise evil plans presumably to effect vengeance, but must silence such urges and show their trust in the Lord by making correct sacrifices as David was doing (vv. 4, 5).

3. Confident trust in the Lord (vv. 6-8)

This stanza begins with a statement of fact, a quotation of the words of pessimistic grumblers, whether among his enemies or among his friends is not made clear. They keep asking how or through whom they would see or enjoy any real good, anything pleasurable or profitable (Hebrew, *tubh*).

David had an answer for such an enquiry – real good (*tubh*) comes about in the reality of God's presence – "Let the light of your face shine upon us, O LORD" (v. 6b). David took up again his prayer and asked that together he and those whom he was addressing might see God's face. In doing so they would really see what they were longing for – true goodness. As evidence that this would be the case, he affirmed his own experience of God's presence and blessing:

You have filled my heart with greater joy

---

[1]There are several possible translations of the first line of v. 4. The Hebrew, *ragatz*, can point to mental agitation and anger, as the NIV translates. It can also focus on physical trembling as the AV suggests.

than when their grain and new wine abound.

For David true joy was not in worldly prosperity as his friends seem to have wanted but in the balm of God's presence and favour.

The climax to the psalm and the nub of its message is in the final verse:

> I will lie down and sleep in peace,
>> for you alone, O LORD,
>> make me dwell in safety.

—v. 8

David was in some kind of trouble, some distress (v. 1), but his faith was such that he could sleep calmly and without the fearful worries and anxieties that could have kept him awake. He was at peace with himself and with his Lord and was not afflicted with a gnawing conscience or with concern about what his opponents might do to him.

This was superb faith, a faith that we, and others, can and ought to make our own. All too often the things that disturb our minds – concerns about health, whether our own or that of someone we love, concerns about our jobs or our relationships or concerns about things we have said or done that make us feel guilty – keep us awake at night. Such things make us feel threatened and insecure.

If, like David, we truly know the Lord and truly trust him, we too can go to sleep without fear and in the assurance that he takes care of us and causes us to dwell in safety.

Psalm 23

Psalm 23 is probably the most familiar of all the psalms. It is often called "The Shepherd Psalm" and has obvious links with our Lord's identification of himself as "the Good Shepherd." Down through the centuries, it has brought comfort, encouragement and peace of mind to multitudes.

The psalmist knew that the Lord, the Supreme Shepherd, was with him in the ups and downs of life. He also knew that because of the Lord's presence important consequences followed. He focuses these in three affirmations:

• I shall lack nothing (v. 1a)

- I will fear no evil (v. 4c)
- I will dwell in the house of the LORD for ever (v.6b).

1. I shall not be in want (vv. 1-3)

David's confidence is based on his experience of the Lord as his shepherd. He uses the shepherd metaphor to show how the Lord had cared for him and how he cares for those who place their trust in him.

In ancient Israel the shepherd metaphor illustrated several key aspects of personal and national life. A shepherd:

- was king over his flock – he controlled it – he led and the sheep followed (cf. John 10:4).
- provided the needs of the flock by leading it to suitable pasture and to water – following him, the sheep find pasture (cf. John 10:9).
- cared for each individual animal – Jesus pictured a shepherd going out on the hills to find one sheep that had got itself lost (Luke 15:1-7 – NB vv. 4, 5a).

Those pictures illustrate how David thought of the Lord. He himself was a king but only under God – the Lord was his shepherd, his king. The Lord provided for him and cared for his every need. He could honestly sing, "**I shall not be in want**" (v. 1) – he would lack nothing he needed.

In verses 2 and 3 he expands the meaning of this:

> He makes me lie down in green pastures,
>> he leads me beside quiet waters
>> he restores my soul.

David was saying:

1. that the Lord provided nurture for him in a way similar to that in which a shepherd provided it for his sheep. He did so by leading them to a place, in which they could eat and drink and where, indeed, they could lie down and rest. Sheep need unruffled water in order to be able to drink. The shepherd finds it and takes them to it. And what a good shepherd did for his sheep, the Lord was doing for David.

Applying David's words to ourselves, we can say that, when we live as subjects of the Lord, when he as king rules over our lives, we have no need to worry about the necessities of life. We too can say, "*I shall not be in want.*" Didn't Jesus tell us not to worry, saying, "what shall we eat?" or "What shall we drink?" "For the pagans run after all these things and your heavenly Father knows that you have need of them" (i.e., "food and drink," – Matt. 6:31, 32).

2.   that the shepherd also cared for each individual sheep and lamb in his flock. Our Lord's story of the shepherd seeking one lost sheep perfectly illustrates this care (Luke 15:1-7). When David became separated from the Lord, by virtue of his sins, the Lord sought him out. He sent Nathan to him and brought him back into the fold and into useful service (2 Sam. 12 and Ps. 51).

3.   that while a shepherd concerns himself with the physical and material well-being of his sheep, our Lord, the great Shepherd, goes further. He is concerned with the inner emotional and spiritual well-being of his children – he restores the soul. When our spirits flag he lifts them up. When our wills are weak, he strengthens them. When our devotion to him wanes, he restores it. He gives us spiritual vitality and moral direction. As David could say, "He guides me in the paths of righteousness (in the right paths) for his name's sake" (v. 3b).

If we really belong to the Lord and long to please him such guidance is vital. We need to know the right paths, especially in a world that has lost its moral bearings and is concerned only to encourage self-autonomy, every person doing what is right in his or her own eyes.

Knowing the Lord as his shepherd, David could, then, affirm with confident faith, "*I shall not be in want.*" Multitudes of believers in this Christian era have affirmed a similar faith – can you?

Before we move on, there is another thought here. David tells us that the Lord makes these provisions, "for his name's sake" (v. 3c). The Good News Bible reads, "for the honour of his name," the New Living Translation, "because of his promises." The sense is that the Lord is honoured – honours himself – by keeping his promises.

The Lord does not only provide food and comforts, restoration and guidance for the benefit of his sheep, his people, but also for the honour of his own name. Because his honour is at stake in a godless world, he is all the more to be relied upon. He will not fail to keep his promises of care and provision for us his people.

With the psalmist, we can indeed sing,

> The LORD is my shepherd, *I shall not be in want.*

2. I will fear no evil (vv. 4, 5)

In these two verses David talked to, rather than about, the Lord and professed his faith with continuing confidence:

> Even though I walk
>   through the valley of the shadow of death,
> *I will fear no evil.*

David is saying that, whatever danger he had to face even the ultimate one of losing his life, he would not be afraid.

Commentators debate about what he meant by "the valley of the shadow of death." Was it a journey through an enclosed valley notorious for attacks by bandits or by wild animals that could pounce from behind vegetation or rocks? Or was it the ultimate crossing over from this earthly life to a realm beyond the grave?

The first interpretation is probably the more correct. David said he did not fear "adversity," which is the opposite of ease or prosperity (Hebrew, *ra'*, denotes not death but adversity). The focus is on trouble that can drag a sufferer into despair, because he can see no way to escape from it. But, even in such dark circumstances, David knew that the Lord was with him – he had no fear of being overwhelmed.

This confidence arose from the Lord's presence with David:

> *I will fear no evil for you are with me.*

He saw himself as living in close company with his shepherd, his Lord, and as a result he could look up to him and be assured of his protection. Again he explained his confidence in terms of the activities of a shepherd:

> Your rod and your staff, they comfort me.

The rod and the staff were tools of the shepherd's trade and, here, are symbols of the Lord's care for his people. The shepherd led his sheep through a dangerous valley by hoisting his staff above the undergrowth so that they could see where he was going. The rod and the staff gave them assurance that they were with him and were being led along the right path. Similarly the Lord's presence with his people brings them comfort and encouragement to follow on in his ways. Assured of this they were comforted (strengthened) – "they comfort me."

Again David goes beyond the normal activities of a shepherd and gives an extra dimension to the protection given by the Lord:

> You prepare a table before me
>   in the presence of my enemies.

When the shepherd was present with his sheep as they ate what he had provided for them, no enemy would dare attack them. Similarly David, who had many enemies during his reign as king, saw the Lord's presence with him as his ultimate protection. No enemy could succeed against him.

But there's still more to David's confidence. He recognised the Lord as the source of his position as king of Israel:

> You anoint my head with oil;
>   my cup overflows.

Anointing with oil indicated appointment to office and in David's case to kingship in Israel. As he had refused to kill Saul, because, as the Lord's anointed, his life was sacrosanct. so he as the Lord's anointed was a protected person. As a result his heart was bubbling over with joy and confidence – he could say, "*I will fear no evil*," ("no adversity").

And we, as believers, have received an anointing from God. John tells his Christian readers: "The anointing you received from him remains in you" (1

John 2:27). That anointing was God's gift of the Holy Spirit to us, when we became Christians, and is the guarantee that he is with us today as he was with David three millenniums ago. So anointed, so possessed by the Holy Spirit, we need fear no evil, no adversity.

3. I will dwell in the house of the LORD for ever (v. 6)

This verse sums up the whole psalm. Because he is assured of the Lord's presence with him, David can affirm that "goodness and mercy" would follow him "all the days of his life."

The word translated "goodness" (*tubh*) denotes the opposite of the adversity (the *ra'*) of verse 4. It implies abundance, prosperity and freedom from opposition. It implies the kind of provision and protection spoken of in verses 2 and 3. That would mean an abundant supply of every essential need.

For sheep this meant the provision of succulent grass and quiet drinking water. For men and women that provision illustrated inner restoration of soul and guidance along the right paths.

The word translated "mercy" is *chesedh*, which is often rendered into English as "mercy," but which essentially means loyal or faithful love. Such love should characterise the parties to a marriage. Faithful and loyal love is a vital element in the Lord's character and David's faith is such that he can confidently declare that the Lord's love towards him would continue faithfully to the very end of his life – "all the days of my life." God's provision and protection would be his for as long as he needed it. This leads to his final affirmation:

> I will dwell in the house of the LORD for ever.

Christians have often interpreted this as David saying he would enjoy eternal life with God, his shepherd, in heaven. But, while the meaning can probably be extended in that way, the primary significance is different – "I will dwell in the house of the LORD *for all my days*."

David uses the same words in both lines of this verse:

> Goodness and love will follow me *all my days*
> and I will dwell in the house of the LORD *all my days.*

In both cases "all my days" translates the same Hebrew phrase and refers to David's life on earth – he would live in and with God's presence. The privilege of having the Lord with him as his shepherd would last throughout his entire life.

But that is not all. David is not just saying that he will continue to enjoy the privilege of God's presence but that he was determined to do so – "I will dwell in the house of the LORD for all my days." This was his commitment to the Lord – he would be among the Lord's people and with them in worship.

For David this commitment will have focused largely on the earthly sanctuary of the Jerusalem temple, but clearly he knew God's presence with him at times when he was not in that building.

Believers in God through Christ must similarly respond to the Lord, their Shepherd. It's not a matter today of spending time at the Jerusalem temple and in observance of its rituals, but of living in fellowship with the Lord in and through the Holy Spirit. Each of us must, like David, resolve to live in that presence throughout our life on earth.

This psalm does of course bring comfort in times of bereavement, but primarily it is a psalm about life. It calls you and me to a wholehearted and permanent devotion to the Lord, to a commitment like that of David –"*I will dwell in the house of the LORD[2] for all my days.*"

Let it be, then, our determination that we too will live in the Lord's presence for all our days, that his house and his presence will be our home for as long as life shall last.

Such then is the message of this wonderful psalm:

- *I shall lack nothing*
- *I will fear no evil*
- *I will dwell in the house of the LORD for all my days*

Is the faith of David yours? Are you determined to live in his presence and under his rule for the rest of your days? If not, then turn to David's Lord and

---

[2]In our consideration of Psalm 27:4 in the next chapter, the significance of 'the house of the Lord' is further discussed.

Shepherd and put your trust in him now. Commit yourself to walk with and to serve him for the rest of your life on earth. Then, like David, you will prove that he is the Good, the Great Shepherd.

CHAPTER 8

IN PRAISE OF THE LORD'S PRESENCE

Many psalms enshrine the firm belief that the Lord was present among his people. That presence had especial reality in Zion, as Jerusalem and its temple were known.[1]

A number of psalms or, at least, passages in them, exult in and either give thanks for or yearn for that presence of God among his people. Those of this type[2] include Psalms 27; 36; 46; 48; 63; 65; 76; 84; 87; 92; 122 and 139. Of these, Psalm 139 is sometimes regarded as a prayer of the presence of God, indeed, as *the prayer of the presence.* The psalmist knew he was in God's presence and that the Lord knew him through and through, yet he prayed that he would search him further and lead him "in the way everlasting" (v. 24).

In some of these psalms the dominant theme is the desire of the psalmist, or of the worshippers whose devotion he expresses, to have fellowship with God in his house, the sanctuary of Zion in Jerusalem, where he was pleased to manifest his presence. Examples include Psalm 27:4-6 (see below) and Psalms 36:7-9; 63:1-2; 65:4 and 92:12-14.

---

[1] Zion is sometimes an alternative name for Jerusalem, also known as the "city of David" (2 Sam. 5:6-10; 1 Kgs. 8:1). In the psalms, however, Zion seems to refer to a particular part of Jerusalem, namely the Temple Mount, the holy hill, which was pre-eminently the Lord's dwelling place (Pss. 2:6, 48:1, 2; 76:2; 132:13-18 etc.)

[2] Some of these psalms are alternatively classified as Songs of Zion in view of the focus on Zion in such psalms (e.g. Psalms 46, 48, 76, 84, 87, 122). Psalm 27 is usually classified as a personal lament psalm (see chapters 10 and 11).

In one or two passages there is clear evidence of a belief that the presence of the Lord brought protection for Zion and for the city and the people of Jerusalem in general. One such passage reads:

> There is a river whose streams make glad
> 　　the city of God,
> 　　The holy place where the Most High dwells.
> God is within her, ***she will not fall***;
> 　　God will help her at break of day.
>
> 　　　　　　　　　　　　　　　　　　—Ps. 46:4, 5

> Those who trust in the LORD are like Mount Zion,
> 　***which cannot be shaken but endures for ever.***
>
> 　　　　　　　　　　　　　—Ps. 125:1; cf. 124:1-5

In this study we will examine Psalms 27 and 122.

Psalm 27

Psalm 27, headed "of David," could be by or about David (Hebrew, *le dawidh*). Alternatively it could be by someone re-enacting his situation. It is in two parts,[3] the first of which (vv. 1-6) is a firm affirmation of the psalmist's trust in the Lord and in the protection afforded by being in his presence and in his house. The second part (vv. 7-14) presents a picture of an author who faces opposition of some kind. But it also exudes a strong and confident trust in the Lord, whose face – i.e., whose presence – the writer earnestly seeks. He could add—"I am still confident of this: I will see the goodness of the LORD in the land of the living" (v. 13). In both sections the writer, indicates that he was under threat from foes and false witnesses (vv. 2-3, 12).

---

[3]Many scholars think the difference between the two parts is so marked that they must have been written by different authors, or, if by the same author, at different times in his life. However, the first section also envisages the author facing threats and violence from enemies and need not be regarded as so different from the second as to demand acceptance of the view that the two have different origins. Thus, both thematic links between the two parts in addition to lexical links (i.e. biblical Hebrew words occurring in both parts) unite the psalm as a unit.

1) David's desire for the Lord's presence

The first section of the psalm (vv. 1-6) is dominated by the writer's deep desire to enjoy the Lord's presence and protection in Zion. The psalm begins with two parallel rhetorical questions, each of which includes a strong profession of the writer's confidence in the Lord, his light, his salvation and the stronghold of his life (v. 1). By "light" he means anything that the Lord sends to bring him joy and happiness and what we would call guidance – God's word was a light to his path (cf. Ps. 119:105; John 1:4-5, 9; 8:12).

Salvation refers to the idea of deliverance from danger and, as verses 2 and 3 indicate, from the assaults of an enemy. The picture of the Lord as "the stronghold" suggests that David had been protected from such danger and knew that he was still being protected by the Lord. Whatever assault was made against him he was confident in the Lord (v. 3b).

On the basis of this strong confidence in the Lord, David proceeds to define the supreme ambition of his life – to be in the Lord's presence, where he knew he would be safe (v. 5) and where he would be lifted up above his enemies. In that situation he would make appropriate sacrifices to the Lord and would sing and make music to him:

> One thing I ask of the LORD, this is what I seek:
>> that I may dwell in the house of the LORD
>> all the days of my life,
> to gaze upon the beauty of the LORD
>> and to seek him in his temple.
> For in the day of trouble
>> he will keep me safe in his dwelling;
> he will hide me in the shelter of his tabernacle
>> and set me high upon a rock.
> Then my head will be exalted
>> above the enemies who surround me.
>
> —vv. 4-6a

For David the one thing that mattered above all others was that he would be privileged to be in the Lord's presence. For this, he tells us, he was praying earnestly—"One thing I ask of the LORD, this is what I seek; that I may dwell in the house of the LORD all the days of my life ..." (v. 4). There is an obvious thought connection with the concluding words of Psalm 23 in which he expressed his determination, his commitment, to live the rest of his days in the presence of the Lord—"I will dwell in the house of the LORD for ever" (i.e., for all the days of my life).

What, we must ask, did David mean by "dwelling in the house of the LORD?" Did he mean that he would take physical refuge from his enemies in the actual building of the temple, which the Lord had made his special dwelling place? Or did he mean that he wanted a spiritual relationship with the Lord, wherever or in whatever circumstances he might find himself?

From what we know of his life-style David certainly did not spend "all the days of his life" in the temple at Jerusalem. He was often away fighting battles and sometimes on the run from rebellions, like that of Absalom. But, perhaps, he was not using his words in an absolute sense of permanent abode in the temple, but saying that as a matter of habit he wanted to worship and to make sacrifices there so as to experience a real living fellowship with his Lord and Master. At the same time his wish involved regular attendance at temple worship – gazing on the beauty of the Lord in the temple and enjoying the protection, the asylum, the Lord would grant him there. He could say, "in the day of trouble he will keep me safe in his dwelling; he will hide me in the shelter of his tabernacle and set me high on a rock" (v. 5).

David was clearly anxious, as he had been in Psalm 23:6, to maintain a close ongoing spiritual relationship with the Lord, one that would enable him to be able in faith to gaze on, i.e., to contemplate in his mind, the beauty of the Lord. This he would do as he sought the Lord in his temple. Making that goal his pre-eminent passion, he was assured that he would enjoy divine favour and protection wherever he might be or whatever troubles might assail him. Thus protected he would be careful to perform all the necessary exercises of Old Testament religion – he would make sacrifices and would sing and make music to the Lord—"at his tabernacle will I sacrifice with shouts of joy; I will sing and make music to the LORD" (v. 7b). He was determined to live in the presence of his Lord.

2) David's prayer for experience of the Lord's presence

The second section of the psalm (vv. 7-13) develops David's theme in a prayer that continues to express his desire for fellowship with the Lord. He hears a call to seek the Lord's face (v. 8a) and responds positively, "Your face, LORD, I will seek." He then pleads that the Lord will not hide his face[4] – his presence – from him or reject him in anger. This suggests to some that doubts and anxieties had entered his mind and that his faith was weaker than in verses 1-6. But, in fact, he still exudes real confidence in the Lord. He knows that the Lord will not reject or forsake him: "Though my mother and father forsake me, the LORD will receive me." The Lord would indeed receive him and lead him in a straight path. His words surely anticipate those of the Lord Jesus, "whoever comes to me I will never drive away" (John 6:37, where the AV reads, "him that cometh to me I will in no wise cast out").

David prayed that the fellowship he enjoyed in God's presence will be worked out in his day-to-day living: "Teach me your way, O LORD; lead me in a straight path" (v. 11). That he would be led in that way was vital in view of the activities of opponents, who were oppressing him through false accusations and even violence. He saw his close relationship to the Lord as the source of an assurance that he would not be handed over to the desires of his oppressors.

Then bursting forth in a final assertion of his faith he says:

> I am still confident of this:
>> I will see the goodness of the LORD
>> in the land of the living.

David may have had confused thoughts – doubts and fears mixing with faith and confidence, but at the end of the day faith was triumphant – he was confident in the Lord and in his presence with him.

The writer to the Hebrews brought the "Zion idea" into Christian thinking. He told his readers that they had come to Mount Zion, to the heavenly

---

[4]The Hebrew, *paneh*, meaning face often stands for a person or his presence. Thus, in the First Commandment, no other gods before me is literally, "before my face" (my *paneh*).

Jerusalem, to myriads of angels and to the church of the firstborn whose names are written in heaven. He was saying that they had come into a spiritual relationship with the inhabitants of heaven, with the angels and the glorified saints already with the Lord – "the spirits of righteous men made perfect." But even better, they and all of us who believe in God through Christ "have come to God, the judge of all men ... to Jesus, the mediator of a new covenant, and to the sprinkled blood that speaks a better word than the blood of Abel" (Heb. 12:22-24).

Whatever else this New Testament passage may mean, it surely tells us that the ultimate meaning of David's picture of "Zion" is spiritual rather than physical or literal. It points not to some future glory for the city of Jerusalem but to the community of those who truly rest in the Lord, who are joined by faith to one another and as members of his church to the inhabitants of heaven. Ultimately they too will join in and enjoy joyful assembly with the inhabitants of heaven.

The final verse of the psalm (v. 14) applies its message, possibly in the first instance to David's own heart, but certainly also to anyone in any age who, like him, faces opposition whether in the form of false accusations or violence. Because he was assured of the Lord's presence with him he was confident he would see the goodness of the Lord (v. 13). He could, therefore, call on himself and on others to wait for[5] – to hope in – to trust in the Lord.

His words echo the encouragement given to Joshua as he took over the leadership of Israel (Deut. 31:7; Josh. 1:6ff.) and are as relevant to us as they were to David. We too must live close to the Lord – in his presence – and, as we wait upon him in trust, be strong and encouraged in him and by his word:

> Wait for the LORD;
>> be strong and take heart
>> and wait for the LORD.

---

[5]The Hebrew verb, *qawah*, can mean, hope for, wait for, expect or trust.

Psalm 122

This is one of the group of psalms called "psalms of ascents" (Pss. 120-134). They are thought to have been designed for singing by pilgrims either as they made their way up through the hills to Jerusalem, which lies some 3000 feet above sea level or as they were actually climbing the temple steps.

In the case of Psalm 122 some commentators think it is a reflection written after the author had attended one of the great festival feasts. Whatever the precise occasion of its origin, it is another hymn extolling God's presence in Zion.

This psalm is also headed, "of David" but some scholars don't think that note is meant to say that David was the author of the psalm. This is mainly because it refers to the temple, 'the house of the LORD" (v. 9a), which had not been built in David's time. However, David had brought the Ark of the Lord and prepared a tent as a temporary tabernacle to house it (1 Chr. 15:1). In doing so he established a focus of the Lord's presence in his newly captured capital, Jerusalem. He could therefore have written this psalm in relation to that rather embryonic house of the Lord.

1. Joy at the opportunity to visit Zion (vv. 1, 2)

Friends, neighbours or family members invited the writer to join them on a trip to Jerusalem for one of the great religious feasts. This brought joy to his heart and subsequently brought him to Jerusalem. He could then say "our feet are standing" or, if the tense of the verb is historic present, "our feet have been standing" in the city of Jerusalem. Whether he was actually there while he wrote, or was somewhere else and reflecting on having been there, his heart was bubbling over with joy. To be within the city's gates was to have access to the earthly presence of the Lord that was thrilling. It was an experience he could never forget and would always extol in song.

2. Appreciation of the glories of Zion (vv. 3-5)

The psalmist describes Jerusalem as a city that is compactly constructed, a comment that makes many scholars think the psalm is post-exilic and refers to the restorations begun by Sheshbazzar and completed by Nehemiah in the hundred years from 529 to 440 BC. Apparently assuming that to be the case, the Jerusalem Bible renders verse 3 as, "Jerusalem restored! The city, one united whole." The main emphasis is that the city was bound together in a unity created by its role as the focal point of Hebrew religious and civil life.

The Israelites regularly went up – ascended – to Jerusalem for the major feasts ordained by God through Moses for the praise of the Lord's name (Ex. 23:14-17).

In verse 5 Jerusalem is presented as central not just to religion – the house of the Lord – but to the administration of justice:

> There the thrones for judgment stand,
>> the thrones of the house of David.

In Deuteronomy 17:8 Moses pointed forward to the establishment of what we might call a "High Court" made up of Levitical priests and a judge who held office at the particular time. This was set up to deal with more difficult civil cases and was to function in the place that the Lord would choose, which is precisely the wording used earlier in the same book of the site of the future sanctuary, which turned out to be Zion/Jerusalem (Deut 12:5).

It would seem that David appointed members of his family to judicial office and that after four years in that role one son, Absalom, led a revolt against his father (2 Sam. 15). Centuries later the responsibility of the king's household – the house of David – to administer justice was emphasised by Jeremiah—"O house of David, this is what the LORD says: "Administer justice every morning …."" Those then serving as judges were clearly failing to fulfil their duties and were in grave danger of divine wrath (Jer. 21:12).

3. Prayer for the peace of Zion (vv. 6-9)

The psalmist calls on his fellow worshippers, and presumably on others, to pray for his much loved city—"Pray for the peace of Jerusalem." He uses the Hebrew word, *shalom*, which means much more than our English word, "peace." He wanted prayer, not just that Jerusalem would be free of conflict, but that, as the place of the Lord's presence, it would enjoy the maximum possible blessings in terms of its overall prosperity and well-being. Against the background of verses 3-5, the prayer he desired from worshippers would have majored on the well-being of the sanctuary, whether it was David's tabernacle or the later temple.

Specific petitions – indeed, specific wordings for prayer – are then offered to the worshipper (vv.6b, 7a and 7b):

- *May those who love you be secure,* that is, may they enjoy prosperity in safety. The prayer is specific to those who love Zion, meaning true believing people of God, those devoted to him and to the worship of his name and of his house.
- *May there be peace within your walls and security within your citadels.* Again the word translated "peace" is *shalom,* meaning total well-being. David wanted prayer that God would protect Zion from its outer wall to its inner core. He wanted prayers that would bring security (Hebrew, *shalvah*[6]) to the city's inner citadels. In verses 8 and 9 David explains why he called for such prayer. His concerns are in somewhat parallel terms:

1. *The well-being of his family and friends*
   David says,

   > For the sake of my brothers and friends,
   > I will say, "Peace be within you."

   He was not extolling Zion and the Lord's presence there for selfish reasons but to encourage prayer for the well-being, the prosperity of others.

2. *The well-being, (the good, Hebrew, tubh) of Zion*
   The prayers, for which David was calling were also to be "for the sake of the house of the LORD our God." Then in the final line of the psalm he dedicated himself to fostering that end: "I will seek your prosperity."

As with Psalm 23, David ends this psalm with a statement of personal commitment. He didn't simply sing about Zion and its glories in the way we

---

[6]This word is similar in sound to *shalom* and seems to come from a related root. The same is true of the second part of the name, Jeru-salem. The repetition of these related words seems to produce word-play based on the assonance between them in verses 6-9.

often sing our Christian hymns – without thinking of the meaning of the words or of their application to our own lives. Rather, the truths he has been affirming about Zion had demanded a response from his heart and mind. David therefore spoke and sang from a heart that was dedicated to the Lord, to his house, to his people and to his glory. For the benefit of his Lord and Master he would strive for the good of his house.

The house of the Lord, the real Zion, that David extolled was a physical building in a physical city, but it was also a place with spiritual significance and in the era of the psalm the focus of God's presence on earth.

In New Testament terms Zion becomes the community of God's people, those who believe in him through Christ, and who in Christ have received the Holy Spirit. Paul refers to that community as "the temple of the Holy Spirit," (1 Cor, 3:16; 6:19; 2 Cor. 6:16) and as "a dwelling in which God lives by his Spirit" (Eph. 2:21, 22; cf. Heb. 3:6b).

Those who belong to that community can exult in the heavenly Jerusalem using the very terms David used in these verses of the city he knew and loved as God's dwelling place on earth. Equally we can use David's petitions for the welfare of that Jerusalem in relation to the well-being of the church on earth and the heavenly city to which we belong and to which we are marching as pilgrims, while still here on earth. For example:

- May those who love God's people be spiritually secure and prosperous in the highest spiritual sense.
- May there be maximum well-being (*shalom*, peace and well-being) within that community.
- May there be security and peaceful unity within the many citadels of the church on earth.

CHAPTER 9

~~~

PRAISING THE LORD AS KING

A number of psalms extol the Lord as King of his people, Israel, and as the universal and eternal King above all earthly and heavenly rulers.[1] The six main examples are Psalms 47; 93; 96; 97; 98 and 99.[2]

The group (Psalms 96-99) shows God's rule manifesting itself in four different ways:

- Psalm 96 stresses his universal glory.
- Psalm 97 pictures the awesomeness of a theophany, an occasion when the Lord, the ultimate King of the universe, manifested his presence on earth.
- Psalm 98 glories in the King's righteousness and in his saving power.
- Psalm 99 presents the Lord as infinitely holy and to be worshipped as such.

In this chapter we select for consideration Psalms 47 and, in outline, Psalm 93.

Psalm 47

This psalm carries the heading, "of the Sons of Korah." The Sons of Korah were thought to be a band of Levites, who were responsible for the arrangement of music in the worship services of the temple. Though several men named

---

[1]Scholars, like Hermann Gunkel, Sigmund Mowinckel and their followers, have postulated that these psalms originated in the context of annual enthronement festivals in Jerusalem that were modelled on those of ancient Babylon. They therefore call them "enthronement psalms." The whole idea is extremely dubious.

[2]Many OT scholars include Psalm 95 among these six psalms which praise Yahweh as King.

Korah are mentioned the Old Testament, it is widely accepted that these "Sons of Korah" derive from the Levites mentioned in 1 Chronicles 6:22.

The psalm calls for jubilant praise of the Lord the King over all the earth. In later times, as part of their new year (*Rosh Hashanah*) celebrations, Jews recited it seven times before the blowing of the ram's horn (the *shofar*[3]).

The psalm is divided in different ways in English Bibles. The word *selah*[4] follows verse 4 and is generally regarded as indicating the end of the first section. The NIV and NLT put a further division after verse 6, while the RSV and NRSV put one after verse 7. The Jerusalem Bible sets the psalm out as five stanzas of four lines each – verses 1 and 2, 3 and 4, 5and 6, 7 and 8 and verse 9 which itself has four lines – making twenty lines in all. In this study we will take verses 5 to 8 as belonging together and forming a second stanza, which very largely repeats and re-emphasises the ideas of the first. Verse 9 then gathers together the various strands of thought to show the implications of the Lord's kingship.

1. All peoples called to honour the Lord (vv. 1-4)

Clap your hands, all you nations (i.e., peoples);
shout to God with cries of joy.

—v. 1

Exuberant and excited enthusiasm for God is what the psalmist wants from all the peoples of the world. His challenge is, perhaps, the most universally applicable found in the Psalms. All nations, all peoples of the earth are called to acknowledge and worship before the King and Lord of all the earth.

Background to the clapping of hands and shouting can be found in 2 Kings 11:12b, where we have the record of the presentation of the seven year old Joash as king of Judah: "they anointed him, and the people clapped their hands and shouted, Long live the king." Here in our psalm the writer calls on the

[3]In Jewish tradition the **shofar** or ram's horn is associated with the binding of Isaac and his willingness to be offered in sacrifice. Its blowing at new year is regarded as signifying the willingness of the Jew to offer himself to serve God.
[4]See above, chapter 7, page 59, for the significance of "selah."

peoples of the world to submit to and acknowledge in a similar way the Lord as their King.

The second line of this verse (v. 1) seems to use words first spoken of Israel by Baalam to Balak of Moab: "The LORD their God is with them; the shout of the King is among them" (Num 23:21b). Israel was then in process of taking possession of the Promised Land – the Lord was with them and there was no way that they could be frustrated. They were on the winning side and they could shout in triumphant celebration "the shout of their King," their victorious God, the Lord. The psalmist wanted peoples everywhere to join in that celebration of the Lord.

Reasons for honouring the Lord (vv. 2-4)

Verses 2-4 develop a three-step argument to show why the Lord should be accepted and honoured as King of all the earth:

- *Step 1 – verse 2*
  Because he is awesome – awe-inspiring[5] – in his universal rule, he is to be revered:

  > How awesome is the LORD Most High,
  >> the great King over all the earth.

- *Step 2 – verse 3*
  Because, in the exercise of his universal kingly rule, he had subdued other nations before Israel. First it was the Egyptians, as Israel had crossed the Red Sea (Ex. 13:17-14:31). Then it was the various tribes of the Caananites, as under Joshua they conquered the land:

  > He subdued nations under us,
  >> peoples under our feet.

- *Step 3 – verse 4*
  Because he had chosen the Promised Land as an inheritance for his people the descendants of Jacob, whom he had especially loved.

  > He chose our inheritance for us,

---

[5]In modern English usage, the AV translation, "terrible," is misleading and should be avoided.

> The pride of Jacob, whom he loved.

The force of this argument is that peoples around the world must give praise and honour to the Lord because of his great goodness to Israel. This develops the idea of Israel as the fulfilment of God's promise to Abraham (Gen. 12:1, 2). He was blessing the nations by making knowledge of himself available to them through his provisions for Israel.

2. The call to honour the Lord repeated (vv. 5-8)

This section begins:

> God has ascended amid shouts of joy,
>> the LORD amid the sounding of trumpets.
>
> —v. 5

These words suggest that Korah – or whoever from his circle wrote the psalm – wanted to stress the way in which the Lord of all the earth had worked miraculous victories for his own people. The verse *may* refer to one or more of the following factors:

1. The belief that the Lord "came down" to effect interventions on behalf of his people (cf. Isa. 31:4d; 64:1, 3). Presumably when an intervention had been successfully completed, the Lord was thought "to go up" from the scene in triumph.

    The author of our psalm has already said that the Lord had subdued nations before Israel (v. 3), meaning that he had accomplished a specific task. The inference is that, having "come down" to perform that task and having successfully completed it, he had now "gone up" in triumph to where he had come from.

2. The bringing of the Ark of the Covenant to Jerusalem after David had defeated the Philistines (2 Sam. 5:17-6:14). The Ark was the focal point of God's presence among his people, who celebrated its ascent to Jerusalem

or Zion "with songs and with harps, lyres, tambourines, sistrums[6] and cymbals" (2 Sam. 6:5).

    When the Ark came up to Jerusalem, the Lord came up with it and David and his people celebrated the occasion. If that event was in the author's mind, the defeat of the Philistines, which preceded it, would be seen as a divine victory from which he had "gone up" in triumph.

3.   Some religious celebration, when the presence of the Lord in the inner "holy of holies" was marked by a blowing of trumpets and when the worshippers joined in singing his praise. Solomon's dedication of the temple, when 120 priests blew trumpets and joined with the whole company of priests and Levites to sing aloud in praise to the Lord, could have been the occasion—"the temple of the LORD was filled with a cloud … for the glory (the presence) of the LORD filled the temple of God" (2 Chr. 5:11-14; cf. Isaiah 6).

Whatever the background to verse 5, the awesome presence of the Lord demanded praise and led in verse 6 to a repetition of the call to praise him as King of all the earth:

> Sing praises to God, sing praises;
>> sing praises to our King, sing praises.

Reasons for singing praise to the Lord (vv. 7-8)

In verses 7 and 8 the author, as he did in verses 2-4, backs up his call to praise by explaining why such praise is necessary. Several reasons for praise emerge:

- *Because the Lord is universal King*

> *For* God is the King of all the earth;
>> Sing to him a psalm of praise.

---

[6] A sistrum was an Egyptian instrument which made music by shaking or rattling.

- *Because God, who manifests his presence with his own special people, is the King of all the earth,* he is to be praised by means of a psalm (Hebrew, a *maskil*[7]).
- *Because the Lord, actually reigns over the nations of the world.* That God's reign is universal and stretches to all nations, calls for a response in terms of intelligent praise, of *maskil.*

While the nations may not realise that the Lord is ruling over their affairs, he, seated on his holy throne, is doing just that (v. 8). Thus the prophet, Michaiah, addressed Kings Ahab of Israel and Jehoshaphat of Judah, who were contemplating a joint attack on Ramoth Gilead, which had fallen into Syrian hands. He advised the two kings against the project by saying that he had seen the Lord sitting on his throne and saying, "who will entice Ahab into attacking Ramoth Gilead and going to his death there" (1 Kgs. 22:19). Thus the Lord seated on his throne was presented as controlling his own people, their international relationships and the nations with which they had contact, whether peaceful or involving war.

3. The implications of the Lord's kingship (v. 9)

The psalmist draws on the logic of what he has been saying to assert that nobles or, more probably, "the willing"[8] from the nations, gather together "as the people of the God of Abraham." The meaning may be that in the psalmist's day there were some people, who were leaders (princes or nobles) that were to some degree willing to acknowledge the Lord and accord to him their worship.

By way of example we think of Naaman the army commander from Syria who suffered from leprosy (2 Kgs. 5). We think of the King of Assyria and his response to Jonah's preaching (Jon. 3). We think also of the responses of Nebuchadnezzar of Babylon and Darius of Persia to the ministrations of

[7]The word *maskil*, appears in the heading of some psalms, e.g., Ps. 45, which, like Ps. 47, is associated with "the Sons of Korah." It seems to mean something like "knowledge" or "understanding" and so may indicate a didactic psalm. In this verse a translation like that of the AV – "sing with understanding" – seems appropriate.
[8]The Hebrew, *nedibhei*, can mean princes or nobles, but its primary meaning is "willing persons" and, despite modern versions, that seems more appropriate to the sense of the context.

Daniel and to the courage of his friends (Dan. 2:46f.; 3:28-30; 4:34-37; 6:25-27). Daniel had emphasised the sovereignty of the Lord over all nations. He told Nebuchadnezzar that the Most High was sovereign over the kingdoms of men and gave them to whoever he wished (Dan. 3:25). His words must have played a part in making Nebuchadnezzar and later Darius *willing* to acknowledge the Lord's sovereignty.

Early in the Old Testament story the Lord had promised to bless all nations through the descendants of Abraham (Gen. 12:2). In addition there was provision in the Mosaic laws for non-Israelites to join God's people and within certain limits to participate in their worship. Later Isaiah envisaged Gentiles seeking the Lord (Isa. 2:3, 11:10, 60:4-7, cf. 42:6, 49:6). Individuals, like the Ethiopian, Ebed-melech, who saved Jeremiah's life, must have been such seekers after the Lord (Jer. 38:1-13).

Thus there was sometimes an acknowledgment of the Lord's kingship from people, who were outside of God's covenant with Israel. It was, however, far from the complete submission that is envisaged here as the psalmist moves into a predictive/prophetic mode. He looks forward to a time when men from every nation will acknowledge the Lord, when, as Isaiah suggested and as Paul affirmed, that at the name of Jesus every knee in heaven, on earth and under the earth should bow and "confess that Jesus Christ is Lord, to the glory of God the Father" (Phil. 2:10, 11; cf. Isa. 45:23).

This expectation is based on what has been emphasised throughout this psalm – the kings of the earth are not self-sufficient sovereigns, not god-kings, but mortals, who ultimately belong to the Lord. He is the One who is greatly exalted and who is to be greatly honoured and praised. He is King of kings and Lord of lords.

Psalm 93

The first thing we notice about this psalm is the absence of a heading. As a result there is no evidence about its origin other than what may be gleaned from its own words. Many scholars think that celebration over the return of Jewish exiles from Babylon is the most likely setting in which it would have been written. There is, however, no specific indication of this in the psalm, though the mention of the Lord's might (vv. 1c, 4) could point in that direction.

In this short psalm of sixteen lines (five verses), the Lord is *spoken about* in the third person (vv. 1 and 4) and is *spoken to* in the first person (vv. 2, 3 and 5). This might suggest that the psalm was used in antiphonal singing in temple worship.

1. The Lord's kingly rule affirmed (v. 1)

> The LORD reigns, he is robed in majesty;
> > the LORD is robed in majesty
> > and is armed with strength
>
> —v. 1a

Kings wear robes that indicate their position and power. So it is with the Lord – he wears, he has put on and proclaims his kingly majesty by the exercise of his power – the Lord "is armed with strength." Because of this supreme strength he has firmly established the earth on which men live and has made it permanent – "it cannot be moved." It is as sure as his own throne. He is King over it and keeps it on an orderly rather than a chaotic course.

2. The Lord addressed in worship (vv. 2-3)

> Your throne was established long ago;
> > you are from all eternity.
>
> —v. 2

As the author approaches the Lord, he acknowledges the eternal nature of his kingship. His sovereignty is eternal and unalterable. The human forces opposed to him are likened to overwhelming floods of water (NIV, "seas"). The repetition of this thought in verse 3 – "the seas have lifted up their pounding waves" – suggests continual opposition to the Lord. The thought seems akin to that of Psalm 2:2-4:

> The kings of the earth take their stand
> > and the rulers gather together against the LORD
> > and against his Anointed One. ...

3. The Lord's power re-affirmed (v. 4)

Again the Lord is *spoken about* rather than *spoken to*. He is mightier than all those who oppose him. He reigns in power over all the earth.

> Mightier than the thunder of the great waters
>> mightier than the breakers of the sea —
>> the LORD on high is mighty.

—v. 4

4. The Lord again addressed in worship (v. 5)

> Your statutes stand firm;
>> holiness adorns your house
>> for endless days, O LORD.

The Lord is eternal and his government of the earth and its peoples is absolutely stable. He does not vacillate and so he and what he ordains are absolutely trustworthy.[9]

His house – undoubtedly, the Jerusalem temple – is characterised by and is adorned with holiness. As the Lord's dwelling place on earth it was a sacred building set apart for the worship of the One who dwelt in it. It was therefore to be treated with proper respect and reverence and used only for its special sacred purposes.

Because the Lord is eternally King of all the earth, there could never be anything ephemeral or temporary about his arrangements (his statutes) for the government of his world and of his creatures. They and his own holy nature are of eternal validity. They are "for endless days" (v. 5c), because he, the Lord, is eternally King (vv. 1-2).

The message of this psalm is, then, that **The Lord is King** and reigns forever over his entire creation. He reigns over the natural realm and over human life. He rules over our world and over our lives today.

---

[9] Alternatively: "who he is and what he ordains are" or "his name/person/character."

CHAPTER 10

PERSONAL LAMENTS I

Dirge or lament songs were mentioned briefly on page 12. In them an individual or a community describes some situation of danger and reacts to it. Sometimes, as in the Book of Job, the main complaint is that God is himself inflicting suffering and sorrow on the psalmist or on those for whom he speaks.

In the case of individuals the suffering can be due to material loss, physical suffering, mental agony, spiritual barrenness or a combination of these. In the case of the community lament the focus is usually on either the oppression of godly people by the unscrupulous or the oppression of the whole community by an enemy.

Lament psalms often begin with a cry to God for help. Sometimes this is linked with a profession of trust in him. Sometimes he is praised in advance for what the suppliant believes he will do. It is as if his reputation is so at stake that he could not do other than deliver the suppliant(s).

In this and the next chapter we examine individual or personal laments of which there are around forty examples in the psalter. Those, usually listed as such, include Pss. 3; 5; 6; 7; 13; 17; 22; 25; 26; 28; 31; 35; 38; 39; 40; 42/3; 51; 52; 54; 55; 56; 59; 61; 63; 64; 69; 70; 71; 86; 88; 94; 102; 109; 120; 130; 140; 141; 142; 143. Many of these psalms also display the characteristics of other psalm-types. Some contain imprecatory passages in which divine punishment is invoked on those who by troubling the psalmist or his people are seen as enemies of God. We will discuss the problems raised by these passages in Chapter 25 below. In this chapter we will, however, concentrate on Psalm 22.

Psalm 22

This is the most quoted psalm in the New Testament, where it is often related to Christ and his sufferings. While it has that predictive aspect and anticipates the sufferings of Christ, it cannot be held that it has no other significance.

It is, first and foremost, a psalm of David spoken and written nearly a thousand years before the coming of Christ, a psalm that had meaning for David and for the men of his day. It is full of David's feelings and his personal pain.

But it is also timeless and has meaning for suffering men and women in every age, not least for suffering believers in our own day. David's faith provides a model for us and for believers in every age. He was brought through adversity and suffering into an enhanced enjoyment of God's presence, quite literally from the "hell" of desolation to the "heaven" of divine deliverance. The message is that all, who truly rely on the Lord, can have a similar experience.

The psalm has two major sections. The first (vv. 1-22) is pure lament, a moan or a complaint, in which the psalmist tells us how he felt about his situation and how he prayed to be delivered from it. In the second (vv. 22-31) David celebrates God's goodness and asks others to do the same.

1. David's lament (vv. 1-22)

1) His problem with God's silence (vv 1-8)

David was in a desperate situation but he doesn't tell us exactly what it was, a fact that contributes to the psalm's timelessness and relevance to every similar situation. In verses 1-5 he complains about what he perceived as God's inaction. He asks, as Job did and as we often do, the often unanswerable *"why* question:"

> My God, My God, *why* have you forsaken me?
>> *Why* are you so far from saving me,
>> so far from the words of my groaning?

> —v. 1

Why, he asks, have you, my Lord and God, given me up to such trouble. The verb he uses (Hebrew, *'atsabh*) often means "to leave" or "to forsake," but it can also mean to hand over, to commit, to release or even to set free. Here

David was not necessarily saying that God had completely forsaken him. Rather his emphasis was that God had deliberately handed him over to adversity and suffering. In quoting these words, Jesus was probably making the same point (cf. Acts 2:23).

Nonetheless David was astounded that his prayers, his crying out (his roaring, AV) by day and night had produced no answer from the One, who was enthroned as the Holy One and as the praise of Israel (v. 2). He was confused because the Lord had responded to the prayers and the desperation of his forefathers. "In you," he tells the Lord, "they trusted and you delivered them ... in you they trusted and were not disappointed" (vv. 4 & 5).

His faith told him to trust in the Lord just as his forefathers had done. Their cries to God had been answered, but his own cries were not being answered. The Lord had, so it seemed, forsaken him and was "far from saving" him, far from the words of his groaning (v. 1b).

He knew that the Lord was the only One with the power and authority to help and save him (v. 3). Quite naturally he asked Why, Why, Why? Why, if earlier generations had enjoyed God's saving power, was God not now consistent and granting him deliverance?

Recalling the deliverances enjoyed by his ancestors drove him to serious self-pity:

> I am a worm and not a man,
>> scorned by men and despised by the people.
> All who see me mock me;
>> they hurl insults, shaking their heads.
>
> —vv. 6, 7

Such an outburst points to a man who was seriously upset and in some anguish. To add to his suffering his opponents were sarcastically lampooning and making fun of his faith:

> He trusts in the LORD;
>> let the LORD rescue him.
> Let him deliver him,
>> since he delights in him.
>
> —v. 8

Those words were picked up and used in a similar mocking way by "the chief priests, the teachers of the law and the elders" who mocked Jesus as he hung on the cross (Matt. 27:41, 42). They are often echoed rather cruelly by those, who ask stressed out or depressed folk in our day to have faith in God and "to pull themselves together" at a time when their spirits are so low and so gripped by despair that their personalities are more or less paralysed. Such people tend to be unable to act on any advice that is given to them and in many cases regard advice as blame that increases their despair. Those who try to help them need to be extremely careful of what they say!

2) He pictures his sufferings (vv. 12-18)

As part of his prayer the psalmist uses a number of pictures drawn from the more fearsome beasts of the animal world to describe his debilitated and emaciated condition. With remarkable frankness he told the Lord exactly what he felt.

He described those, who were troubling him, as bulls, as lions and as vicious dogs. This is vivid poetic language. Strong bulls, reared on the lush grasslands of Bashan, surrounded him (v.12). Roaring lions, like those engaged in tearing apart some unfortunate prey were opening their mouths and threatening to devour him[1] (v. 13). Dogs, probably ravenous wolves, were, he says, waiting to tear him apart (v. 16a).

The threat to David arose from evil men who were acting like wild animals:

> A band of evil men has encircled me,
>> they have pierced my hands and my feet.
>
> —v. 16b, c

In verses 14-18 David again mixed his metaphors as he described how he felt. He felt as if he had become a flabby sack, that is, a skin bottle for wine or water, from which the fluid had been poured out. He felt that his bones had disintegrated and were totally out of joint (v. 14). At the same time he had lost the courage he needed for life and for his role as Israel's king. His heart had

---

[1]Incidentally lions, akin to those of Africa, were common in SW Asia in Bible times and there were still some in Syria in the 1800s AD.

become like wax and had melted away. His strength had gone – dried up like a potsherd, a useless fragment of pottery that would never again become wet from holding water (v. 15a). It left him mangled and pierced, a virtual skeleton fit only for burial!

Worse still these evil men were encircling him and were causing him pain and enfeeblement: "they have pierced my hands and my feet" (v. 16c). The emphasis could, however, be more psychological than physical – they make me feel like a convicted villain mutilated by having my hands and feet pierced or even cut off.

In addition David had lost his appetite and had lost weight. He was visibly emaciated and could easily count all his bones. As a result people were staring at him, gloating over him and waiting to see him die so that they could divide up his garments casting lots to discover who would receive what (v.18). In a word, life didn't seem worth living and he seems to have been envisaging his own death. He even went as far as to accuse God of ordaining that to happen, "You lay me in the dust of death" (v. 15c).

3) He prays for deliverance (vv. 9-11, 19-22)

As David bore the burden of the adversity the Lord had placed upon him, he may have felt abandoned, but underneath his uncertainties and doubts he still had faith in God. He would therefore pray. And he did pray earnestly that God would be near him and, when there was no other helper available, would help him as he continued to face trouble from his enemies.

As he pleaded with God, he acknowledged, in a clear expression of faith, his dependence on God. Despite his sense of desolation, despite the caustic criticism of his enemies, he could say:

> *Yet* you brought me out of the womb;
>   you made me trust in you
>   even at my mother's breast.
> From birth I was cast upon you;
> from my mother's womb you have
>   been my God.

—vv. 9, 10

Even though his experiences were dark and mysterious, he clung to his basic faith. He believed that God had brought him to birth and had sustained his life even since then – he had no God other than the Lord. He had been born into a community that believed in, or, at least, that regarded itself as basically believing in the Lord: "from my mother's womb you have been **my** God." Ultimately he himself was resting in and relying on the Lord and could address him as his strength—"O my strength" (v. 19). He knew that no other source of strength existed.

In verses 11 and 19-22 David pleaded that the Lord would quickly rescue him:

> Do not be far from me,
>> for trouble is near
>> and there is no-one to help.

—v. 11

> But you, O Lord, be not far off;
>> O my Strength, come quickly to help me.
> Deliver my life from the sword,
>> my precious life from the power of the dogs.
> Rescue me from the mouth of the lions;
>> save me from the horns of the wild oxen.

—vv. 19-21

There is a difficulty with the AV and NIV renderings of verse 21. The second line, "Save me from the horns of the wild oxen," reads as parallel to and as repeating the thought of the first, "Rescue me from the mouth of the lions." However, while the verb in the first line is a call for help (Hebrew, *yasha'*, meaning to deliver, rescue or save) that in the second (Hebrew, *anah*, meaning to speak or answer) seems to affirm that an answer had already been received. Translated literally this second line reads, "From the horns of the wild oxen you have answered me." Perhaps, as HC Leupold[2] suggests, the psalmist thought of himself as having been caught up on or about to be gored by the horns of an

---

[2]*Exposition of the Psalms*, Evangelical Press, p. 203.

ox, when suddenly the Lord answered his prayer and delivered him from the danger of death.

Because of this the NRSV treats the first line of the verse, "Rescue me from the mouth of the lions," as the climax of David's lament. It then leaves a break and presents the second line as introducing a new theme and a new man, one who is no longer seeking God's deliverance, but is rather enjoying it.

2. David's exultant praise (vv. 21b, 22)

Joining verse 21b with verse 22 the New Revised Standard Version (NRSV) reads:

> From the horns of the wild oxen you have rescued me.
>> I will tell of your name to my brothers and sisters;
>> in the midst of the congregation I will praise you.

In these lines David has emerged from the darkness of physical and mental agony. Suddenly his heart was lifted from its gloom. Because he had been rescued, he would bear witness to his experience and proclaim the Lord's name to all and sundry, to his family and to the wider family of the assembled congregation of his people. He seems to envisage doing this at one of the great festivals when crowds that gathered in Jerusalem would provide a great opportunity to testify to God's salvation.

3. David's plea for praise (vv. 23-31)

David's faith had conquered his doubt and perplexity. He would not, despite everything that had happened to him, let go of God. Deep down he knew that prayer was not pointless and that God had not withdrawn from or in any sense forsaken him and so he had turned to prayer.

1) Praise from Israel (vv23-26)

David says he will exuberantly declare God's name, that is God's reputation and honour. He will call on the congregation to join him in praising the Lord:

> You who fear the LORD, praise him!

All you descendants of Jacob, honour him!
Revere him, all you descendants of Israel!
For he has not despised or disdained
the suffering and afflicted one;
he has not hidden his face from him
but has listened to his cry for help.

—vv. 23, 24

When David complained that God was not answering his prayers for help (vv. 1, 2), his perception had been wrong – the reverse had been the case. In his time of crisis and trial the Lord had been with him. He had not been abandoned.

Now that the anxiety of the earlier verses had gone and he had been rescued, the psalmist found that praise was his only option. He was assured that God had not despised or deserted him but had been with him and had listened to his cries for help (v. 24).

In verse 25 he says that the praise he would offer would be a fulfilling of vows he had made to God, presumably during his time of crisis. Those vows probably entailed bringing thank-offerings in the form of animals to be sacrificed to the Lord and eaten by worshippers at a festival meal. By virtue of this the poor would join him in giving praise to God – they would "eat and be satisfied" (v. 26a) – and go on to add more praise to the celebration. Because his hope was that they would enjoy ongoing divine blessing, he could say, "may your hearts live for ever!" (v. 26c).

2) Praise from all mankind (vv. 27-31)

The psalmist envisages jubilation extending to "the ends of the earth." He thinks of the whole human race returning from estrangement and alienation to allegiance and adoration: "all the ends of the earth will remember and turn to the Lord, and all the families of the nations will bow down before him."

The point seems to be that the testimony the Psalmist would bring to God's saving intervention in his own life would influence other peoples. They would, always remember his message and would turn around and bow down before the Lord, who has sovereign rights over all peoples:

For dominion belongs to the LORD

> and he rules over the nations.
>
> —v. 28

Verses 29 and 30 convey the exuberant enthusiasm of the psalmist and his hope that his testimony would not only influence the people of his day but those of subsequent generations. His own lifetime would not be long enough for the proclamation of the good news of how God had delivered him. Future generations would worship the Lord (v. 30) and they too would proclaim the story:

> Posterity will serve him;
>> future generations will be told about the LORD.
>
> —v. 30

> They will proclaim his righteousness
>> to a people yet unborn –
>>> for he has done it.
>
> —v. 31

The NEB helpfully renders the final two lines as:

> declaring to a people yet unborn
>> that this was his doing

Such then is the content of Psalm 22.

4. The message of the psalm

This psalm addressed the worshipping people of David's time and it addresses subsequent generations of the Lord's people, who encounter affliction and anguish of soul. It speaks especially to those for whom God seems silent and for whom his help seems non-existent. It says that:

1. We are in error, when we feel that God is not answering our prayers in a way that we would like and that he is leaving us to bear some burden alone. He has promised never to leave us. He is, in fact, with us in the trials that distress us, just as much as in the pleasures that elate us. He is with us all the time, even when we think he has abandoned us.

2.   We, like the psalmist, can call on him and trust him. We can expect and, in his good time, experience his deliverance. Then, like David, we can join with other believers in giving him our thanks and in proclaiming what he has done for us. The second part of the psalm teaches us that praise to God is a priority and that every experience of God's goodness should lead us to paeans of exuberant praise and to bold testimony. Indeed, David gives praise with as much or even more energy than he used to express his complaints and his supplications.

5. The predictive role of the psalm

The psalm has, of course, a clear application to and a clear fulfilment in our Lord's sufferings and death. Its words are presented as pointing to and finding a second, a more ultimate fulfilment in the sufferings of our Lord:

- The Roman soldiers, who disposed of our Lord's garments (John 19:24), were fulfilling verse 18, which says, "They divide my garments among them and cast lots for my clothing."
- Our Lord's cry of dereliction – "My God, My God, why have you forsaken me" – used the very words of the first verse of our psalm. That cry shows that those words had a fulfilment and a meaning beyond the experiences of David.
- The chief priests and elders mocked Jesus using words from the psalm—"He trusts in God. Let God rescue him now …" (Matt. 27:43' quoting Ps. 22:8a).

It is only with awe and bated breath that we can speak of the dreadful moment when Jesus died. We have no idea, and no way of gaining an idea of what he suffered as he bore the load of human sin, the divine punishment for the sins of the world; "He himself bore our sins in his body on the tree" (1 Pet. 2:24). As the hymn has it:

> We may not know, we cannot tell,
>   what pains he had to bear
> but we believe it was for us
>   he hung and suffered there.

As God, his Father, laid that load on him, the opening words of our psalm encapsulated his thought—"Eloi, Eloi, lama sabachthani?"—meaning, "My God, my God, why have you forsaken me?" or "why have you laid this burden on me?" The terror of horrific suffering made him feel alone. Why, Why, Why, he asked, was his Father *imposing* this load on him? It was as if God had forsaken him, but, in fact, that was not the case. God was in his moments of suffering. The heart of the Father bled with his heart. The Father shared in the agony!

But the suffering of death was followed by the victory of resurrection and by a restoration of the joy of his Father's presence and fellowship and soon by elevation through the ascension to the Father's right hand.

Ultimately this is the message of the Gospel, the message we believers are expected to proclaim. And when we emerge from bitter experiences, like those that encompassed David, we should, by virtue of our experiences, be better equipped to call on men and women of the world to "remember and turn to the Lord," and to "bow down before him" (v. 27).

CHAPTER 11

❦

PERSONAL LAMENTS II

Psalm 51

This is one of seven psalms (Pss. 6; 32; 38; 51; 102; 130; 143), which express penitence. It is a moving expression of deep grief over sin.

1. The heading

The psalm is attributed to David at the time, when his adultery with Bathsheba was brought to light by Nathan. Its language certainly fits that situation, because David, having seen the Lord withdraw his Spirit from his predecessor, Saul, would fear that his own sin might also lead to a loss of the Spirit's anointing for kingly office (v. 11).

Some scholars find difficulties in connection with this commonly accepted view of the psalm:

- The confession of sin *against God alone* (v. 4) doesn't exactly fit David's case. He also sinned against Bathsheba and against her husband, Uriah!

  But, since the focus is on the psalmist's relationship to God, this problem is not of great significance. Expressions of penitence are not always complete! A contrite heart is the vital component. Nonetheless the confession of "bloodguilt" (v. 14) could be an acknowledgement of the murder of Uriah.
- Verses 18 and 19 seem to imply that, at the time of writing, the walls of Jerusalem were in ruins a scenario more appropriate to the times of Nehemiah (440BC) than of David half a millennium earlier.

But, while it could be that these two verses were added later to adapt the psalm to express the penitence of the nation and the expectation of its restoration to God's favour, it could also be, as some scholars maintain, Davidic in origin.

• Jewish records showing that the psalm was used in public worship on the Day of Atonement suggest that it related to national repentance and to the removal of accumulated guilt from the nation. Some scholars think that a writer put national contrition into the mouth of an individual who might well have been David.

But it could also be that, because David saw his sin as threatening Jerusalem/Zion and also Israelite national life, he prayed for national as well as for personal forgiveness and restoration.

• The high spirituality of the psalm is said to belong to a later age than that of David and to have been influenced by the ministries of the great prophets. It is argued that only someone so influenced could have had such intense feelings of guilt (cf. Isaiah 6:5; Neh. 8 & 9 etc.). The psalm is seen, therefore, as a later production intended to epitomise national contrition in personal terms.

But there is with this, as with many psalms, a timelessness that prevents us from tying it down to any one particular era. It fits the experience of David, of Isaiah, of Ezekiel or of any other saint of old and it fits our experience today. As someone has said, even the advent of the Gospel has not superseded the spiritual language of this psalm – it merely deepened it.

The psalm is entirely made up of intercessory prayer. Whatever the scholars say about its origin, the psalmist is so burdened by his guilt that he can do nothing other than plead for God's forgiveness. With the possible exception of verses 18 and 19, which may have been added later, it is a unit that does not readily yield clear divisions. Any analysis – the one that follows included – is therefore somewhat arbitrary.[1]

---

[1]Users of the Hebrew Bible should note that the heading, which is longer than usual, is allocated two verses so that our v. 1 is its v. 3 etc.

2. Pleading for pardon (vv. 1-12)

1) The psalmist's basic prayer (vv. 1, 2)

The psalmist grounds his appeal for forgiveness on the character of the Lord, which had been revealed to Moses in the proclamation recorded in Exodus 34:6 & 7: "the Lord, the compassionate and gracious God, slow to anger, abounding in love and faithfulness, maintaining love to thousands, and forgiving wickedness, rebellion and sin.[2]" His only hope lay in the unfailing love and the great compassion of the Lord.

The first four lines are in chiastic form with the fourth line repeating the thought of the first and the third repeating that of the second.

> A) Have mercy on me, O God,
> 　　B) according to your unfailing love;
> 　　B) according to your great compassion
> A) blot out my transgressions
>
> 　　　　　　　　　　　　　　　　　　　　　　　　—v. 1

The meaning of the fourth line is then expanded as its thought is repeated in lines five and six. Thus in verse 2, Blot out my transgressions. (Hebrew, *pesha'*) is expanded:

> Wash away all my iniquity (Hebrew, *'awon*)
> 　　and cleanse me from my sin (Hebrew, *chattah*).

The three verbs, "blot out," "wash away" and "cleanse" all ask for the removal of the stain and guilt of sin and the three nouns, "transgressions," "iniquity" and "sin," are, as we have already noted, the three words the Old Testament uses to give a comprehensive picture of everything that offends God. On each count forgiving grace was needed and on each David requested a radical work of grace to blot out, to wash away and to cleanse him of his sin and guilt. The character

---

[2]These categories of offence are translations respectively of the Hebrew words, *'awon, pesha and chattah. 'Awon* is man's inner corruption, the fallen nature that causes him to offend God. *Pesha* refers to deliberate acts of rebellion, of transgressing God's law. *Chattah*, meaning a 'missing of the mark', is the more general word for the whole gamut of failure to attain to God's standards.

of God – unfailing in love and greatly compassionate – gave David an assurance that the forgiveness he needed would be forthcoming.

2) The psalmist's penitential confession (vv. 3-6)

Again we have skilful parallelism. First, there are three couplets (vv. 3 & 4) each of which is a straightforward synonymous parallelism. Joined together in a constructive fashion, they build up a bigger picture moving from the sinner's wrongs to the absolute rectitude of God's justice :

> For I know my transgressions,
>   and my sin is always before me.
> Against you, you only have I sinned
> and done what is evil in your sight,
> so that you are proved right when you speak
> and justified when you judge.

The remaining two couplets (vv. 5 & 6) repeat the thoughts of the first three except that instead of speaking about transgression (*pesha*) and sin (*chattah*), they focus on the psalmists underlying wickedness, the corruption (the *'awon*) of his heart:

> Surely I was sinful at birth
>   sinful from the time my mother conceived me.

Read literally, the Hebrew is, "I was brought forth in iniquity and in sin my mother conceived me."

These words are widely regarded as forming the clearest statement of 'original sin' in the Old Testament. David was absolutely clear about his condition before God. He was born with a wicked heart, born perverse and dominated by iniquity. He had been such from the moment of his conception. It was not enough, therefore, for him to confess sins. He must also acknowledge the iniquity of his heart that was totally at odds with the truth and the wisdom that belong to God, and also that the Lord desires inner truthfulness in his creatures:

> Surely you desire truth in the inner parts;
> You teach me wisdom in the inmost place.
>
> —v. 6

Aware of the purity, integrity and wisdom of God, David saw himself as a miserable offender. He was like Isaiah, who seeing the glory of the Lord cried out: "Woe to me! ... I am ruined! For I am a man of unclean lips ...my eyes have seen the King, the LORD Almighty" (Isa. 6:5).

3) The psalmist's petitions for restoration (vv. 7-12)

Each of these six verses is a couplet, in which the second line repeats in different words the thought of the first. In addition there is an element of parallelism, between the thoughts of verses 7 and 10:

> Cleanse me with hyssop, and I shall be clean;
> wash me, and I shall be whiter than snow.
>
> —v. 7

> Create in me a pure heart, O God,
> and renew a steadfast spirit within me.
>
> —v. 10

In these verses the psalmist is asking the Lord to remove from him all trace of the stain caused by his sin. In the context of Israelite religion he thinks of ceremonial cleanliness. The background is the use of sprigs of hyssop as sprinkling devices for blood (Lev. 14:6) or for water (Num. 19:18). The rituals in which hyssop was used related to cleansing from leprosy and from the ceremonial defilement of contact with a corpse. David applied them metaphorically – spiritually – to his own sinful condition and to his need for cleansing from the entanglements, the guilt and the penalties, of sin. He was desperate for cleansing – to become inwardly as clean and pure as the whiteness of freshly fallen snow.

Verse 8 tells us that David wanted to be freed from the burden and the pains of guilt. For him it seemed that God had veritably crushed his bones. He had also expressed that pain in Psalm 32:3 and 4, where he tells us that God's hand had been heavy upon him. Here he is desperate to return to a life of true happiness so that even the bones that had been crushed could come back to life and vitality and join in his overall rejoicing:

> Let me hear joy and gladness
>> let the bones you have crushed rejoice.

—v. 8

In verse 9 his prayer seems to become more intense as he asks the Lord not to look at or hold his sins against him. He wants all memory of them to be blotted out:

> Hide your face from my sins
>> and blot out my iniquity.

—v. 9

In verse 11 the psalmist is worried lest he be driven away from the presence of the Lord and away from what was the source of his happiness. He didn't want to be left as a God-forsaken fugitive, cut off from the presence that meant more to him than anything else. We remember his commitment to remain permanently in close fellowship with the Lord—"I will dwell in the house of the LORD for ever" (or "for the rest of my days," Ps. 23:6).

The second line of this verse shows his fear in another way, as he prays that God would not remove his Holy Spirit from him. If that had happened, it would have indicated that David had lost God's favour and his special anointing as king. That would have been disaster and the end of his kingship, as had, indeed, been the case with his predecessor, Saul (1 Sam. 16:14). Hence David's plea:

> Do not cast me from your presence
>> or take your Holy Spirit from me.

—v. 11

In verse 12 he moves on to request that the joy of salvation – something he had obviously enjoyed in the past – would be restored to him. It seems that he had been experiencing the kind of separation from the Lord that the Jews of Isaiah's day knew: "Your iniquities have separated you from your God; your sins have hidden his face from you, so that he will not hear" (Isa. 59:2). He therefore asked

God to restore the relationship he had previously enjoyed with him but which had been destroyed by his sin.

But more than that he wanted to be changed inwardly. He wanted God to give him "a willing spirit," to work within him so that he would become freely and spontaneously desirous of the things that would please God. He wanted to be sustained in – kept permanently in – such a condition.

> Restore to me the joy of your salvation
>> and grant me a willing spirit, to sustain me.

—v. 12

4) The abiding value of the psalmists confession

David's words in the first twelve verses of the psalm can be used by repentant sinners in every age. Since no specific sins are mentioned, they provide every penitent sinner with suitable words with which to confess sinfulness.

In modern evangelical life open profession of penitence like this seems to be a rarity. Past sin is often neither confessed nor acknowledged. Those who testify mostly say that they turned to God in a time of trouble or need and finding that he helped them, they became believers. If that type of testimony means a genuine turning to the Lord, it is wonderful and in no way to be despised or criticised. Indeed, since penitence for sin is essentially inward, a matter of the heart, it may be that it is present in those who do not openly acknowledge it. But, nonetheless evidence of repentance is important. John the Baptist demanded it of his hearers: "Produce fruit in keeping with repentance" (Matt. 3:8). And Paul defined his message to King Agrippa in similar terms: "I preached that they should repent and turn to God and **prove their repentance by their deeds**" (Acts 26:20). The real evidence of repentance is, then, to be gleaned, not merely from a profession of it but from a changed life-style, from the fruit of godly living that it produces If faith in Christ is real it will produce love for him and works that are harmonious with his will.

Nonetheless it has to be said that the biblical picture of repentance is that sins – whether of gross immoralities like those of David, or of the selfish trust in one's own resources and abilities that characterises modern life – are confessed, repudiated and forsaken.

Jesus illustrated this in his parable of the Lost Son (Luke 15:11-32), in which the prodigal came home confessing his sin: "I have sinned against heaven (i.e., against God) and against you. I am no longer worthy to be called your son" (v. 21). Just like David, he acknowledged his sin and his consequent guilt and blameworthiness before his father. In grace that father, like God, extended grace to the penitent and granted him a renewed father-son relationship.

Paul speaks of "godly sorrow" that brings repentance, that leads to salvation and that leaves no regret (2 Cor. 7:10). Repentance begins in such sorrow. The sinner weeps over his sins and, like the tax collector (AV, publican) in Jesus' parable, comes before God crying, "God, have mercy on me, a sinner" (Luke 18:13). Where, we must ask, is there evidence of such sorrow-initiated repentance today? Where, indeed, each of us must ask ourselves, is the evidence of such sorrow in our own hearts?

And we must also ask ourselves if we are still truly penitent? The Christian is indeed expected to live a life of continuing repentance. John tells us that, if we think we are without sin, we deceive ourselves (1 John 1: 8). We will always have sinful natures and specific sins from which we need to repent. But as John could go on to affirm, God has given us a wonderful assurance that in grace he forgives the penitent who confesses his sin to him:

> If we confess our sins, he is faithful and just and will forgive us our sins
> and purify us from all unrighteousness.
>
> —1 John 1:9

Let us make sure, then, that we have truly repented of our sins and truly expressed our sorrow over our inherent wickedness. And let us daily examine our thoughts, our words and our actions and confess to him all that we know to be unworthy of one of his followers. Then in faith let us lay hold of his promise and receive his forgiveness.

At this point the lament element of this great psalm comes to an end. As in most lament songs the emphasis proceeds to a positive expression of confidence in the Lord.

3. The prospects for the pardoned sinner (vv. 13-17)

In these verses the psalmist envisages himself enjoying God's forgiveness and making appropriate responses to it.

1) Serving as a teacher-evangelist

> Then I will teach transgressors your ways,
>   and sinners will turn back to you.
> Save me from bloodguilt, O God,
>   the God who saves me
>   and my tongue will sing of your righteousness.
> O LORD, open my lips
>   and my mouth will declare your praise.
>
> —vv. 13-15

The psalmist is confidently resolved to respond to God's forgiving grace. He will show others the follies of transgressing God's laws. He will not keep the great blessing he has received to himself. He is even assured that his evangelistic teaching will result in many people returning to the Lord. He will therefore use his tongue, his lips and his mouth to declare God's righteousness and his praise.

The prayer of verse 14 is quite intense: "save me from bloodguilt, O God, the God who saves me." Some take this as David confessing that he had murdered Uriah. Others regard it as a more general prayer for deliverance from the guilt of offences that, under Israelite law would have attracted the death penalty. In either case he hopes for forgiveness and strength to declare God's praise.

2) Prioritising inner contrition (vv. 16, 17)

> You do not delight in sacrifice, or I would bring it;
>   you do not take pleasure in burnt offerings.
>
> —v. 16

Some commentators regard these two lines as a blanket rejection of the whole Mosaic/Levitical system of sacrifice. But the fact is that those sacrifices were not provided for deliberate sins, like those of David, and so were not applicable to David's cleansing (See Num. 15:22-31 and Ezek. 45:20). It has even been suggested that, if David had attempted to gain cleansing by that route, he would have been making his sin merely a matter of weakness or failure and denying its real seriousness as deliberate transgression.

This leads into what is the climactic affirmation of the psalm:

> The sacrifices of God are a broken spirit;
>   a broken and contrite heart,
> O God, you will not despise.

                                                                        —v. 17

HC Leupold says that this is one of the deepest expressions of spiritual insight in the whole Old Testament. He adds, "A pardoned sinner alone knows what it means" (Exposition of the Psalms, EP, p. 407). The point seems to be that for wilful sin, such as is confessed in the psalm, God could not be propitiated by animal sacrifice. David's hope, any person's hope, lies in coming before God with a penitent spirit, with a heart that is broken by sorrow and contrition.

That is what the Psalmist brought to the Lord and that is what he tells us we have to bring in order to receive God's forgiveness. The implication is that God will accept the penitence and bring the penitent into a new relationship of peace – of reconciliation – with himself.

The truths of these two verses are terribly neglected in our self-centred world. People today have little realisation of the truth that they are born with sinful natures and that even their best actions fall short of what God requires. They see themselves as essentially good.

With no sense of need to seek God's mercy, they dislike the message of repentance and the requirement to be broken in sorrow before God because of their sin. The truth is that to be right with God we all need to be broken before him, who deigns to dwell only with those who are contrite and lowly in spirit (cf. Isa. 57:15). Pride in oneself, in one's abilities and attainments, has to be replaced by the humility of penitence and the cry for mercy: "God, have mercy on me, a sinner."

Postscript (vv. 18, 19)

Earlier in this study it was noted that these verses may have been added to the psalm at a time when Jerusalem and its walls were desolate, a time like that which confronted Nehemiah around 440 BC. At first sight they seem more fitted to communal than to personal prayer:

> In your good pleasure make Zion prosper;
>> build up the walls of Jerusalem.
> Then there will be righteous sacrifices,
>> whole burnt offerings to delight you;
>> then bulls will be offered on your altar.

This prayer seems to be an acknowledgment that, having been reconciled to the Lord, the psalmist can now seek his favour without fear of rejection because of transgression (Isa. 59:2 etc.). Whatever the life-setting of these verses, they anticipate the Lord's acceptance of his penitent people.

Some scholars have seen the commendatory view of sacrifices in verse 19 as at odds with the emphasis of verse 16, but it has to be remembered that this is an Old Testament writing coming from a time when the old covenant arrangements still applied. Sacrifice in honour of the Lord according to the rules revealed to Moses was therefore perfectly in order for a forgiven person and/or for a restored people.

For Christians the Old Testament sacrifices are no more, because they have found their fulfilment in the infinitely greater sacrifice of Christ. In him there is cleansing from sin (1 John 1:9). Once cleansed, the believer can and, indeed, must offer himself totally and in total commitment to the Lord as a sacrifice of thanksgiving (Rom. 12:1, 2).

We must make sure that the contrition so wonderfully expressed in this psalm becomes an abiding and a genuine element in our walk with God.

CHAPTER 12

COMMUNITY LAMENTS

Some psalms are expressions of national or community distress. In many of them God is challenged to vindicate his honour by delivering his people from whoever or whatever is troubling them.

There are sixteen of these psalms –Psalms 12; 14; 44; 53; 58; 60; 74; 79; 80; 83; 85; 90; 106; 123; 126 and 137. In several of them plural communal references, like "we" or "our" alternate with singular personal ones, like "I" and "my." For example, in Psalm 44 we find:

- v. 1 **We** have heard with **our** ears, O God.
- v. 4 You are **my** King and **my** God ...
- v. 5 Through you **we** push back **our** enemies.
- v. 6 **I** do not trust in **my** bow.

Some scholars think that this happened because of antiphonal singing in which a soloist alternated with a larger choir. Its incidence can sometimes make it difficult to distinguish between communal and personal laments.

For this study we will look at Psalms 74 and 137.

Psalm 74

This psalm carries the heading, "a *maskil* of Asaph." The significance of maskil, which some think is related to a verb meaning "to be wise," is far from clear. It is generally regarded as a musical term of uncertain meaning. Asaph, to whom the psalm is attributed, was a Levite appointed by David as a senior praise leader

(1 Chr. 16:4, 5; cf. 16:39). His sons served as musicians from the time of David till the restoration after the Exile (1Chr. 25:2; Ezr. 3:10 etc.).

Though this psalm is placed among Davidic psalms in Book III of the Psalter, it is clearly much later than David's time. Its references to Israelite humiliation best fit the period after the fall of Jerusalem to Nebuchadnezzar in 586/7 BC. The land was overrun and Jerusalem with its temple was in ruins, a story told in some detail in 2 Kings 25. There was a fear that the adversity of the day might be prolonged or even become worse as the enemy continued to mock and revile God (v. 10).

The psalm has something of a chiastic – A, B, B, A – structure. Its first and fourth (A) sections parallel each other as appeals for God's help. Its second and third (B) sections contrast God's present inaction with his past powerful activities.

1. Appeal for God's help (vv. 1-3 — Stanza A1)

The psalm voices the thought and the feelings of the Lord's people, who felt that he had permanently rejected them and that his anger was smouldering against them. They were, therefore, blaming God for their humiliation and were asking why he was treating them in this way. They seem to have forgotten that they had become apostate and thoroughly unrighteous and had provoked the Lord's anger. They were right in thinking that their humiliation had been brought about by the Lord, but they were totally wrong in not confessing to him their sin that was the cause of what he was doing to them.

Nonetheless they were wise enough to ask that he would remember and return to the people he had redeemed of old (v.2). They didn't pray for restored buildings but for a renewal of the Lord's presence in Zion. In the past he had been present there (v. 2c), and now they pray that he would make his way towards "these everlasting ruins" – the sanctuary the enemy had destroyed (v. 3b) – and make himself present there again.

2. God's present inaction (vv. 4-11 — Stanza B1)

In these verses the depredations of the enemy are described in terms that harmonise with the description of the desolation of Jerusalem by the Babylonians in the Book of Lamentations. That enemy was roaring in triumph among the ruins of the temple, the place where in the past the people had met with God:

- He had set up on that sacred site his own insignia (his emblems) as signs of his victory (v. 4b).
- He had hacked apart the temple's carved panelling and had burned the sanctuary to the ground (vv. 5-7a).
- He had desecrated the dwelling place of the Lord's name (v. 7b; cf. Deut. 12:4-7).
- He had boasted that he would completely crush Israel/Judah and destroy every meeting place for the worship of the Lord (v. 8).
- He had deprived God's people of their own insignia and of miraculous signs that would have indicated his presence (v. 9a). In doing so, he had deprived them of the prophets, who might have predicted how long the agony would last (v. 9b).

Deprived in these ways they could only cry out asking God:

- How long he would allow the enemy to mock him and to revile his name (v. 10).
- Why he was holding back his hand and was failing to destroy the enemy (v. 11).

3. God's actions in the past (vv. 12-17 — Stanza B2)

The psalmist tells God that from of old he had been King[1] and Saviour (v. 12). He had not held back his hand in the past, but had displayed his kingship in effecting salvation on the earth and in particular for his people:

---

[1] The psalmist apparently speaks for the nation – hence "*my* King."

- He had given them victory over the Egyptians by dividing the Red Sea to let them escape from Pharaoh. In the process he crushed the Egyptians, who are, it seems, symbolised by the sea monster and the mythological figure of Leviathan[2] (vv. 13b, 14).

- He provided them with water in the desert and then dried up the River Jordan to let them cross into the promised land (v. 15).

- Behind these provisions the Lord had created the material universe and had established its order – the sun and the moon, day and night and the seasons of summer and winter. By setting the boundaries between the seasons and possibly also those separating land from sea and those separating earth's peoples from one another (vv. 16, 17; cf. Gen. 1:14-19; Acts 17:26).

4. Appeal for God's help (vv. 18-23 — Stanza A2)

The stanza makes six requests, which are cast in both positive and negative terms. In it the people speak and ask the Lord:

- To remember that Israel's enemy was in fact his enemy, one who in opposing them was, in fact, mocking him and reviling his name (v. 18).

- Not to hand over his people ("his dove") to their enemy ("to wild beasts") and not to forget them for ever (v. 19).

- To hold to the promises of his covenant relationship[3] to his people (v. 20). If he didn't do so they would have had to seek asylum in places, where they would suffer violence. There is more detail in Lamentations 5:8-18.

- Not to let the poor and needy, the downtrodden and oppressed victims of war, be put to total shame (AV, "return ashamed"). This is a negative request,

---

[2]The multi-headed monster fairly clearly represents the Egyptians as does Leviathan, a term referring to a twisting aquatic beast, like the crocodile, that was used as a representation of Egypt (cf. Ezek. 29:3-5).

[3]The basic covenant was that with Abraham at the time of his call (Gen. 12:1-3, expanded in Gen. 15 and 17). Subsequently there was the covenant made under the ministry of Moses (Deut. 24:1-8) and later still that with David (2 Sam 7:1-16; Ps. 89:3 etc.). For a fuller discussion of covenant see Chapter 22 below.

but the psalmist also asks the Lord to change their situation into one in which they could praise his name (v. 21).

- The Lord is asked to arise and defend, not so much the cause of his people, but his own cause. Seeing themselves as in covenant with him, they regarded their cause as his cause. The irreligious and unbelieving fools, who had devastated Jerusalem were in fact mockers of God against whom he should be defending himself (v. 22).

- In conclusion the Lord is asked *not* to ignore, not to remain silent in relation to the clamour of those who were in fact his foes and who were making a continuous uproar by shouting aloud their triumph (vv. 23, 24).

Despite the gloom of this lament, there was still an underlying trust in the Lord. The people had no hope beyond or beside him and so were looking to him for relief, for restoration of their beloved city, for its prosperity and for its temple. They were clinging to God's covenant promises but they totally failed to confess and repent of their own sin of breaching that very covenant.

They did not acknowledge the fact that they had violated and broken their covenant with the Lord. They were committed by what their forefathers had promised: "We will do everything the Lord has said; we will obey" (Ex. 24:7). Now, in being exiled and in having their beloved city in ruins, they were suffering the consequences of their persistent failure to obey. Moses and the prophets had threatened that exile would be the outcome of disobeying the Lord (Lev. 26:27ff; Deut. 4:25ff; 29:25ff; Hos. 5:14; Isa. 5:25ff; Jer. 12:14). It was, surely, preposterous for them to ask that the Lord would keep his side of the covenant, when they had broken theirs and were unwilling to repent before him (v. 20). The author of Lamentations did what this psalm does not do. He confessed the sin that was background to the exile: "the crown has fallen from our head. Woe to us, for we have sinned!" (Lam. 5:16).

In his mercy the Lord did hear their pleas, for he brought many of the exiles back to Jerusalem and he caused the temple to be rebuilt and rededicated and then, under Nehemiah, had the city walls repaired. Ultimately his grace outstripped his wrath.

Psalm 137

The events that gave rise to this psalm are clear – Jerusalem was in ruins and the psalmist was either in exile in Babylon or looking back on having been there. Scholars who take the first view are divided about the point, at which, when the temple was in ruins (586-516 BC), the psalm would have been written. Some place it early in the exile when the pain of having been taken captive would have been the dominant emotion of the exiles. Others think that it could have originated towards the end of the exile, say around 550-540 BC. The commoner view, however, is that the past tenses of its verbs suggest that the exile was over and that the psalm originated among returned exiles shortly after they arrived back in a severely devastated Jerusalem.

Whatever its precise date of origin, the psalm vividly portrays the poignant grief of the Jews in exile in Babylon, a grief, which in the final verses (vv. 7-9) turns to anger and imprecation of divine wrath on their Babylonian captors and the Edomites who had helped them.

The psalm falls into three stanzas of three verses each.

1. Grief (vv. 1-3)

Picture the scene. The city of Babylon lay on the eastern side of the River Euphrates. To the north-east was the other great river, the Tigris. There were also numerous irrigation canals in the area, in which the Jewish exiles were imprisoned and enslaved. Sitting beside one of these waterways was a group of Jewish exiles. Perhaps they had come to a quiet place to worship the Lord and Babylonian guards were keeping a watchful eye on their activities.

As they sat down, they were overcome with grief and could only weep as they remembered Zion. Worship, like that of Jerusalem, was impossible. There they had enjoyed the facilities and the rituals of the temple, but here they had nothing other than hot sun and sand, some water and their memories of the city and the way of life, from which they had been torn by their captors: Little wonder they sang:

By the rivers of Babylon we sat and wept

When we remembered Zion.

—v. 1

To add to their misery their captors became their tormentors and demanded that they sing one of the songs of Zion. In sheer mockery they were being asked to sing songs of worship to the Lord – "on of the songs of Zion" – which would almost certainly have been one of the Psalms (v. 4). The Jews found it impossible to oblige - they had hung up their harps on the willow or poplar trees that grew alongside the rivers of the area. For them this was not a time for music or joyful singing:

> There on the poplars we hung our harps,
> for there our captors asked us for songs
>> our tormentors demanded songs of joy;
>> they said, Sing us one of the songs of Zion!
>> How can we sing the songs of the LORD
>> while in a foreign land?

—vv. 2-4

Scripture makes it absolutely clear that the Jews in exile in Babylon were enduring grief as a result of their persistent disobedience. They were reaping what they had sown, but in this lament psalm, as in Psalm 74 (treated above), there is no mention of that fact. There is no contrition and no repentance, just sorrow for themselves in their captivity. This is in contrast to the personal laments we studied in Chapters 10 and 11. David said, "I know my transgressions and my sin is ever before me. Against you, you only, have I sinned and done this evil in your sight" (Ps. 51:3).

Only when Nehemiah completed the rebuilding of Jerusalem's walls (Neh. 6:15) do we find the people of Jerusalem, led by Ezra, making confession of their own and their forefathers sins:

> For many years you were patient with them. By your Spirit you admonished them through your prophets. Yet they paid no attention, so you handed them over to the neighbouring peoples ...

—Neh. 9:30

At the same time it needs to be said that suffering is **not always**, as ancient wisdom often taught and as some people still think, the direct result of the sufferer's own sin. The foolish accusations of Job's friends together with God's verdict on them tell us, that it is wrong automatically to make a direct connection backwards from suffering to sin. Sin may sometimes be the cause of adversity but it is not always so. For this reason Jesus dismissed and counteracted the suggestion that people, who had lost their lives or were otherwise suffering in tragic circumstances were receiving payment for their sins (Luke 13:1-5; John 9:1-3).

2. Reflection (vv. 4-6)

The question of verse 4 – "How can we sing the Lord's song in a foreign land?" – links this section to what has gone before. As a way of tormenting the exiles, the Babylonian guards had asked to hear one of the songs of Zion, but they just could not do this in the situation in which they found themselves. Their voices and their harps had to be silent – how could they, as captive slaves, sing such songs?

We today must acknowledge that those who, for whatever cause, suffer deep grief, often need times of silence and should be allowed to have them – "there is a time to be silent and a time to speak" (Ecc. 2:7b). If we speak, when we should be silent, we too may become tormentors!

Then, in a reflective mood, the author, speaking in the first person gives reasons for the grief he described (vv. 5, 6).

> If *I* forget you, O Jerusalem,
> > may *my* right hand forget its skill.[4]
> May *my* tongue cling to the roof of *my* mouth
> > if *I* do not remember you;
> > if *I* do not consider Jerusalem my highest joy.

---

[4]The Hebrew reads, "let my right hand forget." English versions supply an object – AV adds "her cunning;" NIV has "its skills;" NLT has "its skill upon the harp," while the. NRSV and NEB both have, "let my right hand wither."

A possible explanation of the switch to the first person is that these two verses were written to be sung responsively by a soloist or by a section of the choir, when the psalm was used in temple worship. In pronouncing a virtual curse on himself, the author and/or the soloist would have been expressing undying loyalty to his native land and to Zion, the centre of its religious life.

If the psalm was written after the return from exile, the writer would have been committing himself to carry that loyalty forward into the future in Jerusalem. He wanted to set Jerusalem and all it stood for at or above the head (Hebrew, *rosh*, head) of his joy. He wanted it to be more important than anything else in life. If he or his people should forget the role of Jerusalem and its sanctuary in the worship of the Lord, music and singing would and should be no more – a withered right hand could not play the harp and a tongue stuck to the roof of the mouth could not sing.

These words remind us of the need to be fully committed to the Lord and to his cause. In earlier studies we encountered David's commitment. He said, "I will dwell in the house of the Lord for ever," meaning "I will live in his presence throughout all my days" (Ps. 23:6). The Apostle Paul had a similar commitment that focused on Christ and the proclamation of his gospel: "For to me, to live is Christ and to die is gain" (Phil. 1:21). He was even ready to wish himself under a curse, if in the process he could win his fellow Jews to Christ (Rom. 9:3). In more general terms he pronounced a woe, a virtual curse, on himself when he said, "Woe to me if I do not preach the gospel!" (1 Cor. 9:16). He was totally committed. Such commitment is our model.

3. Anger (vv. 7-9)

In these verses imprecation on himself if he were to become a backslider (vv. 5, 6) passes over into anger against those who had been responsible for bringing the plight of exile in Babylon on the Jews.

The first object of the psalmist's anger is the Edomites, descendants of Esau, who over the centuries had shown considerable antagonism towards the Israelites (Amos 1:11, 12). When the Babylonians sacked Jerusalem, the Edomites helped them (Jer. 52:12-30). Their participation in this sacking forms the main subject of the little prophecy of Obadiah – they had carried out slaughter and other acts of violence against their "brother Jacob" (Obad. 10-14). Here in the psalm their cry on the day of Jerusalem's fall is recorded: "tear it down, tear it down to its foundations!" They had no brotherly love for the Jews!

The final verse vents anger against the Babylonians, who were, of course, the main agents in the destruction of Jerusalem:

> O daughter of Babylon, doomed to destruction,
>   happy is he who repays you
>   for what you have done to us—
> [*happy is*][5] he who seizes your infants
>   and dashes them against the rocks.

Many scholars have found it difficult to reconcile these harsh sentiments – possibly the harshest in the psalms – with the brokenness of spirit evident in the earlier parts of the psalm. Even more difficult is reconciliation with the teachings of the New Testament that require God's people to love their enemies and, in particular, Jesus' teaching about his care for little children (Matt. 19:13, 14).

All we can say is that this is from Old Testament times and long before the completion of divine revelation in Christ. The psalmist was expressing a normal human reaction to the terrible sufferings of his people at the hands of the Babylonians and the Edomites. It was apparently the custom of the age in the near-east to treat the children of conquered nations in the way the psalmist wants God to treat those of Babylon (cf. 2 Kgs. 8:12; Hos. 10:14; 13:16; Nah. 3:10). Indeed, Isaiah had predicted such a fate for Babylon—'their infants will be dashed to pieces before their eyes' (Isa. 13:16). Here the psalmist was simply asking God to bring just retribution on those who had maltreated Judah and who in all probability had themselves destroyed a large number of Jewish infants.

These imprecations, which appear to be a call for cruel justice create a moral problem in relation to this and to a number of other psalms. So far as this study is concerned, we will leave the matter and return to it in more general terms in chapter 25.

---

[5]The words, "happy is" are supplied in the NRSV to clarify the sense.

CHAPTER 13

WISDOM PSALMS

Wisdom was a form of thinking and of teaching common to the entire ancient near-east. There is a great deal of wisdom form in the Old Testament – in the Pentateuch and in what are called 'the Wisdom Books', Job, Proverbs, Ecclesiastes, Song of Solomon – as well as in the writings of some of the prophets.

Twelve psalms – 1; 32; 37; 49; 73; 78; 112; 119; 127; 128; and 133 – are normally classified as wisdom or teaching psalms. They tend to stress obedience to God's law, as do sections of several other psalms that have a different basic emphasis (e.g., 19:7-10). Each psalm has a message, the most famous of all, Psalm 119, stressing in every one of its 176 verses, the importance and the relevance of God's word and of his law. Psalms 37 and 73 grapple with the related problems of why the righteous suffer and why the wicked prosper. Psalm 78 gives instruction on the basis of Israel's past history. Psalms 127 and 128 teach the worth of godliness in family life. Psalm 133 teaches the importance of unity among brothers.

The difference between Old Testament wisdom and that of the wider near-eastern world lies in the fact of divine revelation and of the context in which it arose and was applied. The key issue was reverence for the Lord: 'the fear of the LORD is the beginning of wisdom and knowledge of the Holy One is understanding' (Prov. 9:10, cf. 1 7). In this chapter we will look at Psalms 1 and 78, the latter in outline only. A brief introduction to the teaching methods of the wise is appended to this chapter.

Psalm 1 sets the tone for the whole Psalter by defining in simple language the two paths men can follow – the way of righteousness and the way of wickedness. It acts as a heading for and an introduction to the whole Book of Psalms. Set in that position it shows that, as well as being the hymnbook of God's people in pre-Christian times, it was also a manual of wisdom, counsel and instruction.

Psalm 1

This psalm gives us no indication of the time when it was written or of the identity of its author. Some have attributed it to Solomon, because its emphasis has many parallels in the Book of Proverbs. Others think it was probably written as a heading for the whole collection of psalms in the period after the return from the exile (maybe in the late fifth, the fourth or even the third centuries BC). Still others suggest that it is quoted or, at least, echoed in Jeremiah 17:5-8 and so must have been written and used before that prophecy (c. 597-586 BC). These speculations are totally without proof.[1]

The psalm stresses that life is a serious business in which morality really matters. The heading added to the Jerusalem Bible's translation – "the two ways" – neatly epitomises its theme, which is that God's blessing rests on the righteous and is absent from the wicked. By implication men and women are faced with a choice, to live by God's rules and flourish or to ignore them and perish.

1. The blessedness of the righteous (vv. 1-3)

The first verse is in the form of a beatitude, which is simply a proverb pronouncing a blessing:

> Blessed is the man
> who does not walk in the counsel of the wicked

---

[1]While positing a post-exile date for the writing of Psalm 1 is speculative, its placement as the head of the Psalter, i.e. as an introduction, is argued by many OT scholars on various literary grounds. The purposeful placement of Psalm 1 at head of the Psalter to set a wisdom tone for the Psalter is implied by the author's comments in the paragraph above.

> or stand in the way of sinners
>> or sit in the seat of mockers.

The person the psalmist describes is indeed blessed or happy. The Hebrew word translated "blessed" (*ashre*) derives from a root meaning "to go straight" or "be guided aright."[2] The idea is of taking a correct path across land or sea in order to reach a chosen destination. As a result the traveller would be blessed with happiness. This man is on the right path of life and is being led through the maze of a hostile world to an assured destination. He is truly happy![3]

In the remaining lines of verse 1 this man is marked by the avoidance (absence) of three negative characteristics. He does not:

- *"walk in the counsel of the wicked,"* meaning that he doesn't mould his character on the counsel (teaching/instruction) that comes from the wicked, i.e., those who are adrift from God and, therefore, are not following his ways (AV translates as, "the ungodly").
- *"stand in the way of sinners"* means that he does not make peers of sinners, i.e., of those who fail to live by God's standards.
- *"sit in the seat of mockers"* which means with people, who ridicule what is good or holy, who are contemptuous of God, of morality and, indeed, of any rule or advice that demanded correction of their ways.

The second and third verses present the opposite side of the picture. This man, who is blessedly happy, has a vital positive characteristic – *"His delight is in the law of the LORD, and on his law he meditates day and night."* Here is a man who more than anything else is concerned to know God's law, to think through its significance and to make it the law of his own life. He has internalised its truth

---

[2] The most recent Hebrew lexicon (HALOT) questions whether '*ašrê* is derived from a root meaning "to go straight." Thus, the author's assertions in this paragraph may be plausible, but the derivation of "blessed" from the Hebrew root as proposed is uncertain.

[3] The Hebrew is plural, hence the NRSV, "Happy are those, who…!" It seems to be a plural of intensity signifying not numerical plurality but *intense* feeling – "O how [*very very*] happy are those, who…!"

and its requirements in his conscience.[4] It dominates his thinking and controls his living, as we might say, 24/7 or 24/365, meaning every day of the week or of the year (cf. Ps. 119:9-16 for an expansion of this theme).

Since this is a teaching psalm it is important that we ask ourselves if we have learned its lesson. Do we cherish God's moral law as proclaimed by the Lord Jesus in the same way as the man pictured in the psalm cherished the Old Testament law?

Verse 3 in typical wisdom fashion develops a picture to strengthen the message: "*He is **like** a tree planted by streams of water, which yields its fruit in season and whose leaf does not wither.*" The picture would be familiar to a Jew, because the south and east of his country had much desert land, which would not sustain trees. But beside a river, a man-made irrigation channel or an oasis, conditions were different. There was moisture in the soil and a tree could put down its roots and become a stable feature on the landscape.

Such a tree overcomes the barrenness of the wider environment and "*yields its fruit in season,*" perhaps dates from an evergreen palm tree or, possibly, oranges etc. from a citrus tree, which with a good supply of water became an evergreen – its "*leaf does not wither.*"

The final line affirms that the outcome of a life lived under the control of the word and of the law of the Lord is successful. The man sees whatever actions he performs under that control come to a successful end: "*Whatever he does prospers.*" This reminds us of the Lord's promise to Joshua that obedience would result in success: "then you will be prosperous and successful" (Josh. 1:6-9).

What must be realised is that the psalmist is not saying that whatever a godly man might do, would be successful – his conclusion was limited by and was only valid in the context of the submission to the word and the law of the Lord.

---

[4]It has been suggested that the psalmist has an appreciation of Jeremiah's hope of God's law being internalised in the heart.

2. The picture of the wicked (vv. 4, 5)

The first line of these verses – "Not so the wicked!" – expresses the antithesis – the opposite – of verses 1 and 2. What the righteous man described in those verses is, the wicked man is not! Instead of being like a tree planted near water and bearing good wholesome fruit, the wicked are like useless chaff, which in the processes of threshing is blown away by the wind (v. 4). The picture is one of worthlessness and of total rejection – chaff is a useless part of grain. The implication is that, while the righteous will stand firm in the time of God's judgment, those who act wickedly (Hebrew, the *resha'im*) will not do so—"they will not stand in the judgment." The word, judgment, here may refer to the continuous day-by-day activities of the Lord as Judge of all or to a more ultimate after-life judgment or to both.

In any event divine judgment will clearly show up the nature of those concerned. The two groups will be irrevocably separated and the wicked will have no place in the assembly (congregation) of the righteous (v. 5). Those whose lives displease the Lord will not be counted among his people either in this life or in the life to come.

3. Applying the teaching (v. 6).

This verse begins with the Hebrew conjunction, ki, meaning "therefore," or as the NIV and NRSV have it "for." It links the summary of the psalm and its teaching very closely with what has gone before. It says, "Let the reader/listener take note of the two-pronged message:"

1. *The LORD watches over the way of the righteous*

   Those, who are blessed in the sense that they are living in God's way and following the correct path of life (v. 1), are assured that the Lord knows and watches over them and their way – he keeps them on the right path and will bring them to their desired destination in the congregation of the righteous.

2. *The way of the wicked will perish*

As verse 4 has said, the wicked are like chaff and in the end will, like it, be discarded as useless – their way will perish. They are not on the right path but on one that is under divine disapproval and that will lead them to perdition. They will, indeed, have no place in the congregation of the righteous.

Stark realities indeed! But this is a message that is essential for men and women in every age and, indeed, for us today. We must live in a godly way and exhibit a blameless lifestyle. We must avoid "the counsel of the wicked," "the way of sinners" and "the seat of scorners" (v. 1b, c, d).

The first psalm sets the tone for the whole psalter. It presents the two extremes of human conduct and offers no middle way – the righteous prosper and are blessed, while the wicked perish. It generalised what was *often observed to be true* in human experience, namely, that a wise or righteous way of life brings prosperity, and foolish or godless living brings disaster. By itself Psalm 1 appears to admit of no experiences that differ from that norm. But that is not, in fact, the full message of the psalter, which in other psalms (e.g., Pss. 37 and 73) recognises both that the ungodly prosper and that the righteous suffer adversity.

Our Psalm's picture of righteous living seems to present a standard of behaviour quite beyond the attainment of ordinary mortals. Ultimately, however, the picture finds fulfilment in the person of Jesus Christ, whom John calls, "the Righteous One" (1 John 2:1). His fulfilment of the picture provides hope for those who struggle to be wise and righteous. As Paul says, "he has become for us wisdom from God—that is, our righteousness, holiness and redemption" (1 Cor. 1:30). He is the One, "who had no sin" and the One whom God made "to be sin for us, so that in him we might become the righteousness of God" (2 Cor. 5:21). Those who become reconciled to God through him are transformed and accepted as righteous by him. They don his righteousness and then seek to act in righteousness just as God himself does (cf. 1 John 3:7).

In this psalm the wise teacher focuses on the two extremes of behaviour in order to extol righteousness and to warn against wickedness. In such a short poem he could not say all that could be said about righteous living and we have to link his words with complementary teaching in other psalms (e.g., Pss. 37 and 73 – See our next chapter). In these the fact that the wicked prospered and the righteous often suffered adversities is set in the context of the ultimate issues of divine rule and divine judgment. They tell us that in a little while – later in earthly life or in the hereafter – the wicked will be destroyed and the Lord will deliver the righteous from their grip (Ps. 37:10, 38, 40; cf. Ps. 73:19, 20).

The Book of Job similarly balances the basic assertions of the wise men. It maintains that there are mysterious and rationally inexplicable elements to life – the righteous often suffer adversity but can't understand whence or why it comes – se for example Job's series of "Why questions" (Job 3:11, 12, 20, 23). The fact that Job ultimately accepted God's provisions teaches us that, like him, we can and must trust the Lord even when we are unable to understand his ways (cf. Job 42).

Psalm 78

This is a long psalm of seventy-two verses, which is attributed in its heading to Asaph. It is a wisdom poem reflecting on and drawing lessons from Israel's past history. It called on its readers to avoid the mistakes and the follies of their forefathers, who after Moses' time had consistently forsaken God's ways. Their failure had led to God's rejection of the house of Jacob (Ephraim and the ten northern tribes that retained the name, Israel) and his selection of Judah and of David as its king and shepherd, a role he fulfilled with integrity and skill (vv. 67-72).

The Psalm will, then, have originated after the separation of the Northern tribes from King Rehoboam and probably after the demise of those ten tribes at the hands of the Assyrians in 721 BC.

The psalm has an introduction and a conclusion (vv. 1-8 and 65-72) and five cycles[5] of teaching in which the poet queries the follies of people, who broke their covenant with God by living in unbelief and adding sin to sin (vv. 9-64).

---

[5]Cf. the cyclic speeches in Job and the cyclic visions in Revelation.

1. Introduction (vv. 1-8)

In these verses the writer-teacher sets out his stall – he challenges his readers
to heed his call, in which he will draw out lessons from the dark happenings
of the past, lessons, which he says must be passed on to succeeding generations
(v. 2-4). He calls his poem a parable (Hebrew, a *mashal*,[6] singular, not plural as
the NIV has it in verse 2).

The basis of his parable is the fact that God had established a testimony in
Israel, which he wanted to be passed on down through succeeding generations.
He wanted those generations to trust him and not to be like their forefathers,
who had not been loyal to him (vv. 5-8).

2. Five cycles surveying Israelite history (vv. 9-64)

These form a symmetrical pattern involving respectively, 8, 16, 8, 16, 8 verses.

1) Israel's disloyalty to God (vv. 9-16)
Ephraim, the leading Northern tribe, epitomises the failures of Israel ́s past and
present (vv. 9-11). They had forgotten how the Lord had brought them out of
Egypt.

2) Israel's rebellion against God (vv. 17-31)
This section asserts the continuous sinning of the Israelites, which is loosely
repeated in verses 32, 40 and 55). It focuses on the way the Lord had provided
for his people during their forty years of wandering through the Sinai desert.
His provision and their sins are interwoven to affirm that, while God was
exceptionally kind to them, they were totally ungrateful and put him to the test
(v. 18) by their grumbling. Why they should have been so ungrateful is one of
the great riddles of their history.

---

[6]A *mashal* can refer to almost any unit of wisdom teaching, from a pithy simile or proverb to a
drama as complex as the Book of Job.

3) Israel's hypocrisy before God (vv. 32-39)

Again the inconsistency of Israel is affirmed: "In spite of all this, they kept on sinning" (v. 32). In this section the historical references are not precise. In some cases they could fit the wilderness wanderings, but the period of the Judges seems more likely. That period was marked by repeated divine punishments leading to short-lived repentances that led to major acts of divine deliverance in which he forgave and did not destroy them (vv. 38, 39).

4) Israel's provocation of God (vv. 40-55)

The main concern of these verses is to recite again God's mighty deeds performed against the Egyptians in order to secure Israel's deliverance from slavery. The plagues are mentioned (vv. 43-51) as is the exodus that brought the people across desert and through the Red Sea to the borders of the land promised to them (vv. 52-54). Then, after forty years of wandering in the wilderness of Sinai, he gave them that land and settled them in it (v. 55).

5) Israel's rejection of the Lord (vv. 56-64)

The mighty deeds of the Lord hadn't produced piety in the Israelites. Rather, they had continued to sin against him. Their sins, especially that of Baal worship and its accompanying idolatry, were spiritual treachery that had angered him greatly and had led to his complete rejection of them (v. 59b). At this point "Israel" clearly meant the ten northern tribes. As a result the Lord allowed the Philistines to destroy the sanctuary at Shiloh (1 Sam. 4; cf. Jer. 7:12, 13), which had been the place of his presence among his people up to the time of Samuel. The sacred Ark had been captured and large numbers of the people including many priests were killed.

Conclusion (vv. 65-72)

The teacher, as we can designate the sage-philosopher behind this psalm, has treated us to a picture of unmitigated human failure. He has borne a loud and clear witness to man's fallen condition and to his inability to live up to the divine requirement of righteousness set for all in Psalm 1. It is a message that, if we are honest, will ring bells in our own hearts, for despite all that the Lord has done for us in Christ, we too can be forgetful of his mercies and can live for ourselves rather than for his glory.

In verse 65 the writer uses a bold picture to affirm God's intervention into the situation – he had awoken as from a sleep! He had tolerated Israel's sin for a long time (cf. Acts 17:30), but was doing so no longer. He had rejected the ten northern tribes – referred to as the tents of Joseph and the tribe of Ephraim (v.67). His chosen people were now the tribe of Judah. He had narrowed down the field and would work through that one tribe alone. That choice of Judah is traced back to the selection of Zion/Jerusalem as the site for a permanent sanctuary replacing Shiloh (vv. 68, 69). It is also traced back to the acceptable way in which David had shepherded his people. He had fulfilled his tasks with integrity of heart, i.e., in devotion to the Lord and in loyalty to his covenant requirements (v. 72).

Ultimately we have to think not just of King David of old but of the one a hymn-writer has called, 'Great David's greater Son,' the Lord Jesus Christ, who like David fulfilled the shepherd image and was/is indeed, the Great Shepherd of God's people. As members of that people, we Christians can often in different and more modern ways fail to do God's will. We need to walk with the Lord and to rely constantly on his Holy Spirit to energise us, as we seek to be obedient to his will.

One final point: We have seen that God's chosen people were narrowed down from twelve tribes to one tribe, Judah. Later the Lord narrowed things still further to a remnant of chosen and faithful individuals. Finally, his purposes found focus in a specific person, the Lord Jesus Christ. As Paul tells us, the seed of Abraham, to whom all God's promises relate, is Christ (Gal. 3:16).

Subsequently God works in and through those, who by faith in him become God's children and who collectively are now "in Christ" and his "New Israel." It is the church, made up of believing and born again people, whether Jewish or Gentile, which inherits God's salvation promises. As Paul told the Galatian believers; "If you belong to Christ, then you are Abraham's seed, and heirs according to the promise" (Gal. 3:29).

Appendix

The teaching methods of the Hebrew sages

What the sages of Israel taught was largely a matter of practical insight into human life and the way it should be lived. They then passed on their wisdom in the form of pithy easy-to-remember instructions called mashals (proverbs). The process by which they produced their mashals involved three stages which are explained in Proverbs 24:30-33:

- *Observation*

  The sages were careful observers of what went on around them. In this passage one of their number describes what he saw as he looked into a lazy man's garden:

  > I went past the field of a sluggard,
  >> past the vineyard of the man who lacks judgment;
  > thorns had come up everywhere,
  >> the ground was covered with weeds,
  >> and the stone wall was in ruins.
  >
  > —vv. 30-31

  Observation of what went on in life situations ensured that the sages used ideas and terminology that were meaningful and relevant to those they taught. They knew how to be on the same wavelength as their hearers.

- *Reflection*

  The second step was to think about, to meditate on, what had been observed and to draw out from it a lesson that needed to be taught and learned. Our sage says:

  > I applied my heart to what I observed
  > and learned a lesson from what I saw.
  >
  > —v.32

The product of such meditative reflection was always a firm conviction about a particular aspect of life. These convictions were formulated as proverbs and were the basic element of the sages teaching or counsel.

- ***Instruction***

The sage then put the fruit of his observation and reflection into a unit of teaching – a *mashal* or proverb:

> A little sleep, a little slumber,
>> a little folding of the hands to rest —
> and poverty will come on you like a bandit
>> and scarcity like an armed man.
>
> —vv. 33-34

This, like the many similar sayings of the wise, was a pithy proverb, which ordinary people, most of whom were illiterate, could easily remember.

CHAPTER 14

WISDOM AND APPARENT INJUSTICE

The sages of ancient Israel maintained that righteousness led to prosperity and that unrighteousness produced adversity. This was generally valid and fitted the majority of situations, but it has to be pointed out that there were exceptions to the rule in that some righteous people suffered adversity while others, who were wicked, prospered. These exceptions or seeming exceptions are faced in the three psalms we are about to examine.

Psalm 37

This psalm carries the heading, "Of David," which implies that David was the author, though it is possible that the heading means something like "in the spirit of David" or "from the circle of David."

The psalm was obviously produced in its author's later years: "I was young and now I am old" (v.25a). It presents the mature reflection of a man, who, by virtue of his many years of observing human life had come to a series of conclusions (cf. Job 12:12: "is not wisdom found among the aged?").

The writer presents his conclusions in the form of the twenty-one proverbial instructions that make up this psalm. These are arranged alphabetically according to the standard Hebrew alphabet. Most are in four line stanzas, but in verses 7 and 20 there are three lines, while in verses 14-15 there are five. In addition the verse numbers depart slightly from the acrostic structure of the psalm.

The teaching style in the psalm is direct and similar to that of Proverbs 1-9. It is not clear if the author was addressing one particular person or a group of people. Since the psalm is incorporated in Scripture, we can conclude that he was addressing the LORD's people in every age.

The immediate recipients were worried by the fact that the standard teaching of the sages – that the righteous prosper and the unrighteous suffer – was not universally true. Those who were doing wrong were prospering and the author's righteous pupil was (or pupils were) envious, perplexed and fretful. They probably felt cheated by, jealous of and angry with their unrighteous and prosperous fellow-Israelites.

1. The source of fear

Several verses point to the unrighteous, whose actions instilled great fear and real anger into the hearts of the righteous:

> The wicked plot against the righteous
> and gnash their teeth at them.
>
> —v. 12

> The wicked draw the sword and bend the bow
> to bring down the poor and needy
> to slay those whose ways are upright.
>
> —v. 14

> The wicked lie in wait for the righteous
> seeking their very lives.
>
> —v. 32a

Clearly these wicked men were showing strong and vicious antagonism to the righteous. They were prepared to resort to violence and even to murder. Little wonder the righteous were fired up with anxiety and anger. Little wonder, too, that the godly sage felt it necessary to tell the righteous not to fret or be envious of wicked or evil men (vv. 1, 8; cf. Prov. 24:19).

2. The antidote to fretting

The main concern of the author was to turn his pupil(s) from anxiety and anger to calm reliance on the LORD:

- Trust in the LORD and do good ... (v. 3a).
- Delight yourself in the LORD ... (v.4a).
- Commit your way to the LORD; trust in him (v. 5).
- Be still before the LORD and wait patiently for him (v.7a).
- Refrain from anger and turn from wrath;
     do not fret—it leads only to evil (v.8).

In their original context these great texts challenged the recipients to be faithful to their obligations under God's covenant with them. They were instructed not to set their hearts on material wealth as the wicked were doing, but to give their total loyalty to the LORD and to rely on him completely.

3. The affirmation of ultimate justice

The psalmist-sage affirmed that, while, in the vicissitudes of life, the righteous experienced inequalities and injustices that made them anxious and angry, there were answers:

1) The prosperity of the wicked is only temporary

He argues that the prosperity of the wicked is but temporary. Ultimately they will not enjoy their wealth:

- Like grass they will soon wither,
- like green plants they will soon die away (v. 2).
- Evil men will be cut off (v. 9a).
- A little while and the wicked will be no more;
  though you look for them, they will not be found (v. 10).
- The LORD laughs at the wicked,
- for he knows their day will come (v.13).
- The wicked will perish.
- The LORD's enemies will be like the beauty of the fields
- they will vanish—vanish like smoke (v.20).
- I have seen a wicked and ruthless man
- flourishing like a green tree in its native soil,
- but he soon passed away and was no more;

- though I looked for him, he could not be found (vv. 35f).

The argument is that either later in life or subsequently through death the wicked will lose their cherished wealth. That being the case, the righteous, who may have been suffering adversity, need not fret or be jealous. In the long term perspective, wealth is impermanent and unimportant. It can be taken away and at death it has to be left behind.

2) The righteous are assured of God's blessing

Much, as does the Book of Proverbs, this psalm assured the fretting readers that God would surely honour them:

- Delight yourself in the LORD
    and he will give you the desires of your heart (v. 4).

- Those who hope in the LORD will inherit the land
                        (v. 9b, cf. vv. 11, 22, 29, 34b).

- The days of the blameless are known to the LORD,
    and their inheritance will last for ever.
    In times of disaster they will not wither:
    in days of famine they will enjoy plenty (vv. 18-19).

- I have never seen the righteous forsaken
    or their children begging bread (v. 25).

- The salvation of the righteous comes from the LORD; ...
    because they take refuge in him (vv. 39-40).

What then is the sage-psalmist's answer to the fretting of his pupil or pupils? It is that the prosperity of the wicked is temporary and, at most, restricted to this life. It is not worth fretting over and certainly not something of which to be jealous.

In contrast he assured his pupils that, if they totally committed themselves to the LORD, they would find that he would reward them with permanent occupancy of their land and with an inheritance that will last for ever.

For the writer of this psalm, the inconsistency of the prosperity of the wicked with traditional wisdom is more apparent than real. By stressing its temporary nature and affirming that God's justice will surely overtake the offending unrighteous people and deprive them of their riches, the sage shows that his principles remain valid. He handles the problem by insisting that, since the offending prosperity is merely temporary, there is no real inconsistency at all!

Psalm 49

This psalm is attributed to "the Sons of Korah," who seem to have been a corps of temple singers descended from the group of Levites mentioned in 1 Chronicles 6:22-24. The date, at which it was written, is not known.

This psalm has a theme similar to that of Psalm 37 – wicked deceivers were surrounding and bringing adversities (evils) to the author (v.5) and were putting their trust in their considerable wealth (v. 6). The main focus of the psalmist's concern was the fact that the wealth of these people was overawing and, no doubt, creating a sense of injustice among the ordinary people whom he was addressing.

The psalm divides itself naturally into four sections:

1. The call for attention (vv. 1-4)

These verses provide a typical "wisdom" introduction for the psalm. They are addressed, not to an individual pupil or even to a specific group of pupils, but to the broad sweep of humanity, to "all the inhabitants of the world," the privileged and the underprivileged, the rich and the poor (vv. 1-2).

The author begins by indicating what he is about to do:

- He will speak wisdom and seek to pass on understanding to whoever is listening (v. 3). He will turn his ear (i.e., listen) to some inner source of understanding that would produce a proverbial instruction (Hebrew, a *mashal*). This could have been either his own reflection on what he had observed (cf. Prov. 24:32) or instruction received by divine revelation or both.

- Singing to the accompaniment of his harp, he will expound his answer to the problem (the riddle) on which he was focusing.

2. The problem defined (vv. 5-6)

The writer must have endured some degree of oppression at the hands of those he describes in these verses. He must have had grounds to fear the adversity – the evil he faced – and the evil days brought about by deceivers who were surrounding him.

> Why should I fear when evil days come,
>> when wicked deceivers surround me—
> those who trust in their wealth
>> and boast of their great riches?
>
> —vv. 5-6

The distinctive of these people was the dominance of materialism in their lives. They made a god of wealth and thought that riches would give them pleasure and the expectation of a long life.

3. The reality explained (vv. 7-15)

The author explains that wealth is only of value in this life; it cannot stave off death. No ransom[1] even from the richest man in the world could be a sufficient payment to God to secure the continuing earthly life of any human being (vv. 6-9).

The fact is that men, whether wise or foolish, die and have to leave their wealth to others. Even though plots of land had been named after them, their tombs are their permanent abodes. In fact, "man despite his riches does not endure" beyond the point of his death – he becomes "like the beasts that perish" (v. 12).

At this point the sage is reflecting the pessimistic outlook that finds fuller expression in Ecclesiastes (3:18-22). Human wisdom, even if, as here, it was the

---

[1]In this context the word "ransom" appears to relate only to the preservation of earthly life and not to the removal of sin and its guilt as is the case elsewhere in Scripture.

product of a godly man, could not take him, as it cannot take us, beyond the point of death (ct. v.15).

This pessimism continues through verses 13 and 14. Death and oblivion in the grave are the destiny of all who trust in themselves and their wealth. They will be far from the princely mansions they once enjoyed!

BUT the writer had a great hope in relation to his own destiny. He knew that what human wealth could not do – purchase endless life – God could do and would do for him:

> But God will redeem my life from the grave;
> he will surely take me to himself.

—v. 15

The writer does not describe what being with God would involve and it is hard to know whether his knowledge extended to the idea of a future resurrection. Nonetheless he uses the very verb that Genesis 5:24 used of Enoch – "God took him away." Clearly, even though he may not have known the full picture, he was convinced that God would do more than merely delay his physical death. He was assured of some similar divine translation (cf. Ps. 73:24) and, like Job, could invest the word "Redeemer" with a deeper significance (Job 19:25-27). While the rich oppressors of this world would perish in death, he, the victim of their oppressions, would enjoy God's nearer presence. In the end the destinies would be reversed and the prosperity of the wicked would be shown to be very temporary, while the blessings of the righteous would abide beyond the grave.

4.The resulting proverb (vv. 16-20)

Having thought things through, our sage advises the world of men about how they should regard and react to those who are wealthy and who are arrogant oppressors of poor and insignificant people like himself.

His advice can be paraphrased:

Don't be overawed by (afraid of)[2] those who become rich and who own
palatial homes.

Material wealth is essentially temporary and therefore quite unimportant; it
cannot be taken into or beyond the grave – the rich man "will take nothing
with him when he dies" (v. 16-17). The blessing and the celebrity he enjoyed
in this life will disappear as he, like his ancestors, enters – permanently enters
indeed – the realm of the dead (vv. 18-19). This presents the destiny of foolish
and unrighteous men of the world as a dark hopelessness. It is in stark contrast
to what in faith the writer envisaged for himself (v.15).

The sage's final thrust is a warning that closely echoes verse 12 – A rich man
without understanding (i.e., one who foolishly leaves God and sound wisdom
out of his life) "is like the beasts that perish" (v. 20, cf. Ecc. 3:18-22).

Psalm 73

This psalm is attributed to Asaph, a Levite, whom David appointed as his
worship leader, when the ark was brought to Jerusalem (1 Chr. 16:4-6). It
begins with an ascription of praise to God:

> Surely God is good to Israel,
>   to those who are pure in heart.

Commentators agree that this is the conclusion to which the psalmist had come
after the battle that had raged within his soul had been resolved (vv. 12-15).

The author first explains the cause of his inner conflict:

1. His envy of the prosperous (vv. 2-16)

He had nearly lost his foothold of trust in the God who had been good to Israel:

> As for me, my feet had almost slipped;
>   I had nearly lost my foothold.
>
> —v. 2

---

[2]This use of the Hebrew verb, *yara*, meaning "to fear," connects with and echoes its appearance
in v.5.

The reason for this wavering of his faith lay in what he knew of the prosperous people he had observed. They had an easy life, free from the burdens common to man and marked by callous hearts, proud arrogance and malice. Yet, presumably because of their worldly and material successes, others were attracted to them (vv. 10-12).

The Jerusalem Bible has a good rendering of these verses:

> This is why people turn to them
> and lap up all they say,
> asking, 'How will God find out?
> Does the Most High know everything?

The psalmist himself had been attracted to them and to their way of life. He saw them as always carefree as they increased their wealth (v. 12). Indeed, he had envied them because of their prosperity (v. 3).

But as he did so he had felt plagued – punished, he thought – by his commitment to a life-style that prevented him from becoming rich. He had been keeping himself pure for no gain (vv. 13-14) – there was no material gain from righteous living! What the wicked had gained and, therefore, what he had missed filled and plagued his mind all day long in a manner that became a constant self-inflicted punishment.

A combination of the "God-dimension" in his life and the standard presentation of wisdom (that prosperity comes to the righteous) had created the oppressive confusion he was suffering. He had, however, been afraid to speak openly of his doubts or of envy for the prosperous, because to have done so would have been a betrayal of God's faithful children and ultimately of God himself. His faith was clearly still alive and exercising a restraining influence on his actions, but, as he tried to sort things out in his mind, he found the process not just confusing but oppressive – "it was oppressive to me" (v. 16b).

2. His discovery of reality (vv. 17-20)

The Psalmist-sage appears to have had a sudden change of mind. Instead of continuing to wrestle with his inner conflict, he went into the sanctuary of God, into the Temple, the place that was the focus of God's presence. There, separated from the hurly burly of life with its inequalities and in the quietness of God's presence he got things into perspective.

We remember the LORD's challenge to his people through the prophet, Isaiah: 30:15:

> In repentance and rest is your salvation,
>> *in quietness* and trust is your strength
>> but you would have none of it.
>
> —Isa. 30:15, emphasis mine

We also remember how Jesus sometimes left his disciples and retired to a quiet place in order to engage in private prayerful communion with his Father in heaven:

> After he had dismissed them [the disciples], he went up on a mountainside by himself to pray. When evening came, he was there alone.
>
> —Matt. 14:23

We also remember how he sometimes took his disciples away from (AV, "apart from") the crowds into a quiet place to rest (Mark 6:31) or to receive some special revelation:

> Jesus took Peter, James and John with him and led them up a high mountain, where they were all alone. There he was transfigured before them.
>
> —Mark 9:2ff

And again we read:

> He took the twelve disciples aside and said to them, We are going up to Jerusalem, and the Son of man will be betrayed to the chief priests and the teachers of the law. They will condemn him to death and turn him over to the Gentiles to be mocked and flogged and crucified. On the third day he will be raised to life.
>
> —Matt. 20:17

When our Psalmist entered the sanctuary of God, he suddenly understood the final destiny of those he had been envying. It seems that he was so overwhelmed by the presence of God that his doubts and worries dissolved as he saw things in their true light. The LORD was on the throne and in control of everything and would not let the wicked avoid his ultimate judgment of their lives – "then," says the psalmist, "I understood their final destiny" (v.17b).

He discovered that the wicked, rather than he himself, were on a slippery slope (ct. vv. 2 & 18). They were bound for ruin, because the LORD would arise and treat them as mere fantasies (vv. 18-20). Their wealth was also a phantom that would not last and could not be taken into or beyond the grave (cf. Ps. 49:17).

3. His confession of faith (vv. 21-28)

Whatever the precise nature of his encounter with God in the temple, the psalmist was humbled and brought to a confession of his erroneous thoughts. Just as a direct encounter with God brought Isaiah (Isa. 6:1-5) and Job (Job 42:1-6) to penitent confession, so the psalmist was brought to an acknowledgement of his errors:

> When my heart was grieved (JB, "growing sourer")
>> and my spirit embittered,
> I was senseless and ignorant;
>> I was a brute beast before you.

Instantly things had changed. His faith that had wavered was strengthened in God's forgiveness and acceptance.

He was now in a right relationship with the LORD:

> Yet I am always with you;
>> you hold me by my right hand.
> You guide me with your counsel
>> and afterwards you will take me into glory.
> Whom have I in heaven but you?
>> And earth has nothing I desire beside you.
> My flesh and my heart may fail,
>> but God is the strength of my heart
>> and my portion for ever.

—vv. 23-26

The psalmist-sage was now a different person. He knew that his doubts (about a justice that had permitted wicked men to prosper) were sinful and that penitent confession was the only way to renewed fellowship with God. He also knew, in what seems to have been an advance on the thinking of Psalm 49:15 (above pp. 155-156) that he had real hope of an after-life with God in heaven. Hence his firm decision to press on in faith:

> As for me, it is good to be near God,
> > I have made the Sovereign LORD my refuge;
> > I will tell of all your deeds.

—v. 28

Like David, who said, "I will dwell in the house of the LORD for ever" (Ps. 23:6), he was committing himself to spending the rest of his life in a close relationship to the LORD. That settled, and with the problem of the prosperity of the wicked resolved in the context of his knowledge of God, he formulated a teaching proverb and made it the heading for his poem:

> Surely God is good to Israel,
> > to those who are pure in heart.

—v. 1

His message was, then, that his pupil(s) should maintain a similar faith in God's goodness and make sure that they did so with pure or single-minded hearts. They should not allow doubts or brutish reasoning, such as had almost ruined him, to damage or destroy their trust in the sovereign goodness of God, the LORD.

CHAPTER 15

ROYAL AND MESSIANIC PSALMS

There are eleven psalms – Psalms 2; 18; 20; 21; 45; 72; 89:19-52; 101; 110; 132 and 144 – which in whole or in part focus on the kingship of David and his successors. In some cases they have pointers to or predictions of a future Messiah-King, who would also be a descendant of David.

With the exception of Psalm 45 (see below, chapter 16) these psalms are basically songs of praise or prayer addressed to the Lord. Psalm 21, for example, begins, "O LORD, the king rejoices in your strength."

As our example of this type of psalm we take Psalm 2, which can be classified both as a royal and as a messianic psalm.

Psalm 2

It is widely believed that this psalm was used in the context of public functions relating to kings in David's line, each of whom, like David and Saul before him, were always regarded as "the Lord's Anointed" (1 Sam. 24:16). The most probable context for its ongoing use is thought to have been an accession ceremony or coronation.

1. The author

There is no heading to suggest the author's name and there are no specific identifying events in the text. There is, however, a possible hint in verses 7-9, where the speaker, using the first person, records a decree of the Lord that confirmed the position of a king mandated to conquer and possess other nations.[1] These verses fairly closely repeat the Lord's promise to David recorded in 2 Samuel 7:10-16 and could have been written or spoken by him in appreciation of what the Lord had promised him.

It has to be remembered, however, that the promise was not directed just to David, but also to his son, Solomon, and, indeed, to subsequent kings descended from them. Solomon, as an inheritor of the promise, could have quoted it or a later poet could have put Nathan's words into the psalm so that a later king could speak or sing them at the initiation of his reign. In doing so the new king would present his kingship and the institution of the Israelite monarchy as based on promises God had given David.

The early Jerusalem believers quoted verses 1 and 2, when they welcomed Peter and John after a brief time under arrest. Using words that definitely seem to ascribe the authorship of the psalm to David, they prayed, "Sovereign Lord, … you spoke by the Holy Spirit *through the mouth of your servant, our father, David*" (Acts 4:25, 26).

Some commentators think, however, that the use of the name David in Acts 4 was simply a device to point to the whole body of psalms, which were known as "the Psalms of David." In that event the author of this psalm, who could still have been David, was not being specifically named.

HC Leupold argues that such usage is ruled out in the case of this psalm because the phrase "*your servant, our father David*" is clearly specific to a known individual from an earlier time. Though he doesn't know how those, who prayed after the release of Peter and John, gained that piece of knowledge, Leupold believes that their words, incorporated in the record of the Acts, prove that David was the author.[2] However, others, on the assumption that the psalm was written for singing at a coronation ceremony, find it difficult to accept this view. This is because there were, apparently, no subjugated nations, who could have conspired against David, when he became king. A conspiracy against him

[1]The Hebrew, *choq*, comes from a root, *chaqah*, meaning to engrave and hence to make a decision or issue a command.
[2]HC Leupold, *Exposition of the Psalms*, Baker, Grand Rapids, 1959, p. 45.

would only have become possible in his later years, when he had conquered several people groups – Philistines, Moabites, Ammonites and others.

There is thus quite a strong argument against David being the author of the psalm. However, as Derek Kidner suggests, he could, perhaps, have written it to recall such an occasion as his coronation. Alternatively he could have written it in anticipation of the coronation of Solomon.

If the psalm was written late in David's reign, he could be the king against whom some subject-peoples were rebelling. If it was written in anticipation of the reign of Solomon, then Solomon would be the king in view. Since subsequent kings largely lost the territories conquered by David, they are unlikely to have been those targeted in verses 1 to 3.

Indeed, when Solomon became king several of these subservient groups were ready to rebel against him and against the Lord. Rehoboam, who was Solomon's son and David's grandson, wasn't even able to hold on to the ten northern tribes of Israel! Whatever the situation in view, it is important to remember that the opposition was not just against an earthly king, but against the Lord – "against the LORD and against his Anointed One" (v. 2).

2. The content of the psalm

The psalm divides into four stanzas, each of which contains three verses. It is widely believed to have been written with the intention that it would be sung antiphonally at coronation ceremonies.

The second and fourth stanzas (vv. 4-6 & 10-12) respond to the issues posed respectively in the first (vv. 1-3) and the third (vv. 7-9). It would, therefore, suit antiphonal singing.

1) Gentile antagonism questioned (vv. 1-3)

"Why," asked the psalmist, is there a conspiracy "against the LORD and against his anointed One" (Hebrew, his *messiah*)? The conspiracy was widespread involving kings and other rulers and their peoples (vv. 1, 2). While the picture fits the unbelieving world in every age—men conspire to evade their obligations toward the Lord and toward his Christ—it must initially have been of more limited reference to the lands and peoples that had been conquered by David.

In verse 3 the picture is of such conspiracy developing into active rebellion. The conspirators wanted to throw off the yoke of Israelite domination and their leaders were ready to try to bring that about— "let us break their chains, they say, and throw off their fetters."

Again, in more ultimate terms and in our modern world in particular, there are powerful forces – philosophic, religious and moral—lining up against the Lord and against his Christ. They are becoming exceedingly aggressive in their attempts to discredit the Bible and the Gospel and to oppose those who seek to live by the teachings of Jesus, the Messiah.

2) The answer from heaven (vv. 4-6)

In these verses a soloist or a section of the choir seems to voice what the writer knew to be the answer of the Lord in heaven. It is a declaration of his absolute sovereignty over men and nations. The Lord on the throne of heaven was not cowed or afraid in the face of the angry howling of the conspirators. He was so secure in himself and in his sovereignty that he could laugh at them! But he also acts in wrath against their audacity, rebuking and terrifying them and affirming the position of the king he had anointed to reign in Jerusalem, on Zion his holy hill.

That being the case the king, be it David, Solomon or another, was safe and had no fear of anything the conspirators might do. The Sovereign Lord had placed him in his kingly position and that was that – no power on earth could overthrow what was of the Lord's appointment. And the same is true today. God is still on the throne and he does remember his own. Opponents may scoff or violently attack those who are disciples of his Anointed One, but in heaven he laughs at them and assures them that he knows and is present with his own people. Unless they repent and amend their ways, his wrath will fall on the conspirators at the time of his choosing.

3) The testimony of the king (vv. 7-9)

Again we have a different voice, possibly that of the king himself or of someone representing him. He begins by saying, "I will proclaim the decree[3] of the

---

[3]Hebrew, *choq*. See Note 1, p. 149.

Lord." He is telling all and suncry that he is no impostor, but a king, who sits enthroned by a divine command. They have no right, therefore to challenge his authority. He then cites the promise made to David through Nathan (2 Samuel 7:14) that he would take his son (i.e., Solomon) as his own Son and would be Father to him. The psalmist's quotation is:

> He said to me, You are my Son;
>> today I have become your Father.

$$-\text{v. 7b}$$

In that promise and also in this citation of it we can detect something of the thinking and practice of ancient wisdom in which a teacher was regarded as father and his pupil was his son. Thus the teacher in the Book of Proverbs addresses his pupil as, "my son" (Prov. 1:8 etc..)[4] The king, here probably Solomon, had been brought into an intimate and loving, a privileged relationship with the Lord on the day of his anointing and installation as king. He was now in a special position as a disciple and son of the Lord and was his vicegerent in Israel.

But in Messianic terms these words take on a new and deeper meaning. They point forward to the One who in every way is God's Son, the One, who shares his deity and is equal with him in the divine Trinity. He is the one, who became God incarnate – God manifest in human flesh, the One of whom at the beginning of his ministry God the Father spoke from heaven saying, "This is my Son, whom I love; with him I am well pleased" (Matt. 3:17; cf. Heb. 1:5).

But the Father had also invited the king to ask him for the nations of the earth as his inheritance. Inheritance is something to which a son does, of course, have a right in human life. But here the language bursts out beyond anything that was conceivable for an Israelite king – the inheritance embraced the nations of the world and extended to the ends of the earth. This is echoed in Psalm 22:27, where we read, "All the ends of the earth will remember and turn to the LORD and all the families of the nations will bow down before him." In Isaiah 2:1ff the prophet highlights the fact that God's purpose is that in the "last

---

[4]Compare 1 Cor. 4:15, where Paul, as the one who taught his readers about Christ, calls himself their "father through the gospel."

days" many people will come to the house of the God of Jacob seeking to be taught his ways. The words of our psalmist clearly link in, then, with messianic prophecies that came to fulfilment in Jesus and in the spread of his gospel across the earth (cf. Matt. 29:19, 20; Acts 1:8 etc.).

Ultimately *the* Son, the Lord Jesus, would rule this vast empire with a rod of iron and would wreak severe punishment on his opponents (v. 9). In the Book of Revelation his ultimate rule is presented in terms taken from this verse – he will rule the nations with a rod, a sceptre of iron (Rev. 12:5; 19:15; cf. Rom. 15:12). The iron sceptre, like the shepherd's staff symbolises ruler-ship and firm government, which would involve the punishment of rebels, but also arrangements for the well-being of all the ruler's citizens.

Earlier in the same book (Rev. 2:26, 27) the Risen Lord cited this verse to affirm that those believers in Thyatira, who faithfully lived for him would be given ruling authority over the nations:

> To him who overcomes and does my will to the end, I will give authority
> over the nations. ... just as I received authority from my Father.
> —Rev. 2:26-27

The implication is that faithful Christians are to share in the victory of Christ and will eventually reign with him. Paul put this truth thus, "if we endure, we will also reign with him" (2 Tim. 2:12; cf. Rev. 5:10; 20:6; 22:5).

4) The challenge to rebel conspirators (vv. 10-12)

In this stanza the implications of the three previous sections are applied to the leaders, who had been conspiring and fomenting rebellion against both the king of Israel and against the Lord, his God.

They are challenged to become wise, another indication that the psalm derives from Israelite wisdom teachers. They are instructed to heed the warnings that had been given. They are called to change their ways, that is, to repent and, instead of conspiring to rebel against the king of Israel and the Lord his God, to submit to and serve the Lord. Since the king was God's vicegerent on earth, to serve him was to serve the Lord, or, at least, was the beginning of such service. Hence the challenge of verses 11 and 12:

> Serve the Lord with fear
>> and rejoice with trembling
> Kiss the Son, lest he be angry
>> and you be destroyed in your way,
>> for his wrath can flare up in a moment.

In the first line of verse 12 "the Son," who is to be kissed, seems to be the same person as was addressed by the Lord in verse 7—"you are *my Son*; today I have become your Father." In royal terms it was the king of the day and in messianic terms, the Christ of the New Testament.

Actually, however, the Hebrew word, *ben* (son), which occurs in verse 7, is not in the text in verse 12, where we find a different word, *bar*. In Hebrew this seems to mean something like purity or sincerity. It could be used here to express a call to sincere worship of the Lord and by implication a genuine honouring of and submission to his representative on earth. Accepting this understanding of *bar*, the NEB, RSV and NRSV translate the challenge as "kiss his feet," meaning something like "submit to him worshipfully."

> Serve the LORD with fear,
>> with trembling kiss his feet.
>
> —NRSV

Bar is, however, also the Aramaic word for "son" and would have been widely known among the Jews of later inter-testamental times, when Aramaic – the language of Syria (Aram) – was the language of government in the area (cf. *Bar*- abbas in the Gospels and *Bar*-Jesus in Acts 13:6). It is likely, however, to have been used in earlier times by the peoples, whose leaders were conspiring against the Israelite king and so might quite naturally have been used in that part of the psalm (vv. 10-12), which addressed those leaders. Otherwise the presence of an Aramaic word in an early psalm seems rather unlikely.

The call to repentance is clear – "get right with God by submitting to his authority and to that of his king." Those who failed to become reconciled to him risked destruction at his hand, something that could arise quickly and without warning: "his wrath can flare up in a moment" (v. 12b).

The kings of the earth who were conspiring against the Lord and his Anointed King have been told to repent and submit to the Lord and to the authority vested in his Anointed One. If, instead of opposing the Lord, they take refuge in him they will be on the right path and will be blessed.[5]

In this fourth stanza (vv. 10-12) the psalm has an evangelistic thrust, which in the first instance is directed at the rebels and potential rebels among the nations under Israelite suzerainty. But, since as we have seen, the language of the psalm bursts out of that mould and points forward to the ultimate and only messianic Son of God, it is a call to men of every age and of every people group to acknowledge, to turn to and serve the Lord and his Son with reverent fear.

True blessedness – including the blessing of avoiding the wrath that will fall on impenitent rebels – comes to those who turn to him and live before him as worshipful servants, who "serve the LORD with fear and rejoice with trembling" (v. 11a). The conclusion is in the final line of the psalm, which is in the form of a beatitude that sums up the message of the whole Psalm:

> Blessed are all who take refuge in him (v.. 12c).

—v. 12c

3. A Royal and Messianic Psalm

At Antioch in Pisidia, Paul quoted lines b and c of verse 7 to indicate that for him this psalm had messianic import. The relationship of the Divine Father to the Divine Son in the psalm was in effect a prophetic prediction that received a dramatic fulfilment through the resurrection of Jesus (Acts 13:33). As Paul told his readers at Rome, Jesus "was declared with power to be the Son of God by his resurrection from the dead" (Rom. 1:4). The Father-Son relationship was such that the Son could not be left to decay in an earthly grave (Acts 13:32-37, which refers to Isa. 55:3 and Ps. 16:10 as well as to Psalm 2:7).

Many scholars believe that the psalm is predictive prophecy pointing solely to Jesus Christ. But, as our exposition has shown, there is a clear connection to the kings of Israel. It seems better, therefore, to regard the psalm as primarily a

[5]See comments on Psalm 1:1 and on the blessedness suggested in beatitudes – pages 138 and 139 above).

royal psalm written for and/or about a king of David's line, possibly in the first instance Solomon. But in God's purposes that earthly king is a prefiguring, or, as some prefer to put it, a type of Christ.

Whether the author did or did not know the messianic implications of his words is unimportant. That the divine Spirit controlled his thinking means that what he wrote is more than a poem about an earthly king – it is also predictive prophecy revealing truth about the future Messiah, who would be the very Son of God.

This is, then, both a royal and a messianic psalm.

CHAPTER 16

A ROYAL WEDDING PSALM

Psalm 45

A song for a King of Judah

In this Psalm a wise teacher addresses and instructs an Israelite king and his bride. Scholars view it in three different ways:

1. as an ancient love song, which the psalm's author adapted for use as a wedding song for a king of Judah

2. as messianic prophecy, pointing to the coming of Christ, the King. Thus Hebrews 1:8, 9 quotes verses 6 and 7 as referring to Christ and introduces them with the words, "But about the Son he [God] says ..." This seems to put the stamp of divine inspiration on the psalm's messianic reference.[1]

3. as having two levels of meaning, the primary relating to the marriage of an actual Jewish king and the second being predictive of the promised Messiah, the Lord Jesus Christ, of his everlasting kingdom and of his spiritual relationship with his bride, the church (cf. Eph. 5: 23ff; Heb. 1:8, 9; Rev. 19:7ff; 21:2; 22:17). Accepting this view, as the present writer does, this psalm, like Psalm 2, is both Royal and Messianic. However, in this chapter we will major on what seems to be the primary level of meaning – its addresses to a king (vv. 2-9; 16-17) and to his bride (vv. 10-12) and the description of their bridal procession (vv. 13-15). Nonetheless in verses

---

[1] The notes in the Scofield Bible take this view, but don't specifically mention the fact of a king's marriage!

6, 7 and 17, we will see something of how the king's marriage fits into messianic prophecy and points to the promised Messiah.

1. Its setting

The heading seems to instruct a leading musician concerning the tune to be used with the psalm. The NIV translates the Hebrew, *shoshannim* ("lilies"), as "to the tune of lilies." Some connect this to the fact that the female lover in another love song is called a "lily of the valley" (S. of S. 2:1, 2) but, since *shoshannim* is also in the heading of Psalm 80, which is not a love song, this is doubtful.

The heading also indicates something of why it was written. In the NIV it is introduced as *A maskil,* which is thought to suggest something like "a contemplation" or "an instruction" and as *shir yadidoth,* meaning as the AV has it, "a song of loves." The NIV renders this as "a wedding song," while the RSV and NRSV have "A love song."

The psalm is addressed to or is a song about an unnamed king: "I address my verses to the king" (v. 1b, RSV – the Hebrew reads, "I speak my works to the king," NIV – "for the king"). The psalm relates to and celebrates his marriage and the prospect that he and his bride would raise a family (cf. v. 16 – "Your sons will take the place of your fathers").

The permanence of the king's throne suggests that the marriage of a king of Judah, descended from David, rather than of an Israelite king,[2] was in view. Several suggestions have been made as to the identity of the king – Solomon and Jehoram are the favourites. However, neither they nor any other king can be convincingly affirmed and it is probably best to leave the question unanswered.

2. Its structure

It is thought by some that the existence of a prologue (v. 1) and an epilogue (v. 17) suggests that, on the occasion for which the psalm was written, these sections were either sung by a leading chorister or by a prophet holding an official position at the king's court, more or less as a chaplain to his majesty. In

---

[2]The throne in the northern kingdom, Israel, was constantly subject to assassinations and so had no settled or fixed dynasty.

that event, as well as being a "Royal Psalm," this song might have been designed for liturgical use and could be classified with the group of such psalms that will claim our attention in chapters 17 and 18.

Between the prologue and the epilogue the psalm divides into three main sections that together form a rather non-symmetrical chiastic structure (see above, chapter 1, pp. 17-19). Verses 2 to 9 and 13 to 16 address the bridegroom-king and the central section, verses 10-12, address the princess-bride. This structure can be set out as follows:

> A. Address to the king-bridegroom (vv. 2-9)
>> B. Address to the princess-bride (vv. 10-12)
> A. Address to the king-bridegroom (v. 13-16)

3. Its content

This psalm begins with a one verse introductory prologue and climaxes in a concluding epilogue, which also forms one verse.

1) The prologue (v. 1)

The psalmist vividly describes his inspiration – his heart is stirred – is bubbling over – with a great, an exciting theme (v. 1a). The subject that excites him is the marriage of the king, because of which (vv. 2-16) he is about to recite his poem either to or for the king (v. 1b). He likens his nimble tongue that is ready to speak the words of the psalm, to the fast-moving pen of a skilful scribe or, as the NRSV has it of "of a ready writer." He is saying that he was speaking with real enthusiasm, because he held his king in great respect and was happy to extol his excellence and majesty.

2) Address to the king-bridegroom (vv. 2-9)

(1) The most excellent of men (vv. 2-5)

First the king is addressed as "the most excellent of men" (v. 2a). The Hebrew word translated, "most excellent" (*yapar*) basically means "specially beautiful" – hence the NRSV, "the most handsome of men." But it was not just physical attractiveness that was in view. This king's words and actions showed that God had anointed him with grace. He was a gracious ruler, whom God had blessed and who was worthy of the honour being given to him on his wedding day. That God had blessed him "for ever" (v. 2c) confirms that we are dealing with a king of David's line, because it was to David that God promised an everlasting kingdom (2 Sam. 7:13-29; cf. Pss. 18:50; 89:2-4).

In verses 3-5 the king is instructed to take his proper ruling role – girding his sword and clothing himself in a way that befitted and displayed his exalted position.[3] But first and foremost he is to use his authority and strength in the cause of "truth, humility and righteousness." Then in the second place he is bidden to do what every ruler is expected to do – is, indeed, required to do – defend his people against their enemies (v. 4c, 5).

(2) The most favoured ruler (vv. 6, 7)
The king's throne and his person are honoured in language that shows him uniquely favoured by God. He has a throne that will last for ever! At the same time his righteous character ensured him of a status above that of his companions, which could mean "fellow-monarchs."

Your throne, O God will last for ever and ever;
  a sceptre of justice will be the sceptre of your kingdom.
You love righteousness and hate wickedness;
  therefore God, your God, has set you
    above your companions
  by anointing you with the oil of joy.

The first line of these two verses, "Your throne, O God, will last for ever" (v. 6a), has been the subject of much discussion and debate. It reads as an address to God Almighty rather than to an earthly king. The word "God" (Hebrew, 'elohim), suggests a divine person and lends weight to the idea that the psalm focuses on a divine Messiah, whose coming at a then future time had been predicted by

---

[3]The first line of verse 4, "In your majesty ride forth victoriously," inspired HH Milman's hymn, "Ride on! Ride on in majesty!"

several prophets (cf. Isa. 7:14; 9:6; 11:1-6; Jer. 23:5; Zech. 3:8; 6:12). The writer to the Hebrews applied these very words to Christ in order to affirm his unique status as the Son of God (Heb. 1:8, 9).

But did the writer of the psalm have that insight several centuries before the Messiah of the New Testament arrived? If, like Isaiah or Jeremiah, he was a prophet he could well have been inspired to speak predictively of the Messiah, who would be more than a mere man – a King, indeed, but One who would be divine and have an eternal throne.

However the rest of the psalm seems to refer to a human king and to his bride. Indeed, in verse 2 the king is addressed as "the most excellent *of men*." He was a man, whom God had blessed and was not, therefore God! In addition verse 7 clearly distinguishes between that king and God, his God, who had anointed him with the oil of joy, thus giving him real happiness on his wedding day (cf. Ps. 23:5b). Clearly, then, someone distinguished from God is addressed in this section of the psalm: "God, *your* God, has set *you* (this human king) above your companions" (v. 7).

Who then is that king, who is addressed as *'elohim* in verse 6? Is he a second divine person – the promised Messiah or is he a human king, who is addressed here as *'elohim?*[4]

The Hebrew word, *'eloha* (plural, *'elohim*), means strength or power. When it occurs in the plural and is the subject of a singular verb, it always refers to God, the Sovereign Lord.[5] When the same plural form, *'elohim*, is used with a plural verb it almost always refers to heavenly beings – angels – that are lower than God and that exist to serve him. *'Elohim* is also used of human persons. For example, we read of human judges, who were designated "the *'elohim*" in Exodus 22:8 and 9 (see NIV footnote). Again we read, "You made him (man) a little lower than the angels" (Hebrew, "the *'elohim*", Ps. 8:5). And in Psalm 82:6-7 we read, of men of whom the Lord said, "You are gods (*elohim*)." Clearly this

---

[4]The RSV, "Your divine throne endures for ever and ever," was an unsatisfactory attempt to evade the problem.

[5]The plural. *'elohim*, when used of God is "a plural of intensity" signifying that all power and wisdom etc. are concentrated in the Lord (cf. the Hebrew, *mayyim*, a plural meaning intense waters, or "the sea").

refers to powerful human beings – those who "would die *like men*" and were, therefore, men.

Clearly then the Hebrew word, *'elohim*, was used in three ways, of the Almighty Sovereign Lord, of angelic beings and of men who were in positions of power.

That being the case, there is no incongruity in our psalmist addressing his beloved king, whom he wished to honour on his wedding day, as a powerful or mighty one, an *elohim*. In using *'elohim* of a man, the psalmist was not investing him with deity but simply designating him as a powerful man. On this basis verse 6a could be rendered, "Your throne, *O mighty one*, will last for ever and ever." This king was set above his companions and on his wedding day, had been anointed with the "oil of joy" (v. 7).

What is clear is that the ruler in view had been greatly blessed with God's favour and blessing (v. 2bc). Not only so, but his character was absolutely impeccable because he loved righteousness and hated wickedness (v. 7a).

While such a picture was undoubtedly true of our king-hero, it is also singularly appropriate for the One who ultimately fulfils the role of being God's anointed Messiah. As the writer to the Hebrews makes clear the words of the psalm that apply to the king *also* apply to God's Son, the messiah-king. He is, as Revelation 5:12 puts it, worthy "to receive power and wisdom and strength and honour and glory and praise," words that virtually repeat a similar ascription of worship to God, the Father, in the previous chapter (Rev. 4:11).

(3) The groom and his bride are ready (vv. 8, 9)

In these two verses a picture of the marriage ceremony begins to emerge – the king is decked with robes and perfumes and stringed instruments are playing music appropriate to a marriage situation. He is ready for his marriage:

> All your robes are fragrant with myrrh
> and aloes and cassia;
> from palaces adorned with ivory
> the music of the strings makes you glad.

To complete the picture, honoured women, some the daughters of other kings, act as "bridesmaids." Beside the king stands his bride, attired in a garment adorned with gold from Ophir and obviously ready to be married to him.

3) Address to the princess-bride (vv. 10-12)

The psalmist – or perhaps a leading chorister or a court prophet using his words – now addresses the princess who is about to become the queen-consort. Adopting the stance of a wisdom teacher-sage he calls her, "Daughter" (cf. the use of "Son" in Proverbs 1:8 etc.).

The mention of "Daughters of Tyre" in verse 12 has been taken as indicating that the king's bride was from that country, but it is possible that the psalmist was speaking of Tyre as a rich neighbour, from which the new queen could expect friends bringing gifts. Equally men of wealth, (possibly, in view of the poetic parallelism in the verse, also coming from Tyre), would seek her favour.

In the first instance the bride is instructed to begin a new life as the wife of her royal master, here new lord,[6] the king. In effect she was to apply to herself the instruction given to Adam that a marriage creates a new family unit in which husband and wife were to become and to live as one flesh, as one person. While Genesis 2:24 imposed this obligation on the husband and made it a responsibility of males, this passage shows that it applies equally to females. In marriage women, like men, have to leave father and mother and become one flesh with their husbands.

That this king was enthralled by the beauty of his bride (v. 11a) meant that she should respond to him in an appropriate way. She should honour him because he was her lord[7] (v.11b) This anticipates the instructions of Paul and

[6]The Hebrew root is 'adon, meaning owner, master, lord or, in the context of marriage, husband. Thus Sarah called Abraham, her 'Adon (Gen. 18:12, AV, "my lord," NRSV, "my husband," NIV, "my master").

[7]The Latin Vulgate translated this line as "honour him for he is your Lord God." This has no support in any known Hebrew manuscript. The Hebrew is not YHWH, the four letter name of the LORD, but 'adonai, meaning master and in the context of marriage meaning head of the family unit. There is no suggestion here that the king was divine.

Peter in the New Testament – Wives must submit to and respect their husbands – "Wives, submit to your husbands as to the Lord" (Eph. 5:25-33) – "Wives be submissive to your husbands" (1 Pet. 3:1). Only by giving herself totally to her husband could this bride or, indeed, any bride, be assured of her husband's undivided admiration and devotion.

4) Second address to the king-bridegroom (vv. 13-15)
The king is told:

1. *That the bride is preparing herself well for the wedding.* The princess has prepared herself for her marriage and is described as 'all glorious within' which is usually taken to mean, "in her chamber." Her gown is interwoven with gold from Ophir (v.9b).

2. *That the bridal procession is on its way.* Dressed in her wedding garment elaborately embroidered with gold and accompanied by her ladies-in-waiting (her bridesmaids), she is being led in procession with joy and gladness to his palace (v. 14). There would be a considerable entourage of excited people singing nuptial songs and proclaiming to all and sundry that the bride was on her way to the king. The psalmist speaking directly to the king tells him that this is actually happening.

    It is sometimes said that a bridal procession heading to the home of the groom is not in harmony with the picture of the bridegroom's procession in our Lord's parable of the ten virgins (Matt. 25:1-13). It is thought that the procedure then was that the groom went in procession with his entourage to the house of the bride and that she with her family and bridesmaids processed back to the groom's home. But in the case of a king's marriage, it might have been contrary to decorum for the groom to go in procession to the bride's home. In any event, this bride might not have had a home in Jerusalem to which such a procession could have gone.

3. *That the king has bright prospects (v.16).* The king's marriage will be fruitful – he will create a new family. His sons would take the place of his fathers and become the main focus of his interest and affection. He would look

forward to making them prince-rulers and through them spreading his influence throughout the land.

5) Epilogue

The psalmist now climaxes his message in words that may have been designed to be sung by a designated chorister or even spoken by a court prophet: It is even possible that if the psalmist was also a prophet – a spokesperson for the Lord – he himself spoke to the king with words he had received directly from the Lord in heaven. Those words are:

> I will perpetuate your memory through all generations
> > therefore the nations will praise you for ever and ever.

The declaration that endless praise would be given to the king is unusual and suggests to some that they are addressed to God or to a divine Messiah (see on vv. 6 and 7 above). However, the poet, in his endeavours to honour the earthly king he seems to love greatly, may well have used hyperbole – a verbal exaggeration to increase effect (cf. John 21:25) – and meant his words for that king rather than for the Lord or for a yet future Messiah.

But at the same time our author has again uttered words that also point to an ultimate fulfilment in the eternal Son of God, who is truly worthy of the praise spoken here. The king of the day, whoever he was, stands as a type, an advanced portrayal, of the King that was to come and that did come as a babe in Bethlehem several centuries later.

The language of the psalmist has a double meaning. It primarily describes an immediate situation, namely the marriage of a Jewish king. But it also points to something and to someone greater – to the coming of God's ultimate anointed King, Jesus our Lord and Saviour. His memory would truly be perpetuated through all generations – he is to be praised for evermore and in a much more permanent manner that any other king of David's line.

Summary

The presence of this psalm, like that of the Song of Solomon, in Scripture shows that the joys of human love and marriage have a place in the purposes of God for his creatures. The creation ordinance is that a man is to leave his father and mother and be joined to his wife so that the two become one flesh (Gen. 2:24). In that relationship they are expected to produce offspring: "Be fruitful and increase in number; fill the earth and subdue it" (Gen. 1:26).

The union of husband and wife, which is so prominent in this psalm, finds a parallel in the union of Christ with his church (e.g., Eph. 5:22-33; Rev. 21:2). In this context the call to the princess to leave her father's house (v. 10) can be taken as a picture pointing forward to the call of Christ to his followers that they should turn away from earthly pleasures and even from their natural families in order to follow him with their whole hearts.

> Anyone who loves his father or mother more than me is not worthy of me; anyone who loves his son or daughter more than me is not worthy of me; and anyone who does not take his cross and follow me is not worthy of me. Whoever finds his life will lose it and whoever loses his life for my sake will find it.
>
> —Matt. 12:37-39; cf. Luke 14:26, 27

CHAPTER 17

LITURGICAL PSALMS

Some scholars think that a number of psalms were written for or, at least, were used antiphonally[1] as part of the liturgical[2] worship of the Jerusalem temple. The parts seem to have been sung by different persons or by alternating groups of singers.

Some scholars think, however, that the evidence for antiphonal liturgical singing in the temple has often been overstated. There may be some truth in their view, but nonetheless the concept does have merit and deserves some consideration at this stage in our studies. In this and the next chapter we will examine two psalms (12 and 15) that fairly clearly could have been designed for liturgical use.

Psalm 12

1. Introductory considerations

1) The heading
The heading to this psalm, as translated in the NIV, indicates that it was written "to" or "for" the chief musician – the director of music – upon or on account

---

[1] Antiphonal speech involves two or more persons (or groups of persons) responding to each other as they recite or sing parts of a work prepared for such usage.

[2] The English word, liturgy, is derived from the Greek verb, *leitourgeō*, meaning to serve or worship. In Old Testament studies liturgy refers to the form and order of worship services in the Jerusalem temple.

of (Hebrew, *le*) the *sheminith*. The meaning of this word is unclear but it may be related to *s'hemonath*, which is the numeral, eight. Some think that an eight stringed instrument is in view, others that the reference is to a section of the choir, made up of eight bases or eight sopranos (cf. 1 Chr. 15:19-31). The best we can say today is that *shemenith* is a musical term of uncertain meaning.

The heading also attributes the psalm to David – "a psalm of David." That the Hebrew preposition translated "of" has a wide variety of meaning including "to," "for" and "concerning" could indicate that this is a psalm about rather than by David. Most scholars believe, however, that it asserts that David was the author.

2) The structure

Psalm 12 provides vivid examples of the artistry of Hebrew poetry. In its eight verses it has nine two-line couplets,[3] in each of which the second line closely parallels the first. Thus in verse 1, as shown by the italics and the underlinings, we have two synonymous thoughts expressed in different words:

> Help, LORD, for **the godly** <u>are no more;</u>
>   **The faithful** <u>have vanished from among men.</u>

The psalm presents us with a dramatic dialogue, or, if as may be the case there are more than two speakers, a colloquy.

Many scholars see the psalm as dividing itself into three sections, set in a chiastic[4] or cross-over/reversal order, for example, ABA. The three sections are seen as containing respectively:

> A) The suppliant's prayer for help (vv. 1-4)
>   B) The Lord's word of promise (v. 5)
> A) The suppliant's prayer of response (vv. 6-8)

Others feel that it is better to think of five sections, which are shown in the table below – an A, B, C, B, A arrangement. The parallels in the five point chiasmus are indicated by underlining and by bold or italic type:

---

[3]Verse 5 has four lines made up of two couplets.

[4]A chiasmus is a cross-over arrangement of parallel ideas.

A) *The suppliant's plea* to the Lord (vv. 1, 2)
  (he is disturbed by the failings of his society)
  B) The supporting prayer (vv. 3, 4)
    (spoken by a prophet or sung by choir)
    C) **The word of the Lord** (v. 5)
    (centrepiece, answering the suppliant)
  B) The supporting comment (v.6)
    (spoken by a prophet or sung by the choir)
A) *The suppliant's trust* in the Lord
The suppliant grasps and trusts God's promise.

The psalm, set out in this pattern is printed on page 179.

2. Exposition

1) –A – The suppliant's plea (vv. 1, 2)

The psalmist, assumed by most Bible scholars to have been David, was distressed and virtually overwhelmed by the situation around him. He, therefore, cried to the Lord for help and deliverance. He asked that he and, indeed, the poor and the needy, who were being unscrupulously oppressed, would be saved from the activities of the ungodly people around them:

> Help, LORD, for the godly are no more;
>   The faithful have vanished from among men.
> Everyone lies to his neighbour
>   Their flattering lips speak with deception.
>
> —vv. 1, 2

Reverence for God had ceased to exist – the godly were conspicuous by their absence! Faithfulness or integrity between fellow-human beings had vanished – no one could be trusted to speak the truth. Deception, especially, it seems, in the form of flattery was the order of the day. The emphasis was on deliberately false speech – the offenders in view were abject liars.

Some scholars have thought that the psalmist may have exaggerated somewhat the failings of David's time in order to heighten his sense of helplessness. If, indeed, the psalm originated with David, there is a fairly grim picture of the lawlessness and deception of his times in chapters 11 to 21 of 2 Samuel. The goings-on in that period would certainly have distressed him on many occasions and would have led him to cry out to the Lord for help as is the case here – "Help Lord," would have been his desperate cry.

If, however, the psalm were to have been written at a later period, this picture of the psalmist's world has parallels with that of the period just before the Jews were carried into exile in Babylon. Habakkuk describes it thus: "Destruction and violence are before me ... the law is paralysed, and justice never prevails. The wicked hem in the righteous so that justice is perverted" (Hab. 1:2-4). Clearly then, some four centuries after David's time, dishonest speech was dominant and was distorting the rule of law and the exercise of justice as had been the case in the days of the psalmist.

The picture suggested by David's words is not very different from that of the world in which we live today. Men and women live without even a thought of God and so see no need to imitate his ways in godly living. They think that what is right is what they think to be so, especially if it happens to work for their own benefit. They acknowledge no absolute moral standards and insist that no one, human or divine, and no set of rules whatever their origin has any right to say what is morally right or wrong for them. They regard themselves as totally self-autonomous and do what is right in their own eyes (AV, cf. NIV, "what they see fit" Deut. 12:8; Jud. 17:6; 21:5).

This being the dominant philosophy of life, faithfulness and personal integrity are in many cases conspicuous by their absence. People break the Ninth Commandment by telling lies or by putting a deceptive "spin" on things in order to hide something that is either dubious or untrue. As in the Psalmist's day, their lips speak with deception.

2) – B – The supporting prayer (vv. 3, 4)

There is uncertainty as to who spoke or sung these two verses, when the psalm was used in a service of worship. It could have been a section of the choir or a temple official – a priest or a prophet.

Many commentators and the translators of modern English versions seem, however, to assume that they are a continuation of the psalmist's plea of verses 1 and 2:

> May the LORD cut off all flattering lips
> > and every boastful tongue
> that says, We will triumph with our tongues;
> > we own our lips—who is our master?

Actually, instead of being addressed to the Lord these two verses speak about him in the third person. The AV translates the Hebrew quite literally—"The LORD shall cut off all flattering lips." If this is the correct understanding of the text, these two verses are a statement of fact and of faith, spoken by a third party to encourage the suppliant to believe that the Lord would intervene to answer his prayer and solve his dilemma.

If, on the other hand, these verses do, as many think, continue the prayer of the suppliant, they involve not a mere statement of fact but an imprecation, i.e., a calling down of divine judgement in relation to those, whose utterances vexed the suppliant and operated against justice for the poor and the needy (cf. v. 5). The imprecation,[5] if that is what we have, would not seem as harsh as some we find in other psalms, where the requests are for the elimination of an enemy, sometimes by what to us might seem to be a cruel method. Here, as in verses 1 and 2 there could be an element of hyperbole (exaggeration for the sake of effect), and the psalmist's aim may simply have been to secure divine help in causing the deceivers to cease from their lying flatteries and to start speaking the truth.

The second line of verse 4 discloses the underlying problem afflicting the flatterers. They were proud of themselves and of their words, which they thought were absolutely true and such as would win any argument that might

---

[5]Imprecation in the psalms will be discussed next (chapter 17).

arise! At the same time they were early proponents of the self-autonomy, that is so loved in our contemporary post-modernist society. No-one and no law of God or of man had any right, they thought, to prescribe what was morally right or wrong for them. Like those of whom we read in Judges 21:25, they were open to no correction and did what was right in their own eyes. They were their own masters and particularly so in relation to the words they used: "We own our lips—who is our master?"

3) – C – The Lord's response (v. 5)

This is the centrepiece of the psalm – a word that came from the Lord in answer to the psalmist's plea. It reads:

> Because of the oppression of the weak
>   and the groaning of the needy,
> I will now arise, says the LORD,
>   I will protect them from those who malign them.

Many scholars think that this word from the Lord was spoken by a prophet, who attended the service of worship in the temple for that purpose. That probability, as was noticed earlier, has given rise to the classification of the psalm as a "prophetic oracle psalm."

Other scholars prefer to think that the Lord's word came directly to the psalmist, whom they thus cast in the role of a prophetic spokesman for the Lord. Since it was, indeed, the role of prophets to declare what God revealed to them, there is no theological reason to doubt that a prophet could have been involved at this point. Indeed, as we read in Amos 3:7, "the Sovereign LORD does nothing without revealing his plan to his servants the prophets." But whether the prophet involved was the author of the psalm or someone else is beyond final proof.

If David was the author of the psalm and this word of the Lord came directly to him, it would mean that, as well as being king, he was also a prophet, a spokesman for the Lord. In that event the roles of prophet and king were less rigidly separated than some Christians have thought.

As to its content this message from the Lord has two parts:

1. An acknowledgement that the flatteries, that worried the psalmist, resulted in the oppression of weak and needy people. Their activities denied them justice and kept the poor in poverty and the needy in need.

2. A promise of help and deliverance. The Lord was answering the psalmist's cry of distress. He said, "I will now arise, ... I will protect them from those who malign them" (v. 5b). He would reverse the harm that was being done to poor and needy people. The precise nature of the protection is not spelled out, but it obviously related to the psalmist's complaint about lying and deceptively flattering words. He would protect him from the flattering deceptions they were propounding, to damage the reputation of those who were complaining about the morality of the current society.

4) – B – The supporting comment (v. 6)

This verse in the NIV reads:

> *And* the words[6] of the LORD are flawless,
>   like silver refined in a furnace of clay,
>   purified seven times.

In the Hebrew text this verse is not connected to the previous one by a conjunction, as the NIV suggests by its addition of the English word, "And," which has been printed in italics above. The verse rather stands separately as a statement distinct in its own right. But who was the speaker – the psalmist, a prophet or a section of the choir? Since the Lord is being spoken about in the third person, he obviously was not the speaker.

Some scholars regard this verse as part of the psalmist's response to and acceptance of God's promise (vv. 6-8). If that was the case, it was the first strand in his expression of a new level of faith – he now knew that he had received a message on which he could rely at all times.

However, this verse, like verses 3 and 4, is sometimes thought to have been spoken by a prophet or sung by a section of the choir in order to supplement and reinforce what the Lord had said. Such an understanding of the text seems

---

[6]The RSV, NRSV and NLT helpfully interpret the Hebrew, *amaroth* (words), as "promises." In the context the Lord's word (v. 5) was a word of promise.

more likely, since the verse refers to the Lord in the third person and so was neither spoken by him nor spoken to him in prayer.

The verse is best understood as a comment designed to affirm the absolute veracity and reliability of what the Lord had just said and in doing so to encourage the suppliant to trust what the Lord had said. As a result he would be left with no excuse for unbelief. In the light of verses 7 and 8 it clearly had that effect – he was now wholeheartedly trusting the Lord.

There is a deliberate contrast in this verse between the flawless and pure words of the Lord and the deceitful lies of those, who were the source of the psalmist's anxieties (v. 2). The contrast couldn't be stronger for the words of God are likened not just to refined silver, but to silver that had been put through the refining process seven times and so was as pure as pure could be. The Lord's words are therefore free of deceit or flattery – they are really true.

5) – A – The suppliant's new attitudes (vv. 7-8)
In verse 7 the psalmist shows that he had genuinely laid hold of God's promise and was now relying on it. He was again speaking *to* the Lord and affirming that he could now face a godless world with confidence in the Lord's determination to protect him and in his ability to effect that protection on a permanent basis:

> O LORD, you will keep us safe
> and protect us from such people for ever.

The Hebrew is more literally, "You, LORD, will keep them (i.e., the poor and needy of v. 5), safe (and) preserve him (i.e., individual victims) from this generation[7] for ever." The NIV and RSV translations follow the Greek Septuagint Version of c. 200 BC and read "us" for "them" and for "him." Whatever the correct reading the affirmation is that the Lord would do what he had promised to do (v. 5).

In verse 8 this confident faith is set in the context of the psalmist's world: "the wicked freely strut about when what is vile is honoured among men." A corrupted society provides room for wickedness. Some translators insert the

---

[7]The word, generation, (Hebrew, *dor*) has something of an ethical emphasis, which is captured by the NIV's 'such people', meaning the flatterers of verses 1 and 2.

relative pronoun, "*who*" to show the connection with verse 7. We could, then, paraphrase verses 7b and 8 as:

You, O LORD will keep them (us) safe;
   you will always protect us from this generation,
     from those *who*, as wicked men, strut about freely,
       when the wickedness of the sons of men is praised.

The psalmist is again highlighting the situation that perplexed him in verses 1 and 2. A relaxed view of morality had allowed wickedness to flourish. And despite the Lord's promise the wickedness hadn't gone away! There is no indication that the prayer requesting that the flattering lips might be cut off (v. 3) had been literally answered! The flatterers were still doing damage to the poor and needy! But, in an unchanged world the suppliant of the psalm had himself been changed. He had been confronted by the Lord, whose word had penetrated his heart. He was now resting on God's promises of protection for the oppressed and, no doubt, also for his own safety.

The lesson for us surely is that, when we are in touch with the Lord and take on board his promises, we can face a constantly hostile world, in which wickedness is honoured and encouraged, without being overwhelmed or made downcast by it. Sin and wickedness, cruelty and oppression will be with us as long as fallen mankind is on the earth, but overarching everything for the believer is the sovereign rule of God and his constant care of his children. The psalmist had come to a place of trust, in which, despite all that was going on around him, he knew that the Lord would keep him and his fellow-sufferers safe.

We remember our Lord's great prayer:

> My prayer is not that you take them (those the Father had given him) out of the world but that you would protect them from the evil one. … Sanctify them by the truth; your word is truth. As you sent me into the world, I have sent them into the world.
>
> —John 17:15-19

We Christians are in this world – sent into it by a commission of our Lord. In it, as was the case with Jesus' early disciples, we need God's protection from its evils and from its evil-doers. We get this protection through his sanctifying word, which we, like the psalmist, must take on board and trust. His promises are flawless – pure and reliable – like silver refined seven times over.

In our modern world we, like David, can, and must, trust the Lord and rely on his promise to protect us, whatever the antagonisms we may encounter in the world around us.

Psalm 12
Set out as a Chiastic – an ABCBA type – Poem

- **A) The suppliant's plea** (vv. 1, 2)

  [*He was disturbed by the failings of his society*]

> Help, LORD, for the godly are no more;
>> the faithful have vanished from among men.
> Everyone lies to his neighbour;
>> their flattering lips speak with deception.

  - **B) The supporter's prayer** (vv. 3, 4)

    [*Spoken by a prophet or sung by choir ?*]

>> May the LORD cut off all flattering lips
>>> and every boastful tongue
>> that says, We will triumph with our tongues;
>>> we own our lips—who is our master?

  - **C) The Sovereign's word** (v. 5)

    [***The centrepiece*** *– The Lord's answer*]

>> Because of the oppression of the weak
>>> and the groaning of the needy,
>> I will now arise, says the LORD.
>>> I will protect them from those who malign
>> them.

  - **B) The supporter's comment** (v.6)

    [*Spoken by a prophet or sung by the choir ?*]

>> The words of the LORD are flawless,
>>> like silver refined in a furnace of clay,
>>> purified seven times.

—vv. 1, 2

- **A) The suppliant's trust** (vv. 7, 8)

  [*He grasps and trusts God's promise*]

> You, LORD will keep them safe,
>> You will always protect each person from this generation,

from those, who, as wicked men, strut about freely
and by whom the wickedness of the sons of men is praised.

—vv. 7 & 8, my paraphrase

CHAPTER 18

AN INSTRUCTIONAL LITURGY

Psalm 15

Many scholars think this psalm was designed to be sung in the context of pilgrims approaching the gate of the temple. As they did so, they asked for the conditions on which they would be permitted to enter the Lord's sanctuary (v. 1). In what many regard as a liturgical response a priest, a prophet or, perhaps, the choir itself defined the conditions of heart and life required in those who would have fellowship with God (vv. 2-5).

The heading connects the psalm with David, who is widely accepted as being the author. The use here of the word "tent" (Hebrew, *ohĕl*, NIV, "sanctuary") could be confirmation of that authorship – it suggests that the psalm was written in relation to worship in the tent constructed by David to receive the Ark of the Covenant on its arrival in Jerusalem (2 Sam. 6:17). It was, of course, the place of God's presence among his people in David's time. In the first instance the psalm is likely to have been used in relation to access to that tent sanctuary. Later worshippers would, no doubt, also have used it as they approached the temple built by David's son, Solomon.

Psalm 15 is in strong contrast with Psalm 14, where the picture is of evildoers, who both believed and behaved foolishly. They said that there was no God and proceeded to suppress and oppress the poor. In contrast this psalm presents a picture of those, who speak truth, do no wrong to their neighbours and live in fellowship with God (vv. 2, 3). Such people, it affirms, have a stable lifestyle and true security before God – they "will never be shaken" (v. 5d).

In the opening question, "LORD, who may abide in your tent?" Who may dwell on your holy hill? (NRSV)— the Lord was being asked to identify who would be entitled to be in his house. From the answer that the LORD gave it is clear that the thrust of the question related not to ritual enactments, but to the moral and spiritual qualities of heart and life that fit a person for fellowship with God. There are parallels to this in Psalm 24:3-6; Isaiah 33:14-17 and Micah 6:6-8.

This psalm, together with those parallel passages, tells us that true Old Testament religion was not the mere outward conformity to law and tradition that we meet in the Pharisees of our Lord's time. It was, as books like Deuteronomy and Jeremiah also show, a matter of inward spirituality and morality. The fact that legalism came to dominate later Judaism must not blind us to the inward nature of true Old Testament faith and religion. Mere observance of laws (legalism) without a proper inner devotion of the heart was a departure from true Old Testament religion.

1. The Question posed (v.1)

> LORD, who may dwell in your sanctuary?
>   Who may live on your holy hill?
>
>   —NIV

The singer or speaker addressed the Lord directly. He wanted to know who might be eligible to come before the Lord, in the place where he had made himself present. Though the two questions are parallel to each other, they contain different metaphors which are somewhat obscured by the NIV. He wants to visit – to sojourn temporarily as a guest – in God's house, his tent.[1] But he also wants to dwell – to settle down more permanently as a resident – on the Lord's holy hill, on Zion, the site of David's tent sanctuary and subsequently of the temple.

---

[1] The Hebrew word, 'ohĕl, translated in the NIV as "sanctuary," means, a tent, and is the word used throughout the Old Testament for the tabernacle that was constructed soon after Israel received the Ten Commandments at Sinai (Ex. 26ff).

The first verse of the psalm clearly enshrines, then, the desires of the psalmist and of worshippers who used his words. They wanted the Lord to tell them what qualities of life he required in them in order that they might be fitted to meet with him in the place he had chosen to manifest his presence. And that, as verses 2-5 tell us, is exactly what he did! He answered their request.

2.The Question answered (vv. 2-5b)

The Lord's answer begins with a general statement of the type of character and life-style that God requires of those he accepts into fellowship with himself: (v. 2 a, b):

> He whose walk is blameless
> and who does what is righteous.

The Lord wants fellowship with those who live consistently within the parameters set by his laws. He wants people of moral integrity who are not liable to be blamed for breaking his laws. The Hebrew word translated "blameless" is *tamim*, which means wholeness, completeness, or freedom from defect and so points to perfection. The AV rendered it as "uprightly," which is as near as any version gets to the meaning. AF Kirkpatrick comments that it includes "whole-hearted devotion to God and complete integrity in dealing with men."[2]

The parallel second line puts the emphasis in different words – the man who is blameless/upright (*tamim*), does what is right, what is *tsĕdĕq*, meaning equitable, fair, just or righteous. Such a man lives a life modelled on that of the Lord, "the Righteous One," who acts equitably, a God of justice, who shows no favouritism (Acts 10:34 etc.) and judges all men in accordance with truth and righteousness (Gen 18:25; cf. Pss. 7:11; 19:9; 145:17; John 17:25; Rev. 16:5-7). Justice, fair play and doing what is right or righteous are vital attributes of God and are also at the heart of Biblical morality. They are qualities of life required of those who would live in fellowship with the Lord.

---

[2]Kirkpatrick, *The Psalms*, CUP, 1902 and subsequent editions, p. 70.

The emphasis presented in these general terms (v. 2 a, b) is developed or expounded in five more two-line couplets[3] (v. 2c-5b). They involve ten lines, which some scholars regard as an attempt to copy the form but not the contents of the Ten Commandments. Here we maintain the five-couplet format, in which the emphasis of the Ninth Commandment is prominent:

1) Integrity of speech (v. 2c and 3a)

> [He] who speaks the truth from his heart
> and has no slander on his tongue.

The quality of speech in view is not merely factually accurate, but, unlike the flatteries mentioned in Psalm 12, is genuinely heartfelt – the speaker's heart is in what he says. That being so he does not use his tongue to spread false rumours about or to slander others.

2) Integrity in relationships (v. 3 b & c)

> [He] who does his neighbour no wrong
> and casts no slur on his fellow-men.

This couplet builds on the one that precedes it and says that the blameless man doesn't use his tongue to calumniate (Hebrew, *ragal*, means "backbite against") or damage those neighbours with whom he maintains social intercourse (Hebrew, *re'eh*, which NRSV translates as "friends"). In even broader terms he will not rake up muck that would be slanderous against a neighbour and destructive of his relationship with that neighbour.

3) Integrity in moral values (v. 4 a & b)

> [He] who despises a vile man
> but honours those who fear the LORD.

At first sight the clause, "who despises a vile man" (NIV), appears to contradict the immediately preceding line, which reads, "and casts no slur on his fellow-

---

[3]The verse divisions and numbering in this section are unfortunate because some couplets are partly in one verse and partly in the next! Each couplet would stand out more clearly if it were a verse on its own.

man." However this couplet may simply say how a godly person thought of the life-styles of those around him. Some he esteemed lightly because of their bad behaviour and others he honoured because of their reverential trust in (their fear of) the Lord.

The English versions from the AV to the NIV may, perhaps, make the language too strong here. The author may have been using hyperbole as a device to highlight the contrast he was making without wishing to express malice towards those who didn't fear the Lord.

There is an alternative reading in an ancient Jewish translation into Aramaic (a Targum). It seems to have influenced the rendering in the Anglican Book of Common Prayer, which in a quaint way describes the acceptable sojourner in the Lord's sanctuary as, "He that setteth not by himself, but is lowly in his own eyes: and maketh much of them that fear the Lord." This suggests that, rather than despising or even lightly esteeming others, the writer was despising himself – setting no store by his own worth' – and that those who later used his words were doing the same. This certainly harmonises with what has gone before, but some commentators think it rather overstates personal humility and makes the righteous man into a spineless "Uriah Heap" type of figure.

Most exegetes believe, however, that what we have here is an honest statement of how the psalmist felt about his unrighteous neighbours – he esteemed them lightly. In stark contrast he honoured those who feared and walked with the Lord. His attitudes were an expression of the integrity of his heart in relation to moral values – he had little or no time for those who were displeasing to the Lord and he had all the time in the world for those who feared the Lord and walked in his ways. He had integrity and consistency in his moral value system.

4) Integrity of his promises (v. 4 c & d)

> [He] who keeps his oath
> even when it hurts.

When Israel was about to enter the Promised Land, the Lord gave permission for his name to be used in the swearing of oaths: "Fear the LORD your God, serve him only and take your oaths in his name" (Deut. 6:13). This meant that, when they needed to affirm that they were speaking the truth, they could swear oaths using the sacred name Yahweh (or Jehovah). In effect, they would call down his curse on them, if they spoke carelessly or failed to honour their promises. To swear an oath falsely was to profane the LORD's name[4] (Lev. 19:12). Oaths taken in that way were regarded as absolutely binding (Num. 30:2) – as a result one ancient sage said, "it is better not to vow than to make a vow and not fulfil it" (Ecc. 5:5).

The truly godly man is one who fulfils the commitment of his oath "even when it hurts." He doesn't opt out of what he has promised when things turn out to his hurt or detriment. As the law of Deuteronomy 23:21-23 put it, "Whatever your lips utter you must be sure to do, because you made your vow freely to the LORD your God with your own mouth."

It was however acknowledged that sometimes people made oaths rashly or under duress. From such oaths the law provided a way of release by the offering of an appropriate sacrifice of atonement (Lev. 5:4 ff.). And on the purely human level, the wise author of Proverbs prescribed that a person who found himself trapped by what he had said to a neighbour should endeavour to free himself from his commitment by going immediately, without even daring to sleep, to that neighbour and asking for release and freedom—"Go and humble yourself; press your plea with your neighbour ..." (Prov. 6:1-5).

Where a promise made on oath had been broken or, for some reason, had not or could not have been fulfilled, pleading to be released from it would probably involve the offer to pay compensation to the disappointed party. Alternatively some compensating penalty could be imposed. In either case the man of honour had to go through with the consequence of his failure and so keep his integrity even though it involved cost to himself.

Overall the thrust of this section is that the man of God must be careful about the promises or commitments that he makes, especially when he invokes

---

[4]Peter's denying on oath that he knew the Lord Jesus, when in fact he did know him, is an example of swearing falsely (Matt. 26:69-75).

the name of the Lord in an oath.[5] His dealings with those to whom he has committed himself must be characterised by honour and integrity whatever the cost to the person himself: "he keeps his oath even when it hurts."

5) Integrity in acquiring wealth (v. 4 c & d)

The person, who will have access to the Lord's sanctuary, will be one who both uses and acquires his wealth in an honourable – a truly moral – way. That being the case, he will also be a person,

> Who lends his money without usury
> and does not accept a bribe against the innocent.

Usury was a misuse of one's money by lending to another person at an exorbitant rate of interest. It seems that in the ancient world the rate could be as high as 20-25% per month! This led to the prohibition of all usury in the case of loans made to fellow Israelites. But the rules had not always been kept and Ezekiel had to condemn the men of Jerusalem for "taking usury and excessive interest" and so making unjust gain from their neighbours by extortion (Ezek. 22:12).

Scripture teaches that there are several illegitimate ways of acquiring wealth. One is by stealing, which was forbidden by the seventh commandment. Another was resort to what we call gambling – the spreading of a table in devotion to the pagan deities called Fortune and Destiny (Isa. 65:11, 12). But neither of these is mentioned in our psalm, where the focus is on usury and bribery.

A bribe is money or favour given in order to procure some service or advantage for the giver that would not otherwise come to him. Those who demand or take bribes are motivated by selfish desire and are, as Jesus put it, serving money (Mammon). Bribery is always a perversion of justice as one person gets an advantage over another (See, Ex. 23:7, 8; Deut. 16:19; 27:25; 1 Sam. 8:3; Amos 5:7-12).

---

[5]Jesus discouraged the making of oaths and said his followers should have such integrity in their speech that oaths would be unnecessary – "Simply let your 'Yes' be 'Yes' and your 'No', 'No'; anything beyond this comes from the evil one" (Matt. 5:37).

Those, who would be qualified to spend time in the Lord's presence, were those who did not take the excessive interest that is usury and that did not resort to the giving or receiving of bribes. They were people marked by moral integrity in their acquisition of wealth.

Here then we have a five-fold integrity – integrity in relation to speech, to relationships, to moral values, to commitments and in the acquisition and use of wealth.

6) The question transcended (v. 5 c & d)

> He who does these things
>   will never be shaken.

This is the conclusion to the psalm, but more than that it is a promise that the questioner will receive even more than he requested (v. 1). He is promised secure and permanent tenure on God's Holy Hill – he "will never be shaken" (NRSV, "moved").

Thus the aspiration of the psalmist and of later worshippers to be admitted to God's earthly dwelling place for the purpose of worshipping him produced a promise that transcended the request of verse 1. There was a promise of fellowship with the Lord that would be permanent or, at least, that would last for as long as the conditions of verses 2 to 5b were evidenced in the life of a worshipper.

Underlying all Israelite religion was the love and grace of God, who chose his people not because they were good or righteous but simply because he loved them. Just as the Ten Commandments were given, not to present a series of works that would earn salvation, but to show his saved/redeemed people how they should live, so it was with these conditions. They are not works that earn God's salvation, but a life-style that was and still is essential to the continuing enjoyment of fellowship with him.

3. Anticipations of the New Testament

The qualities of life highlighted and indeed advocated in this psalm can be seen as anticipating the teachings of our Lord and of the apostles. For example:

- *"He whose walk is blameless and who does what is righteous"* (v.2 a,b), finds an echo in Jesus' words, "Unless your righteousness surpasses that of the Pharisees ... you will certainly not enter the kingdom of heaven" (Matt. 5:20; cf. 5:6, 10; Eph. 1:4; 1 Thes. 3:13).
- *"Who speaks the truth from his heart ..."* (v. 2c-3c), has echoes in Matt. 5:33-37 – "Simply let your 'Yes' be 'Yes', and your 'No', 'No'; anything beyond this comes from the evil one" (cf. Eph. 4:25; Col. 3:8, 9).
- *"Who honours those who fear the LORD"* (v. 4b), is echoed in the actions of Maltese people, who honoured Paul and his companions "in many ways" (Acts 28:10).
- *"Who keeps his oath ..."* (v. 4c,d), resonates with our Lord's instruction to avoid (unnecessary) oaths – "I tell you, Do not swear at all ..."(Matt. 5:33-37; cf. Matt. 23:16-22; James 5:12).
- *"He who does these things will never be shaken"* (v. 5 c, d) is echoed in 2 Pet. 1:10 – "For if you do these things, you will never fall."

That there are such strong echoes – virtual quotations of our psalm in the New Testament surely indicates that its teaching is abidingly relevant and, therefore, relevant to all who today profess to follow Christ. The question each of us must ask ourselves is, 'Do I maintain the kind of integrity that is set out in these verses?' If I am not doing so, it is surely time that I examined my lifestyle and sought to put it right before God.

PART II

TOPICS ARISING FROM THE PSALMS

CHAPTER 19

THE THEOLOGY OF THE PSALMISTS

The psalms are a unique resource. They record, in a fuller way than any other book of the Bible, how men of the old covenant era expressed and maintained their relationships with the Lord. In the process they also inform us of those men's theology, i.e., their beliefs about God.

We must always remember that the psalmists lived and wrote over an extended period of, perhaps, half a millennium. They did so as Old Testament saints, who did not have the fuller revelation of God that we Christians have received through Christ and in the New Testament. We will, therefore, find that the message of some Old Testament texts are not in continuity with New Testament revelation. One example is the use of imprecation, which seems seriously out of harmony with the demand of Jesus that the people of God love their enemies as well as their neighbours (Matt. 5:43-48).

This contrast illustrates the importance of what is called "progressive revelation," which recognises that God revealed himself and his purposes progressively to men and women in ways that fitted their situations and their knowledge of him at a particular time. As a result we find, for example, certain Old Testament practices which have been transformed either by later Old Testament revelation or by the gospel of Christ. The imprecatory passages of the psalms and, indeed, of other Old Testament writings belong to the Old Covenant order that has been superseded in Christ and the New Covenant. With that in mind, we can proceed to examine the theology of the psalmists, that is their beliefs about the nature and character of God.

1. Sovereign over all creation

The psalmists acknowledged God, Yahweh, the LORD, as the Creator of everything that exists. For them he was "the Maker of heaven and earth" (Ps. 134:3) and the one who formed the mountains by his power (Ps. 65:3). They believed that he created not just the world in which men live but also the heavenly bodies, the sun, the moon and the stars and the heavens that are his own dwelling place. In a word, they insisted that he created everything that exists. They, therefore, called on the whole creation to praise him, because as one anonymous psalmist tells us:

> He commanded and they were created.
> He set them in place for ever and ever ...
>
> —Ps. 148:1-6; cf. 89:11-13

As Creator, God occupied an awesome place in the thinking of the psalmists. He was the owner of and the sovereign ruler over everything he had made:

> The earth is the LORD's, and everything in it,
>   the world and all who live in it.
>
> —Ps. 24:1

Psalm 47, which is a psalm of praise to the LORD as King, develops the theme in Chapter 9 above:

> How awesome is the LORD Most High,
>   the great king over all the earth!
>
> —v. 2

> For God is the King of all the earth;
>   sing to him a psalm of praise.
> God reigns over the nations;
>   God is seated on his holy throne.
>
> —v. 7

> for the kings of the earth belong to God;
>   he is greatly exalted.
>
> —v. 9

2. A personal God

The God of the psalmists is a living person: "The LORD lives" (Ps. 18:46). A person is a being with powers of thinking (rationality), feeling (emotion) and willing (volition). A person is also a being whose actions are subject to moral evaluation as right or wrong, good or evil.

Again and again the psalmists address God as a person – "you" – "Praise awaits **you**, O God, in Zion" (Ps. 65:1; cf. 4:1; 5:3; 8:1; 9:1; 10:1; 42:1 etc. etc.). When they speak about the Lord, they refer to him in personal terms – as "him" or "he"—"Give thanks to the LORD, for **he** is good" (Ps. 136:1; cf. 18:1-50; 29:6). As such a person, the Lord is:

- **Omnipresent** – he is a spiritual being who is not limited by spatial considerations. He is present everywhere and so is always able to guide his servants. He is never inaccessible to them. Little wonder David asked, "Where can I go from your Spirit? Where can I flee from your presence?" (Ps. 139:1-12).
- **Omnipotent** – he is all-powerful – the mighty one who is able to do whatever he wills (Ps. 115:3).
- **Omniscient** – he is all-knowing: "he knows the secrets of the heart" (Ps. 44:21b). He has knowledge beyond man's comprehension—"You know when I sit and when I rise." (Ps. 139:1-6).

As such a person the Lord has revealed himself and his will to men, declaring his glory through his works of creation:

> The heavens declare the glory of God;
>> the skies proclaim the work of his hands.
> Day after day they pour forth speech;
>> night after night they display knowledge.
> There is no speech or language
>> where their voice is not heard.
> Their voice goes out into all the earth,
>> their words to the ends of the world.
>
> —Ps. 19:1-4

He also revealed himself through the words he gave to men. As Psalm 147 says, "he sends his command to the earth; his word runs swiftly. ... He has revealed his word to Jacob, his laws and decrees to Israel" (vv. 15-20). His words are, of course, words of instruction and are nowhere more firmly extolled than in Psalm 119, in which every verse – all 176 of them – mention the revealed word of God which is referred to in terms like law, statutes, precepts, decrees and commands. The message of the psalm is that the man, who walks according to God's revelation of himself in his Law is the one, who is really blessed (v. 1).

3. Sustainer of all life

Two passages highlight God's constant provision for his creation, Psalms. 65:9-13 and 104:10-30. In these David and an anonymous psalmist respectively sing praise to the Lord for his abundant provision of the needs of the earth and its flora, fauna and human departments. These all, the living creatures of land and sea, "look to you to give them their food at the proper time" (104:27).

Similarly David expressed his faith in God's adequate provision for all living things in Psalm 145: "You open your hand and satisfy the desires of every living thing" (v. 15, cf. Ps. 23 and chapter 9 above).

4. Ever present with his people

In Psalm 3 David asserts that he felt safe because of the Lord's presence with him —"You are a shield around me, O LORD; ... I will not fear the tens of thousands drawn up against me on every side" (vv. 3-6). The same thought dominates the central section of Psalm 23—"I will fear no evil, for *you are with me*" (v. 4a). When, at another point in his life, David had to confess his terrible sins of adultery and murder, he pleaded earnestly that the Lord would not deny him his presence—"Do not cast me from your presence or take your Holy Spirit from me" (Ps. 51:11).

The focus in the psalms, as in the rest of the Old Testament, is often in terms of the Lord's face or countenance (*panim* in Hebrew). When David asked, "How long will you hide your face from me" (Ps 13:1b) he was lamenting the fact that at that moment he felt cut off from God's presence. In contrast in Psalm 22:24b he expressed the opposite reality, namely that God had not deserted his afflicted servant: "He has not hidden his face from him but has listened to his cry for help." In Psalm 24 David speaks of the Lord blessing those who seek his face (i.e.' his presence) and in Psalm 27 he prayed, "Do not hide your face from me.... Do not reject me or forsake me, O God my Saviour." Then in confident faith he added, "Though my father and mother forsake me, the LORD will receive me." Clearly closeness to the Lord and enjoyment of his presence meant everything to David.

There was a parallel emphasis on God's presence with his people, Israel. The anonymous author of Psalm 67 prayed, "May God be gracious *to us* and bless *us* and make his face (his presence) shine *upon us*" (v. 1). David prayed that God's ways would be known to other peoples and that they would come to fear him and join in his praise (Ps. 77:2-7).

In the collection of psalms, known as "Psalms of ascents" (Pss. 120-134) the focus of the pilgrims ascending to Jerusalem was on meeting with the Lord in Zion, his house. He was regarded as specially present there (Ps. 132:13, 14):

> For the LORD has chosen Zion,
> > he has desired it for his dwelling:
> This is my resting place for ever and ever;
> > here I will sit enthroned, for I have desired it.

In another of these psalms, Psalm 124, which we considered in chapter 6 above, David glories in the Lord as the defender of his people: "If the LORD had not been on our side, when men attacked us, ... the raging waters would have swept us away. ... Our help is in the name of the Lord." Such an expression of faith assumes the LORD's presence with those he had delivered.

Another psalmist, Asaph, also connected the face (the presence) of the Lord with deliverance or salvation: "make your face shine upon us that we may be saved" (Ps. 80:3, 7). The same connection of God's presence undoubtedly underlies the deliverances for which thanksgiving is demanded in Psalm 107 (See chapter 6 above).

5. Sovereign over human history

The psalms that acknowledge and praise the kingly role of the Lord (chapter 9 above) are affirmations that he is the ultimate controller of human history. He is "the King of all the earth." As such he reigns over the nations and the kings of the earth belong to him (Ps. 47:7-9). In Psalm 93 the Lord is presented as "the Most High **over** all the earth" (v.9). His sovereignty is such that he can laugh at and rebuke those who gather against him (Ps. 2:4-6).

In Psalm 44:1-3 the conquest of the land occupied by the Israelites is attributed to the Lord. It was by his hand and because of his presence with them and his love for them that the land had become theirs—"It was not by their sword that they won the land … it was your right hand, your arm and the light of your face, for you loved them" (v. 3).

In greater detail Psalm 105 surveyed the history of God's people from the call of Abraham to the Exodus from Egypt (vv. 8-41). The course of that history is entirely attributed to the Lord's planning and action and to his faithfulness to his covenant promises: "for he remembered his holy promise given to his servant Abraham" (NB vv. 8-11). The psalmist's call was that his people give thanks to the Lord and remember the wonders **he** had done for them throughout their history (vv. 1, 5).

In sovereign power the Lord had brought the Israelites out of Egypt (105:37, 38). He drove the Caananites out of their land and gave it to Israel (Ps. 44:1-3; cf. 111:6). Centuries later, when those people were in serious trouble and were driven from their land and into exile, they cried to him and, as sovereign over the nations, he heard their cries and delivered them from their distresses (Ps. 107:6, 13, 19, 28, 33-42).

6. The morally perfect One

The perfection of God's character is often subsumed in the words "holy" and "holiness." To be holy (Hebrew, *qadosh*) means to be separated from something and to be set apart to or consecrated to someone or something else. The vessels of the tabernacle were holy in the sense that they were set apart from common use and for specific use in the religious rituals of the sanctuary where God was pleased to make his presence known (cf. Ex. 40:9, 10). Similarly a betrothed woman was holy in the sense of not being available to other suitors because she was consecrated to the one to whom she was betrothed. In relation to God, holiness refers negatively to his total separation from all that is imperfect, impure, unrighteous or evil and positively to his total perfection in terms of his character and behaviour. He is morally perfect.

One psalmist called for worship at the Lord's footstool and added, "he is holy" (Ps. 99:5), and David addressed the Lord as "the Holy One." In Psalm 22:3 he said, "You are enthroned as the Holy One." David was saying that the LORD is free of evil and is morally perfect in all he does—He rules in holiness, "seated on his holy throne" (Ps. 47:8). He speaks with integrity, swearing by his holiness and saying, "I will not lie to David" (Ps. 89:35). His activities that gave salvation to Israel were achieved by his right hand and holy arm (Ps. 98:1), which means that he gave victory within the canons of his own holy character.

In parallel with this, the psalmists often assert that the Lord is righteous (Hebrew, *tsadiq*, meaning just, equitable, fair, true or innocent). We read of David addressing him as the "righteous God, who searches hearts and minds" (Ps. 7:9; cf. 119:37) and declaring, "the LORD is righteous, he loves justice …" (Ps. 11:7; cf. 33:5). Similarly David says, "my tongue will speak of your righteousness" (Ps. 35.28). Asaph adds, "the heavens proclaim his righteousness, for God himself is judge" (Ps. 50:6). Because God's righteousness is everlasting his commands are always right: "your statutes are for ever right" (Ps. 119:144) – "all your commands are righteous" (119:172). The Lord is then both holy and righteous, morally perfect.

7. Holding men to account

The first psalm contrasts the righteous and the wicked and affirms that there is a difference between them in terms of their acceptance by God. The wicked will not stand in the judgment – they will have no place in the company of the righteous and will ultimately perish. This is the psalmist's way of saying that the Lord governs his creatures on a moral basis. He is a moral being and has made men in his image and, therefore, as moral beings whom he can judge righteous or unrighteous, good or evil.

When he penned Psalms 32 and 51, David was deeply conscious both of his accountability before God and of the justice with which God had judged him for his sins of adultery and murder (cf. 2 Samuel 12). He knew he had offended the Lord and needed his forgiveness:

> When I kept silent,
>   my bones wasted away
>   through my groaning all day long.
> For day and night your hand was heavy upon me; ...
> Then I acknowledged my sin to you ...
> I said, "I will confess my transgressions to the LORD"—
>   and you forgave the guilt of my sin.
>
> —32:3-5

> I know my transgressions,
>   and my sin is always before me.
> Against you, you only, have I sinned
>   and done what is evil in your sight,
> so that you are proved right when you speak
>   and justified when you judge.
>
> —51:3, 4

The imprecatory passages, which we will discuss in chapter 25, show an underlying awareness of man's accountability before God. Why, otherwise, would the psalmists have asked the Lord to exercise retribution on those they regarded as having sinned against him as well as against themselves? The same is true of Psalms 37 and 73, both of which grapple with the problems created by the fact that righteous men often suffered adversity, while the wicked prospered, a fact that seemed to call in question the justice of God's providence. The answer given in Psalm 37 was that such travesties of justice would be short lived and that in the end the wrongs of this life would be put right:

> Evil men will be cut off ...
>   a little while, and the wicked will be no more: ...
> All sinners will be destroyed;
>   the future of the wicked will be cut off.
>
> —Ps. 37:9, 10, 38

> Surely you place them on slippery ground;
>> you cast them down to ruin.
> How suddenly are they destroyed,
>> completely swept away by terrors!

—Ps. 73:18, 19

The psalmists believed, then, that the Lord calls men who do evil and those who oppress the righteous to account for their actions and be subject to his wrath.

> Those who are far from you will perish;
>> you destroy all who are unfaithful to you.

—Ps. 73:27

8. Loving and compassionate

The psalmists thought of the Lord as a God in whom faithful love was an essential element in his nature and character. They did not, however, come up to the level of the apostle John, who could say most emphatically, "God is love." Nonetheless they knew him as one who loved his people – he loved the descendants of Jacob, who was also called Israel (Ps. 47:4).

Being compassionate or merciful, the Lord forgave the sins of his people, people who, in spite of all his goodness, had kept on sinning (Ps. 78:32, 38). David addressed him as "a compassionate and gracious God, slow to anger, abounding in love and faithfulness" (Ps. 86:15; cf. 111:4; 145:8).

In a host of passages the psalmists use the Hebrew word, *chesedh*, of the Lord. The AV mostly translated this word as mercy, but in the main its nuance is that of faithful or steadfast love and covenant loyalty. The God who chose the Israelites in faithful love, kept the promise he had sworn to their forefathers (Deut. 7:8). Keeping his covenant, he still loved them and was still faithful to the covenant he made with Abraham and confirmed to Jacob (Ps. 105:8-11). Indeed, he remembers his covenanted love for ever (Ps. 111:5b, cf. chapter 21). He was a God of love.

Psalm 89:1, 2 sums up what the psalmists believed:

I will sing of the LORD's great love (*chesedh*) for ever;

with my mouth I will make your faithfulness known
through all generations.
I will declare that your love stands firm for ever,
that you established your faithfulness in heaven itself.

Forgiving the penitent

In a number of psalms, especially, for example, Psalms 6; 32; 51; 106 and 130, we have references to the forgiveness of penitent sinners. The first of these does not specifically mention sin, but the idea that God would forgive him seems implicit in David's request that the Lord would not discipline him in wrath, but would rather extend mercy to him (6:1-3). His open confession in Psalm 51 has already been the focus of our attention (Chapter 11 above) and so has his heart-felt expression of thanks for God's forgiveness in Psalm 32:1-5 (Chapter 5 above). The author of Psalm 130 – a psalm of ascents sung by pilgrims approaching Jerusalem and its temple – was evidently both penitent and assured that God would forgive him, when he wrote:

> If you, O LORD, keep a record of sins,
>   O Lord, who can stand?
> But with you there is forgiveness;
>   therefore you are feared.

—vv. 3-4

Psalm 106 gives expression to confession of the nation's sin—"We have sinned even as our fathers did; we have done wrong and acted wickedly" (v. 6). The verses that follow (vv. 7-43) detail some of the nation's sins from the time when they were enslaved in Egypt to the captivity of the Jews in Babylon. This section concludes with this telling comment, "they wasted away in their sin" (v. 43c).

The final section is an affirmation that the Lord had heard his people's cries for deliverance and in his great love had even moved their captors to have pity on them. Their request that the Lord would deliver them from the penalty of their sins was answered as he had gathered them from the nations into which they had scattered. The great burst of praise in the final verse (48) is an acknowledgment that they had been forgiven and restored. Psalm, 107, repeatedly and emphatically gives thanks for that very restoration.

That God is able and willing to forgive those who come before him in true penitence is an expression of his love.

Conclusion

The psalmists' view of God has the essentials, the seminal ideas not just of Old Covenant theology but also of New Testament or Christian theology. Any valid study of the Christian doctrine of God begins with the teachings of the Old Testament, which are so well highlighted in the Psalms, and then adds what our Lord taught about God as his own Father and as the Father of those who put their trust in him.

The LORD, Yahweh/Jehovah is Creator of all, a living personal being who provides for and sustains all creation and controls individual and communal history. He is the morally perfect one who holds men to account, who forgives the penitent and whose love is steadfast and unfailing. He is the God, who revealed himself in even fuller glory in the person of the Lord Jesus Christ, our Saviour.

He is also our God, the God and Father of our Lord Jesus Christ and our Father in him.

CHAPTER 20

THE PSALMISTS' ANTHROPOLOGY

In the previous chapter we were concerned with the beliefs of the psalmists about God – their theology. In this chapter we examine their anthropology, that is, what they believed about the nature of man and the way in which he should relate to God.

1. Man is God's creature

Man's position as a creature of God is more assumed than proclaimed, but it lies behind and conditions all the thinking of the psalmists about themselves and about their fellow human beings. The logic of their assertion that God is the Creator of and the Sovereign over all that exists (above chapter 19) is that man is included in that "all." He is a creature of God and lives under his sovereign rule.

Reflecting on the glory of the Lord displayed in the heavens (Ps. 8: 1-3), David asked himself a crucial question: "what is man that you are mindful of him, the son of man that you care for him?" Looking at the heavens in their superb majesty and looking at puny man,[1] he just couldn't understand how the God, who created such glory in the sky, could be interested in and actually care for such an insignificant creature as man. But he knew that the Lord does so and had made man just a little lower than the angelic beings, who inhabit the heavenly realms. He had even "crowned him with glory and honour," making him ruler over the works of his hands and over all the lower elements of living

---

[1] Hebrew, *ĕnosh*, a fragile, mortal and relatively insignificant person.

creation (vv. 5-8). In these verses David was obviously picking up the thought
of Genesis 1:28-30 to affirm that, while man was insignificant in comparison to
the majesty of the Lord, he was still a creature of great significance and worth
(below Section 5).

2. Man is made in God's image

While, in Psalm 8, David did not specifically say that man had been created in
God's image, he clearly believed that to be the case. By using words from the
creation story (vv. 6-8), he was endorsing its truth, including the fact that man
had been created by God and fashioned in his own image.

God, as we saw in chapter 19 is a personal being – he thinks,[2] feels[3] and
exercises will by making choices and performing actions[4] that can be morally
evaluated. He is the supreme person and the archetype of all personality. As
such he always does what is right: "none can compare to you" (Ps. 40:5c, NRSV).

The psalmists knew that they and their fellows were also persons, who
were made in God's image. They were thinking, feeling, acting beings, whose
lives were also subject to moral evaluation. Unlike God, however, they often
acted in ways that were immoral and wrong.

The psalmists demonstrated their personalities through their thoughts
expressed in what they said and wrote. They showed emotions, like love (Pss.
18:1; 116:1) and sorrow (Pss. 13:2; 116:3). They exercised their wills by making
choices and by then acting them out by, for example, singing of God's praise and
teaching his wisdom. They made moral judgments about their own thoughts
and actions and about those of others. David, for example, called on the Lord
to contend with those whom he judged to be wrongly contending with him,
seeking his life and plotting his ruin (Ps. 35:1-4). In another psalm he spoke of
those who never thought of doing a kindness but hounded to death the poor

[2]See e.g., Ps. 92:5, "how profound your thoughts" (cf. Ps. 139:17 etc.).
[3]He loved Jacob and Zion (Pss. 47:4; 78:68). He expressed emotions, like love (Pss 86:15; 111:4
etc.) and anger (Pss. 21:9; 95:11 etc. etc.).
[4]His deeds, for example, are remembered – "he performs miracles" (Ps. 77:11, 14) – his deeds
are seen in the deep etc. (Ps. 107:24). He is a God of action, whose ordinances are altogether
righteous (Ps. 19:9).

and the needy and the broken-hearted (Ps. 109:16). Such people's thoughts were the cause of their evil actions.

Because God and man as persons have capacities in common – thinking, feeling and willing – they can communicate with each other and in a very real sense know each other. The psalmists were able, whether in praise, prayer or complaint, to speak to the Lord in a way that showed they knew him intimately. At the same time they called on other men to enter into a relationship, in which they too would know him: "Be still and know that I am God ..." (Ps. 46:10).

The reverse aspect of this truth is that man is known by God. As Psalm 44:21 puts it, "he knows the secrets of the heart." Thus David could say:

> O LORD, you have searched me
>   and you know me.
> You know when I sit and when I rise;
>   you perceive my thoughts from afar.
> You discern my going out and my lying down;
>   you are familiar with all my ways.
> Before a word is on my tongue
>   you know it completely, O LORD.
>
> —Ps. 139:1-4

The "knowledge of God" in the psalms will receive fuller treatment in Chapter 25 below.

3. Man has obligations before God

The psalmists recognised that man's god-ward obligations were at two distinguishable levels. There were universal obligations resting on every human being through what are often called creation ordinances and there were specific additional obligations resting on the Israelites, who, as a people, had a special covenant relationship with the Lord.

In some cases the psalmists focused on both areas of responsibility in the same psalm (e.g., Ps. 66). They even used God's dealings with his covenant people alongside his awesome deeds in the world at large to affirm his sovereign power and as the basis for an appeal that world-wide obedience be given to him.

1) Universal (Creation ordinance) obligations

The bottom line was that God, the ultimate judge, holds all men responsible for what they think and do and rewards them on the basis of their morality, be it good or bad. In a psalm attributed to David we read, "The LORD reigns for ever. ... he will judge the world in righteousness" (Ps. 9:7, 8). Asaph says, "He summons the heavens above and the earth, that he may judge his people: ... The heavens proclaim his righteousness, for God himself is judge" (Ps. 50:4-6; cf. 7:8, 9 etc.). His judgments extend to all peoples – "He will judge the world in righteousness" (Ps 96:14).

The second psalm (see Chapter 15 above) asks why the peoples of the world and their rulers plot against the Lord (vv. 1-3). The Lord, we are told, is amused and rebukes them in anger, terrifying them with a threat of his wrath (vv. 4-6). The clear implication is that those rebellious peoples had obligations towards the Sovereign God of all the earth. In the final stanza (vv. 10-12) their kings are called to submit to and serve the Lord lest he become angry and destroy them.

Psalm 66 opens with a call to all peoples of the earth to sing with joy to God. This is surely a call to recognise the sovereignty of him who eternally rules mankind, whose eyes watch over the nations. Especially significant for our purpose at this point is the injunction of verse 7c: "let not the rebellious rise up against him." The rebels in view were from nations, over which the Lord acted as a moral watchdog (v. 7b, cf. Ps. 11:4) and who are therefore urged to acknowledge him by singing praise to him (vv. 1 and 8).

Neither psalm spells out the specific moral or legal obligations that the peoples of the world should have been obeying. But in calling on all mankind to submit to and sing the praises of the Lord the psalmists certainly indicate that all peoples of the earth were obligated before him.[5]

---

[5]Scripture shows that the Creation ordinances applied to all mankind.

2) Israelite covenant obligations

In the time of the psalmists the obligations of Israel as God's covenant people arose from the laws received and covenant commitments made at Sinai[6] (Note Ex. 20-24). The key words are, "We will do everything the LORD has said; we will obey" (Ex. 24:7). Loyalty to the covenant commitment made at Sinai demanded obedience to the laws God had given them as a code of conduct appropriate for those he had redeemed from the slavery of Egypt.

David was quite clear that his people knew the terms of God's covenant: "The LORD confides in those who fear him; he makes his covenant known to them" (Ps. 25:14). The psalmists also knew that he would remain faithful to his side of the bargain: "he remembers his covenant for ever" (Ps. 105:8; cf. 111:5, 9).

The Israelites were often guilty of breaking their covenant obligations before the Lord: "their hearts were not loyal to him, they were not faithful to his covenant" (Ps. 78:37). In contrast the psalmists were concerned to maintain their own integrity as obedient servants of the Lord. David, for example, says, "I have kept the ways of the LORD; I have not done evil by turning from my God. All his laws are before me; I have not turned away from his decrees. I have been blameless before him and have kept myself from sin" (Ps. 18:21-23). He also says that in keeping God's commands there is great reward (19:7-11). Then in Psalm 26:1 he even asks the Lord to vindicate him by virtue of the fact that he had "led a blameless life!"

This emphasis seems to contrast rather sharply with David's confession of sin in psalms like Psalm 51! However, the two strands of thought have to be regarded as complementary and have to be held in balance. We can say that David and the others, living in the context of Old Testament life, were not so much asserting their moral perfection as placing themselves within the company of those who were enjoying God's favour, including the favour of forgiveness. They were men who were living in accordance with the divinely inspired wisdom they had received and were enjoying blessing, because they

---

[6]Note Exodus 20-24 and our next chapter.

"did not walk in the counsel of the wicked," but rather delighted "in the law of the LORD" (Ps. 1:1-3). As the opening lines of Psalm 119 put it, they walked blamelessly according to the law of the Lord: "they do nothing wrong; they walk in his ways" (vv. 1-3). This does not mean that they were morally perfect and never failed in their pursuit of righteous living. They sometimes sinned and needed forgiveness, which was available to them within the terms of their covenant.

4. Man is a sinful being

The various penitential psalms (Pss. 6; 32; 38; 51; 102; 130 and 143) present a picture of man as a sinner either in need of or rejoicing in God's forgiveness. David's confession in Psalm 51:5 highlights the fact that sin is inherent in human nature: "Surely, I was sinful at birth, sinful from the time my mother conceived me." But David not only confessed his inherent sinfulness – his fallen nature – he confessed that he was given to acting foolishly: "You know my folly, O God, my guilt is not hidden from your eyes" (Ps. 69:5). He knew that sin, as a matter of his inner heart, could cause a break in his communion with the Lord (Ps. 66:18) and that no-one living was or could be "righteous before God" (Ps. 143:2). David knew that God is always right and fully justified when he passes judgment on a person's sin (Ps. 51:4b). Man is a sinner both by nature and in practice. He is guilty before God, his Maker.

1) He is liable to punishment

The psalmists didn't hesitate to speak of the wrath of God that is attracted to sinners because of their sinful thoughts and actions. The Lord is presented as reacting in anger to those who behaved sinfully. They would be rewarded as they deserved!

Psalm 1 sets the tone: "the wicked will not stand in the judgment, nor sinners in the assembly of the righteous" (v. 5). In Psalm 34 David asserts that "the face of the LORD is against those who do evil, to cut off the memory of them from the earth" (v.16). The anonymous writer of Psalm 94 concluded:

> He will repay them for their sins

and destroy them for their wickedness,
the LORD, our God will destroy them.

—v. 23

In most cases it is clear that the wrath of which the psalmists wrote was thought
to be experienced here on earth, either during the lifetime of the sinners or
in the deaths that terminated their lives. In Psalm 78:31, for example, God's
wrath had cut down in death the sturdiest youths of Israel. It is not presented
as something they would experience after death. In Psalm 88:7 the author says
that God's wrath was then lying heavily upon him. He was experiencing it as
he wrote, not expecting it after his death. This seems to be true of the other
references to God's anger – it imposes punishment and even death within the
sphere of life on earth (see, Pss. 2:5; 12; 21:9; 59:13; 79:6 etc.).

Psalm 37 grapples with a problem that troubled many in Bible times – the
problem of the wicked prospering while the righteous suffered adversity and
became jealously fretful. From his own experience David, as an old man, had
a philosophy that enabled him to cope with what appeared to be an injustice
on God's part. He advised a fretting friend to wait on the Lord and assured him
that while there was a future for the man of peace, sinners would be destroyed.
They might flourish for a time but in the end they would be cut off – they
would pass away and be no more (vv. 34-38). They would get their due reward.
Psalm 73 tackles the same basic problem and concludes that those who are far
from God will perish – God will destroy them (v. 27; cf. Pss. 54:5; 145:20).
The imprecatory passages in a number of psalms (Chapter 19 above) call down
God's wrath on sinners. In Psalm 69 David prayed that God would pour out
his wrath on his enemies and blot them out of the book of life (vv. 22-28). He
wanted them destroyed.

Clearly, then, the psalmists believed that God held men accountable for
their actions and would punish – destroy – those who were unrighteous and
wicked. But did this mean punishment in this life or in an after-life? It is difficult
to answer that question. The Hebrew verb translated "destroy" in Ps. 73:27,
(tsamath) is relatively rare and can mean "silence," "cut off" and "destroy." It
is also used to indicate human actions – with the Lord's help David had cut
off some of his enemies (Pss. 18:40; 69:4). Similarly the Lord's destruction of

the wicked could, then, have been viewed as happening before or at death and without any suggestion that they would take place in an after-life.

2) He is unable to cure his sinfulness

The psalmists believed that nothing a man himself could do would wipe away his sinfulness and his guilt before God. Nothing he could do for himself – even offering sacrifices according to the Mosaic Law could not bring about his deliverance from sin and its guilt: "You do not delight in sacrifice, or I would bring it." What God wanted was a broken and a contrite heart, a heart that knew the sinfulness of sin and that was turning away from it and turning to God in penitence and faith (Ps. 51:16, 17). Similarly no one could do anything to effect reconciliation to God for another person: "No man can redeem the life of another or give to God a ransom for him" (Ps. 49:7). In a word the psalmists believed that personal redemption and justification before God was a matter not of human effort, but of God's gracious provision.

Hence David's cry for God's mercy: "Have mercy on me O God,... blot out my transgressions. Wash away all my iniquity and cleanse me from my sin" (Ps. 51:1, 2). For this cleansing he was absolutely dependent on God graciously dealing with his sin and his guilt. And when that happened he could only burst out in a song of praise:

> Blessed is he
> > whose transgressions are forgiven,
> > whose sins are covered.
> Blessed is the man
> > whose sin the LORD does not count against him
> > and in whose spirit is no deceit.
>
> —Ps. 32:1, 2

5. Man is of worth to God

Though the psalmists presented man as a sinner, they knew that God could and did grant forgiveness to penitents. They knew that man had real worth in God's eyes. Sinful men, who turned to him in repentance, had hope of redemption and thus of a new, a right relationship with the Lord.

That God valued men is shown in the various references to his redeeming works for them. He would not have gone to the lengths he did to guide, to protect and to renew individuals and his own people, Israel, if they had not been exceedingly valuable to him.

David prayed to the Lord as his **Redeemer**[7] (Ps. 19:14) and asked that the Lord would in mercy **redeem** Israel (Ps. 25:22). In a time of trouble, when enemies were trying to destroy him and his people, David prayed, "Come near and rescue me; **redeem** me because of my foes" (Ps. 69:18; cf. 25:22; 44:26; 74:12-14; 78:5; 106:10; 111:9; 130:8 etc.).

In Psalm 107, "**the redeemed of the LORD**" (v. 2) are those who had been scattered abroad at the time of the Exile. Now, having been freed to return to their own land, they were "**the redeemed**" (Hebrew, the *ge'ûlîm*) who were repeatedly called on to give appropriate thanks to the Lord (Ps.107:1, 8, 15). In several psalms redemption relates to the deliverance of individuals and of the nation from sin and its penalties – for example, "He himself will *redeem* Israel from all their sins" (Ps. 130:7, 8).

Those who redeem something consider what they redeem to be of real worth. Similarly the God, who redeems men, must consider them to be of real value. It was, of course, our Lord, who put the ultimate value on human beings: "more valuable than the birds of the air" (Matt. 6:25-27) and more valuable than "the whole world." "What good is it," he asked, "for a man to gain the whole world, yet forfeit his soul (his self)?" (Mark 8:36, 37 etc.).

---

[7]Hebrew noun, *go'el*, means a person who frees another either by avenging some wrong he had suffered or by paying a ransom somehow equated to the worth of the other. The verb, *gaal*, means to act as a redeemer.

CHAPTER 21

COVENANT IN THE PSALMS

An appreciation of 'covenant' is fundamental to a proper understanding of the relationship between God and his people. From the creation to the cross and beyond that to Christian experience, God has made and honoured commitments through a series of promises or covenants.

1. Covenants in Old Testament times

In Old Testament times, as today, a covenant was an agreement between two parties, which in some way bound them to each other. The Hebrew for a covenant (a treaty or agreement) is *berith*, which is thought to be derived from a verb meaning 'to bind' and so to refer to a binding agreement. A covenant involved both privileges and responsibilities and was confirmed or made binding by solemn promises, which were often given on oath.

In Scripture covenants were of two main types:

1) Negotiated or bilateral covenants

In these two more or less equal parties negotiated about and agreed on how they would relate to each other. These covenants were ratified by formalities, which could involve oaths, ceremonial meals, the passing of gifts or money from one party to the other, or the erection of some permanent monument to remind the parties of what they had agreed.

Old Testament examples include:

- Abraham's treaty with Abimelech, which was sealed with an oath (Gen. 21:22-34).
- The treaty that settled the dispute between Laban and Jacob. This was ratified by the erection of a monument and by sharing in a meal (Gen.31:22-55, NB vv 44-54).
- Joshua's "treaty of peace" with the deceiving Gibeonites. The Israelite leaders ratified this by making an oath (Josh. 9:1-15).
- The compact between David and the Israelite people, by virtue of which he became their king (1 Chr. 11:1-3).
- The covenant binding David to Jonathan (1 Sam 23:18).

2) Imposed or unilateral covenants

In these a dominant – a suzerain – party *imposed* its will on a subordinate one, i.e., its vassal. Examples include:

- Joshua's imposition of the status of wood-cutters and water-carriers on the deceptive Gibeonites (Josh. 9:16-27). It is noteworthy that Joshua and his fellow-elders kept their earlier covenant commitments (v. 19).
- Jehoiakim, son of Josiah, was the victim of such a covenant imposed on him by Pharaoh Neco, king of Egypt (2 Kgs. 23:34-37).
- During Jehoiakim's reign Nebuchadnezzar of Babylon invaded Judah, ended the Egyptian suzerainty and made Jehoiakim his vassal for three years (2 Kgs. 24:1).
- Three months after Jehoiakim's death in 597 BC Nebuchadnezzar's forces again besieged Judah. As a result Zedekiah became a client king under Babylonian suzerainty. However, after nine years he rebelled and provoked a further Babylonian invasion that led to his capture and two years later to the Jewish exile in Babylon (2 Kgs. 24:18-25:26; cf. Ezek. 17:11-21).

3) Marriage covenants

Marriage covenants were essentially parity agreements between families but were often more or less imposed on both bride and groom. In some cases, like those of Joseph and Samson the will of the groom was taken into account.

Three passages indicate that the making of a marriage covenant involved the presentation of a gift (Hebrew, *mohar*, AV, dowry, NIV, price or bride-price) by the prospective husband and his family to the father of his intended bride (Gen. 34:12; Ex. 22:16; 1 Sam. 18:25). In the third instance Saul demanded, not money, but 100 Philistine foreskins from David! The content of the *mohar* seems to have been agreed and paid in part or in full at the point of the couple's betrothal. They were then committed to and were in covenant with each other.

Two references to marriage as a covenant relate to a bride or a groom breaking their commitments. An adulteress is described as having "left the partner of her youth and [having] ignored the covenant she made [with him] before God" (Prov. 2:17). And men are charged with breaking faith with the wives of their marriage covenants to which the Lord was regarded as being witness (Mal. 2:14).

There is no record in Scripture giving the terms of an Israelite marriage covenant. But from Jewish literature originating at Elephantine in Upper Egypt in the 5th century BC, we learn that the groom made a formal declaration, possibly an oath, about the bride: "She is my wife and I am her husband from this day and for ever." Since the Elephantine Jews had fled from Judea at the time of the exile, we can safely assume that such wording had been used there in earlier times.

2. God's gracious covenant promises

Since God was sovereign Lord of all the earth and its peoples, his covenants were more akin to the imposed suzerain-vassal type. He acted unilaterally, announcing his promises and imposing his terms on the human recipients of his love and grace. The unfolding Old Testament story is the progressive revelation of his covenantal grace in a series of steps, which point forward to and find fulfilment in the coming of Christ and the new Covenant:

1) The covenant with Noah

This promise was made before the flood (Gen. 6:18-22). On its subsequent inauguration God said that there would never again be such a flood. The rainbow was a sign that it had come into operation (Gen. 9:8-17). This covenant was unconditional and was to last forever.

2) The covenant with Abraham

In this God, as suzerain, unilaterally promised that the descendants of Abraham and Sarah would multiply and possess the whole land of Canaan—"she (Sarah) will be the mother of nations, kings and peoples will come from her" (Gen. 17:19, cf. 12:2). Male circumcision, carried out on Abraham, and on all the males in his household and subsequently on those descending from him was required as the sign of participation in its blessing. When Israel was enslaved in Egypt, the Lord remembered and kept his promises made in this covenant (Ex. 2:24; cf. 6:4, 5).

3) The Sinai Covenant

Israel, having escaped from the bondage of Egypt, met with the Lord in an awesome theophany at Sinai (Ex. 19-24). This marked the inauguration of a new covenantal relationship with God. Moses, who had met with the Lord on the mountain, read the commandments God had given him to the people (Ex. 20:1-17). He followed this with a package of sundry laws giving directions for dealing with the problems of social life (Ex. 21:1-23:33).

The Lord thus laid down conditions for the enjoyment of his blessing and showed the kind of behaviour that was appropriate for those he had redeemed as they travelled to and later lived in the land he had promised to Abraham's descendants. That promise was re-iterated (Ex. 23:27-33) showing that this Sinai covenant built on that made with Abraham and that the Lord fully intended that his people would inherit and occupy the promised land. The conditions attached to the Commandments and the subsidiary laws of the Covenant related both to individuals and to the nation.

A covenant ratification ceremony followed (Ex. 24:1-8). Animals were sacrificed and their blood was sprinkled half on the altar – i.e., for the Lord – and the other half on the people thus symbolising the bond that now joined the two parties. In all of this the initiative came from God. This was a unilateral covenant made in grace by the sovereign Lord and accepted willingly by the recipients, who had no opportunity or occasion to bargain with him as with an equal party! All they could do was take the role of vassals and say submissively, "We will do everything the LORD has said; we will obey" (24:7). Sealed in blood, this was a promise covenant, to which stipulations were attached.

4) The Covenant with David

When King David settled in his palace in Jerusalem, he called Nathan to discuss the fact that the Ark of the Lord was housed in a tent rather than in a permanent palace. Overnight Nathan received guidance from the Lord – David was not to be the builder of God's house – that role would fall to his son and successor,[1] who turned out to be Solomon (2 Sam 7:12-14). In addition the son of David would be established on a throne that was to be everlasting:

> Your house and your kingdom shall endure for ever before me; your throne will be established for ever.
>
> —2 Sam. 7:16

Three caveats were added to these promises. Two were positive and one was negative:

- The first was positive: "I will be his father and he shall be my son" (v. 14a). The meaning of this was that God would be his teacher or mentor and that he, as son, would be God's pupil or disciple. In Psalm 89:26-29 these words are applied to David as well as to his kingly descendants. In the ultimate New Testament fulfilment. Jesus was Son of God in an absolutely unique sense.
- The second was negative and imposed conditions on David's successors: "When he does wrong, I will punish him with the rod of men" (v. 14b).
- The third was positive – "my love will never be taken away from him" (v. 15). The message was that, while God would use human forces to correct future

---

[1]Note that David's first wife, Michal, never had a child (2 Sam. 6:23). Thus David, like Abraham, received God's promise of a son, when it would have seemed that he had no immediate prospect of having one!

kings who didn't keep the terms of this covenant, he would still surround them with his love (vv. 11-16). He would not give up his chosen nation.

These promises gave rise to the hope of a future Messiah that appears, not just in the prophetic books but also in a number of psalms. That expectation was an expression of faith in the Lord as a God who kept and would continue to keep his promises.

5) Promises of a new covenant

The history of the Israelites in the Promised Land was marked by repeated failure to fulfil the obligations imposed on them at Sinai. They broke the first commandment by giving themselves to the worship of pagan deities, mainly the local Baals of Caanan. Because they had turned to worthless idols and to those who prophesied by Baal, they had turned away from God, their Father and the Husband to whom they were bound by the solemn covenant of Sinai. They were guilty of committing "spiritual adultery" by virtue of their turning to the Baal cults of Caanan (Jer. 2:1-37; 3:6; 3:19-20 etc.).

By failing to live up to their covenant obligations, they evoked God's anger and triggered their own exile. Yet the Lord remained faithful – he still loved them – and he planned restoration under a new order, a new covenant arrangement, the obligations of which would not be a matter of laws external to those required to obey them, but internal, written on their very hearts:

> The time is coming, declares the LORD,
>   when I will make *a new covenant*
> with the house of Israel and with the house of Judah. ...
> This is the covenant that I will make
>   with the house of Israel
>   after that time, declares the LORD,
> I will put my law in their minds
>   and write it on their hearts
> I will be their God
>   and they will be my people ...
>   —Jer. 31:31-34; cf. Ezek. 36:24-32; Joel 2:25-32

Thus the covenant principle, initiated in God's promises to Noah, developed progressively, step by step. It moved from the promise that the descendants of Abraham would have a land for their dwelling to promises of a continuing dynasty for the House of David and on to the ultimate spiritual fulfilment in Jesus Christ, who under the new covenant established a new spiritual and eternal kingdom.

3. God's covenants in the psalms

The Psalmists believed that these covenants were the basis of Israel's position as God's people. Asaph, for example, described the Israelites as those who had made a covenant with the Lord by sacrifice, an obvious reference to the ceremony recorded in Exodus 24:1-8 (Ps. 50:5). Later in the same psalm he quoted the Lord as castigating the wicked, who in a hypocritical way were daring to take God's covenant on their lips (v. 16, cf. 78:10).

1) God's faithfulness to covenant is affirmed

In a number of psalms it is affirmed that God remembers and therefore keeps his covenant promises forever:

> He remembers his covenant for ever,
>> the word he commanded, for a thousand generations,
> the covenant he made with Abraham,
>> the oath he swore to Isaac.
> He confirmed it to Jacob as a decree,
>> to Israel as an everlasting covenant:
> To you I will give the land of Caanan
>> as the portion you will inherit
>
> —Ps. 105:8-11

The affirmation that the Lord "remembers his covenant for ever" occurs again in Psalms 106:45 and 111:5. In Psalm 132:12 the conditional element in the covenant with David is stressed: "if your sons keep my covenant … then their sons shall sit on your throne for ever and ever."

The psalmists knew that their people, including the kings descended from David, had failed to observe the obligations that rested on them by virtue of

God's covenant promises. As noticed above, the covenant with David imposed conditions on his successors – If any of them forsook God's law, they would be punished (2 Sam. 7:14). However God would not cease to love them, because of the oath he had sworn to David. He would be faithful to his covenant undertakings (vv. 30-37, cf. 1 Sam. 7:15-16).

Two Hebrew words draw our attention to God's faithful adherence to his commitments.

(1) chesedh [2]

This word occurs nearly ninety times in the psalms. The AV mostly translated it as "mercy," which for us tends to denote a relaxation of punishment. Essentially, however, the word focuses on a faithful carrying out of one's commitments. Used of the Lord it says that he keeps his promises. The NIV sometimes translates *chesedh* by "love" (e.g., Pss. 26:3; 36:7; 40:10; 63:3; 88:11a; 89:33; 103:4). In other cases an adjective is added – David, for example, speaks of God's "*wonderful* love" to him (Ps. 31:21). In other cases we find "his *unfailing* love," which stresses his faithfulness to the promises he had made in covenant (e.g., Pss. 17:7; 33:5; 51:1b; 52:8; 107:8; 15). The RSV and the NRSV consistently translate *chesedh* by "**steadfast** *love*," which rightly emphasises the fact that God remains constant in his love for his people and in his determination to keep the promises he had made to them.

(2) emunah [3]

This word occurs thirteen times in the psalms. The AV, NIV and RSV/ NRSV all translate it by "*faithfulness.*" David, for example, speaks of the Lord's *faithfulness* (Ps. 40:10) and Ethan says that he will make the Lord's *faithfulness* "known through all generations" (Ps. 89:1). In extolling the Lord's covenant promise to David, the same psalmist mentions his *faithfulness*, his *emunah*, on five occasions (vv.1, 2, 5, 8, 33). Other occurrences of this word are found in Psalms. 36:5; 85:11; 119:75, 90 and 143:1. In Psalm 89:14, the related word,

---

[2] Or *hesed*.
[3] Or *'ĕmûnāh* , *'ĕmet* , *'ĕmun*.

emeth, is also translated by "faithfulness" as is another cognate, *emun,* in Psalms. 89:49b; 98:3 and 100:5b.

4. Israelite failure to keep covenant

In a psalm, attributed to David, the author laments that his people had ceased to be faithful to their obligations to the Lord: "The godly are no more, *the faithful* have vanished from the earth" (Ps. 12:1). Psalm 78, which seems to be from several centuries later, catalogues how, despite the Lord's great acts of kindness to them, the Israelites committed a multitude of covenant-breaking sins: "they did not keep God's covenant and refused to live by his law" (v. 10) and "their hearts were not loyal to him, they were not faithful to his covenant" (v. 37).

The Israelites had made a habit of putting the Lord to the test by rebelling against him, as if probing to see whether he would or would not punish them! They were disloyal and unfaithful and angered the Lord by resorting to pagan worship in Baalistic high places (vv. 56-64). Finally, the Lord rejected the ten northern tribes led by the Ephraimites and began to concentrate his care and interest on the southern kingdom of Judah and its kings descended from David[4] (vv. 65-72). For some 135 years, Judah was, in effect, a continuing "remnant" of God's covenant people. But even its people, the Jews, lost his favour because of following the example of and committing the very sins of their northern cousins. They too had to be sent into exile, never again to be a national entity under the rule of a Davidic king.

An anonymous psalm (Ps. 106) was apparently written at or about a time when the Jews were scattered abroad and were under the control, of foreign peoples. This could have been during the Exile, which began with deportations to Babylon in 597 and 586 BC or, possibly, shortly after it officially ended in 539 BC.

Like the author of Psalm 78, this writer confessed that he and his people had persistently sinned against the Lord and against the covenant commitments

---

[4]Psalm 78 would seem to have been written after the demise of the Northern Kingdom at the hands of the Assyrians (721 BC) and before the ravaging of the temple by the Babylonians in 587/6 BC (vv. 67-69).

their forefathers had made: "We have sinned, even as our fathers did; we have done wrong and acted wickedly" (Ps. 106:6). Having outlined their offences in the time of Moses, the psalmist surveyed the covenant-breaking actions of the Israelites in the succeeding centuries (vv. 34-46).

> They did not destroy the peoples [of Caanan]
>   as the LORD had commanded them,
> but they mingled with the nations
>   and adopted their customs.
> They worshipped their idols,
>   which became a snare to them.
> They sacrificed their sons
>   and their daughters to demons...
> They defiled themselves by what they did;
>   by their deeds they prostituted themselves.
> Therefore the LORD was angry with his people
>   and abhorred his inheritance.
> He handed them over to the nations,
>   and their foes ruled over them.
> Their enemies oppressed them
>   and subjected them to their power...
> Many times he delivered them,
>   but they were bent on rebellion
>   and they wasted away in their sin
>
> —vv. 34-43

Conclusion

The subject matter in this chapter will have shown us that the psalmists had a strong faith in the Lord as a God, who kept the undertakings he had made, when he entered into covenant with his people. Those divine undertakings included threats of punishment and even of loss of the land if they should disobey the stipulations laid on them. This, in fact, is what they did and, though ultimately he had to deprive them of their land, he delayed that punishment for centuries – he afflicted them again and again and, when in distress they cried to him, "he remembered his covenant and out of his great love relented" and caused them to be pitied by their captors (Ps. 106:44-46). He was a covenant-keeper, while the Israelites were covenant-breakers!

Even when one psalmist felt the Lord had abandoned both the king and his people (Ps 89:38-51), he was still focused on God's covenant, which promised David's descendants a permanently "firm throne" (89:3-4, 28-29). At the time he wrote the situation seemed completely at odds with that covenant promise (vv. 38-45). It even seemed that God was spurning and rejecting the king of the day (v. 38). This psalmist with a directness, like that of Job or Habbakuk, accused the Lord of doing just that: "You have renounced the covenant with your servant" (v. 39). In the process of experiencing suffering the psalmist must have thought that to be the case. But, in fact, what the Lord had been doing was fully in keeping with the terms of his covenant commitment that he would punish any successor of David who did wrong (2 Sam. 7:14-15).

Finally, this same psalmist pleaded that, in loyalty to his covenant promises, God would intervene. "Where," he asked "is your former great love, which in your faithfulness you swore to David?" (Ps. 89:49). He wanted God to remember the sufferings of his "anointed one," the king of the day. Despite his erroneous perceptions and his protests, he still had faith in God's covenant promise.

The psalmists themselves were, then, men who knew of God's covenant and who sought to uphold the commitment their forefathers had given to its terms. They trusted the Lord in a way that faithless Israel had failed to do.

CHAPTER 22

THE PSALMISTS' KNOWLEDGE OF GOD

A number of our earlier studies have shown that the psalmists were personally devoted to the Lord. They appreciated him and gave him their praise and their thanks (chapters 4 and 5). They happily professed their trust in him (chapter 7). They were dependent on his word and his wise instruction (chapter 13). They accepted his kingship over them and over their people (chapters 14 and 15).

But there was something even deeper to their relationship with the Lord. Not only did the psalmists know and react to facts about him, they knew him and loved him in a person-to-person manner. They were truly spiritual in the sense that from their inner selves, their spirits, they communed with him, the ultimate and eternal Spirit. They knew him.

No study of the psalms would be complete without an examination of how the psalmists expressed their personal knowledge of the Lord. It is to that examination that we turn our minds in this chapter.

1. The grounds on which they knew God

The possibility of communion with God arises from the nature of God and the nature of men. Genesis tells us that God made man "in his own image" (Gen. 1:27). Whatever else this means, it surely tells us that in his essential being man has attributes that reproduce attributes of God. Man is not God, but, nonetheless, he has been created to act in a way that makes him God's counterpart – his image – on earth.

Scripture makes it clear that God is personal spirit. He is the ultimate person and the ultimate Spirit (John 4:24). Men are also personal spirits, and it is clear that the image of God is in that dimension rather than in man's physical make-up. God is the prototype and man is the likeness, the copied image. The fact that man has been made in God's image means that God and man are so constituted that communication between them is possible, so possible indeed that each can know the other. Because God is spiritual and personal and man, made in his image, is also spiritual and personal, he and man can communicate with and come to know each other in a way that would not be possible if one or other were non-personal.

The image of God in man was, of course, marred by the Fall (Genesis 3; Rom. 5:12-19 etc.), but that does not mean that it then became non-existent. God's word to Noah after the Flood re-affirmed the fact (Gen. 9:6) and Paul and James both spoke of fallen man as made in "the image of God" (1 Cor. 11:7; Jas. 3:9).

All human beings are, then, made in and continue to bear God's image. Because the psalmists were spiritual and personal beings, it was possible for them to call on the Lord and to enter into a personal relationship with him. They could know not just facts about him but be acquainted with him on a person-to-person basis. In their writings they didn't need to argue for the possibility of knowing God. They simply displayed the reality that they knew him by the way they thought and acted.

2.The Psalmist's knowledge of God

In harmony with what has just been said the psalmists only rarely used the verb "to know" (Hebrew, *yada*) to affirm their knowledge of the Lord. Indeed, the only precise case of such usage is in Psalm 9, where, addressing the Lord, David could assert:

> Those who know your name will trust in you,
>> For you, LORD, have never forsaken those who seek
>> you

—v. 10

In the Old Testament to have knowledge of the Lord's name was, in fact, to know and to be in a personal relationship with him. Thus, in allowing Moses to know his unique name, Yahweh or Jehovah the Lord was taking Moses into intimate one-to-one fellowship with himself (Ex. 3:14). Similarly David could affirm that those who knew God's name were those who showed that they knew him in a personal way by having sought him and by trusting in him and relying on his faithfulness.

The call of Psalm 46:10, "Be still and *know* that I am God," affirms that for the author and for those he addressed it was possible to know the Lord. More importantly it presents an invitation from the Lord to know and rest in him as the exalted Lord of the nations, of the whole earth and especially of one's own life.

While the psalmists didn't frequently trumpet the fact, they had ways to express the fact that they knew God. Their thanksgivings, for example, were based on an intimate relationship with him. Thus David, praising and thanking the God, who had forgiven his sin, demonstrated that he had an understanding and a real relationship with the one he knew as the Lord. It was an intimate "I-You" or, as some still prefer to put it, an "I-Thou" relationship:

> Then I acknowledged my sin *to you*
>> and did not cover up my iniquity.
> *I* said, *I* will confess my transgression to the LORD—
>> and *you* forgave the guilt of my sin.
>
> —Ps. 32:5

The other penitential psalms operated on the basis of a similar relationship – the penitent knew the one from whom he sought forgiveness:

> I confess my iniquity;
>> I am troubled by my sin. ...
> O LORD, do not forsake me;
>> be not far from me, O my God
> Come quickly to help me, O LORD, **my Saviour**.
>
> —Ps. 38:18-22; cf. Pss. 51; 130; 143

The same is true of the many passages that exude trust in the Lord. In a prayer recorded in Psalm 4 David told the Lord that many people were asking, "Who can show us any good?" (v.4). His own response was to tell the Lord that he trusted in him to do real good. Because he knew the Lord and knew he could rely on him to do him good, he could say, "I will lie down and sleep in peace, for you alone, O LORD, make me dwell in safety."

Psalm 23 is, of course, a similar expression of trust by one who knew the Lord as his Shepherd (see chapter 7 above). David knew that with his personal relationship to the Lord he would not be allowed to be in want, he need fear no evil and he could live the rest of his days in God's house, that is in his presence and in fellowship with him – he knew his God!

A further line of evidence is found in those passages in which the psalmists express deep longings for God: For example, Psalm 42 begins:

> As the deer pants for streams of water,
>   so my soul pants for you, O God.
> My soul thirsts for God, for the living God
>   When can I go and meet with God?

And then in Psalm 43, which is clearly linked to Psalm 42 we read:

> Send forth your light and your truth
>   let them guide me;
> let them bring me to your holy mountain,
>   to the place where you dwell.
> Then will I go to the altar of God,
>   to God *my* joy and *my delight.*
> I will praise you with the harp, O God, *my* God.

—Ps. 43:3, 4

In similar vein the psalmists pleaded for divine instruction:

> Show me your ways, O LORD,
>   teach me your paths;
> guide me in your truth and teach me,
>   for you are God my Saviour,
>   and my hope is in you all day long.
> Remember, O LORD your great mercy and love,
>   For they are from of old.
> Remember not the sins of my youth
>   and my rebellious ways;

> according to your love remember me
>> for you are good, O LORD.
>>>> —Ps. 25:4-7; cf. Pss. 27:11; 142:1-7

Such pleadings with God would only have been possible on the part of men who had a living relationship with God and who truly knew him.

The tragedy of the godless world around them was that men and women didn't seek the Lord. Because they didn't call on him, they hadn't begun to know him. Instead they had all turned aside and had become corrupt. Not one of them was doing good (Pss. 14:2-4; 53:2-4). One imprecatory prayer highlights the same emphasis: "Pour out your wrath on the nations that *do not know you* ..." (Ps. 79:6, NRSV).

3. The Lord's knowledge of men

If the psalmists but rarely use the Hebrew verb, *yada*, to refer to their knowledge of God, they use it again and again of the Lord's knowledge of men. Sometimes modern versions, like the NIV, translate it into English by phrases like "watch over" or "take care of," but essentially its focus is on God's awareness and his intimate inter-personal relationships with his faithful people. Thus Moses asked that the Lord would teach him his ways so that he might know him and continue to find favour with him (Ex. 33:13).

Some examples will show how the psalmists used yada to focus on God's knowledge of, indeed, his complete knowledge of men:

> The LORD watches over (Hebrew, *yada*, knows) the way
>> of the righteous.
>>>> —Ps. 1:6

> I will be glad and rejoice in your love,
>> for you saw my affliction
>> and knew the anguish of my soul.
>>>> —Ps. 31:7

> He knows the secrets of the heart.
>>>> —Ps. 44:21

> You know my folly, O God;

> my guilt is not hidden from you.
>
> —Ps. 69:5

> The LORD knows the thoughts of men;
>   He knows that they are futile.
>
> —Ps. 94:11

Taking these examples together we learn that God knows everything that can be known about men – their strengths and their weaknesses, their struggles and their frustrations, their follies and their sins. He knows the very worst about them and still loves and cares for them – and indeed for us!

The ultimate depiction of God's infinite knowledge of his creatures is found in Psalm 139 and its implications are quite irresistible:

> O LORD, you have searched me and you know me.
> You know when I sit down and when I rise;
>   you perceive my thoughts from afar.
> You discern my going out and my lying down
>   you are familiar with all my ways.
> Before a word is on my tongue
>   you know it completely, O LORD.
> You hem me in—behind and before
>   you have laid your hand upon me
> Such knowledge is too wonderful for me,
>   too lofty for me to attain.
>
> —vv. 1-6

"Where," the psalmist went on to ask rhetorically, could he go to escape from God's Spirit and from his presence (v. 7)? Where, in effect, he asked could he go so that God would not know, would not be aware of his thoughts and his actions? His answer was that there was nowhere in all the universe. Nothing is hidden from God. He knows everything, he is omniscient and the psalmist can only pray that God would apply his infinite knowledge to search him and test his thoughts and his ways[1] and so lead him in "the way everlasting."

---

[1] It should be noted in passing that Psalm 139 is a strong rebuttal of the arguments of what, in the late 20th and early 21st centuries, became known as "Open Theism." This maintains that God's

Conclusion

The psalmists knew their God and knew that he knew them. Applying this to ourselves in the Christian era we can do no better than cite the words of Paul as he sought to warn his friends in Galatia against sliding back into the slavery of Judaistic dependence on works rather than on faith:

> Formerly, when you did not know God, you were slaves to those who by nature are not gods. But now that you know God—or rather are known by God—how is it that you are turning back to those weak and miserable principles.
>
> —Gal. 4:8, 9

Dr. James Packer's comments are superb, and, though they are not based on a consideration of the psalms, they are surely true of how the psalmists knew the Lord. They are equally apposite to all who truly belong to the Lord:

> What matters supremely is not, in the last analysis, that I know God, but the larger fact that *He knows me*. I am graven on the palms of his hands. I am never out of his mind. . . . I know him because he first knew me, and continues to know me. . . .
>
> This is momentous knowledge. ... There is *unspeakable comfort ...* in knowing that God is constantly taking knowledge of me in love and watching over me for my good. There is *tremendous relief* in knowing that his love to me is utterly realistic, based at every point on prior knowledge of the worst about me, so that no discovery now can disillusion him about me and quench his determination to bless me. There is certainly *great cause for humility* in the thought that he sees all the twisted things about me that my fellow humans do not see. ... There is, however, equally *great incentive to worship and love God* in the thought that for some unfathomable reason, he wants me as his friend, and desires to be my friend and has given his Son to die for me in order to realise this purpose.
>
> —JI Packer, *Knowing God*, 1973, p.37. Emphases mine

---

knowledge is limited, that he leaves much of what happens or will happen to human decisions and that he even delights in the information we feed to him! This great psalm leaves no room for such thinking.

CHAPTER 23

⤳⤳⥱⤳⤳

PROSPECTS OF LIFE AFTER DEATH

The psalms were written in Old Testament times, mostly before clearer revelations about life after death were given to some of the writing prophets and in particular to Isaiah and Daniel. Neither, of course, did they have the benefit of the even fuller revelations of the New Testament. As Paul put it, it was only in the Lord Jesus Christ that "life and immortality' were brought to light through the gospel" (2 Tim. 1:10).

What the psalmists knew of the mystery of life after death is inevitably, therefore, somewhat uncertain, unclear and enigmatic. At times what they said is difficult to interpret and sometimes seems inconsistent with or, indeed, contradictory of other statements in the book.

1. Death is an unavoidable terminus

A number of psalms speak of the inevitability of death and the grave (Hebrew, *Sheol*).[1] Solomon's colleague, Ethan the Ezrahite, asks, "What man can live and not see death, or save himself from the power of the grave?" (Ps. 89:48). Describing his own experiences when he was on the run from Saul, David said

---

[1] The basic meaning of *Sheol* is thought to be hollowness – so the word can mean a grave hollowed out of the earth: "You have delivered me from the depths of the grave" (Ps. 86:13). The word was also used of the state of death – to be in Sheol was to be dead! It was a place of silence and darkness. Later it came to be used of an underworld abode of the dead, where the departed were but weak shades or shadows of their former selves. It is sometimes presented as a place to which the wicked are sent, perhaps prematurely, as judgment for their sins – "like sheep they are destined for *Sheol*," i.e., for the grave (Ps. 49:14a).

that he had been on the very edge of death – "the cords of death entangled me … the snares of death confronted me." (Ps. 18:4, 5; cf. 116:3). The death he had feared would have meant silence and impotence with no speech, (Ps. 28:1) and no strength (Ps. 88:4; cf. Ps. 90:3: "You return men back to dust").

Death was a condition from which, up to that point in his life, David had been spared. He could, therefore, tell the Lord, "You have delivered me from the depths of the grave" (Ps. 86:13). He was not saying, however, that he would never go to the grave. Indeed, he also said that no ransom could ever be paid that could avert death and the decay that follows it (Ps. 49:7-9).

There is, then, no suggestion in these passages that the psalmist's own soul or the soul of any one else would survive beyond the death or the grave.

2. Death as the end of personal existence

When the psalmists said that those who die go down into a pit or a grave, they were thinking primarily of burial in the earth, where all human physical remains decayed. One psalmist, Heman, the Ezrahite,[2] saw himself as "set apart" to be with the dead, lying in a place of destruction, where God's love is not declared and his wonders are not known (Ps. 88:3-12). Heman seemed to have no hope at all of continuing existence after death.

At times David, the greatest of the psalmists, also seems to have thought that death would take him to a realm (*sheol*), where he would not even have the capacity to think. In that vein he told the Lord that the departed neither remember nor praise the living:

> No-one remembers you when he is dead.
> Who praises you from his grave (Hebrew, *sheol*)?
>
> —Ps. 6:5

---

[2]Solomon's wisdom is said to have exceeded that of a group of sages including Heman and another Ezrahite called, Ethan (1 Kgs. 4:31). Most scholars regard them as belonging, not to the time of Ezra (late 5th century BC), but to that of Solomon 500 years earlier. However, since Kings was not completed till at least 450 BC (2 Kg. 25:27 – the 37th year of the exile), its author/compiler could have been contrasting the wisdom of his own and Ezra's day (c. 444 BC) with that of Solomon.

In Psalm 39 David again seems to have been thoroughly pessimistic about the after-life. He pleaded with God to hear him and to ease the pressure on him before he would depart and be "no more" (vv. 12-13). But does this mean that he thought death would mean total and final annihilation? Possibly so – he was so greatly distressed that he had to ask the Lord to show him how and when his life would end. This suggests that his apparently impending death was dominating his mind. His only hope was that the Lord would hear his cry for help and give him a period of joyous relief before he would finally depart. Then his earthly life would have ended and he would not be around any longer. The expectation of an after-life, if it was present at all in David's mind, was extremely faint.

In Psalm 49, a Son of Korah expressed an even more pessimistic view of those who die. "Man," he said, "is like the beasts that perish" (vv. 12b, 20b). However, the context shows that he was primarily referring to the fate of rich people, who trusted in themselves—"like sheep they are destined for the grave (*sheol*), where their forms will decay in the grave (*Sheol*)." This suggests that, in his mind, there was a distinction between the fate of the rich and foolish – an early death (v. 14) – and that of the wise and upright, who, like himself, could hope that God would redeem them from the grasp (Hebrew, *miyadh*, from the hand) of death (v. 15). Taken literally, this says that God will so hold him as to protect him from death and the grave.

> God will redeem my life from the hand of the grave
> for he will take [hold of] me.

There seems to be no linguistic basis for the two additional words in the NIV, which reads, "he will take me *to himself*," or even for the RSV and NRSV readings "he will receive me."[3]

The strong probability is, then, that here the psalmist was thinking of this life and that his hope was that the LORD would intervene to redeem him by giving him more time on earth before he died.

---

[3] At this point some translators seem to have become the victims of a temptation that often takes hold of more conservative believers – they read more meaning into a text than it actually contains! While the Hebrew verb, *laqach*, can mean "receive," here it more probably has the force of God taking hold of and keeping the writer out of Sheol.

In many instances, then, the psalms present death as followed by an absence of thought and communication – "It is not the dead who praise the LORD, those who go down to silence, it is we [the living, who fear the LORD (v. 13)], who extol the LORD..." (vv. 17, 18). The rhetorical questions of Psalm 88:10-12 expect negative answers and affirm that the LORD does not show his wonders to the dead or expect them to rise up and praise him. His love is not declared in the grave (Hebrew, *Sheol*) or his faithfulness in the place of "Destruction" (Hebrew, *Abbadon*[4]), the place of darkness and oblivion.[5] The implication seems to be that existence as a thinking, feeling and willing person is ended by death. Even a man's communion with God seems to have ended.

This is not, however, the end of the story in the Psalms. There are, indeed, pointers to a belief in or a least a hope of an after life in several psalms.

3. Possible pointers to belief in an after life

A more positive strand of thought seems to emerge in at least four passages, but, when we examine the relevant texts, we find that in most cases they too speak *primarily* of the survival of earthly life rather than of life after death. However as was often the case with the prophets their writers spoke more than they knew and their words were taken up in the New Testament as having a second meaning that related to life after death.

Four passages call for our examination:

1) Psalm 16:9-11

David affirms his determination to maintain a close relationship to the Lord (v. 8) and says that in that relationship his body would rest secure because the Lord would not abandon him to the grave (*Sheol*), nor let his Holy One see decay. He went on to say that the Lord had made known to him the path of life – the path of continuing life in the body rather than the path that leads to decay in

---

[4]*Abaddon* means the grave in which the body decays after burial. It lacks the emphasis of *Sheol* (in its later occurrences) as the residence of the soul after death and so tends to have the implication of destruction or even extermination.

[5]Hebrew, *nishya*, means forgetfulness, i.e., presumably a place where the residents have no memory and are not remembered.

the grave. He was filled with joy and pleasure because of the Lord's presence with him.

Peter quoted these verses in his great speech on the day of Pentecost and treated them as a prediction that was fulfilled by our Lord's resurrection (Acts 2:25-28). When he preached at Pisidian Antioch, Paul also cited the line, "You will not let your Holy One see decay" (Ps. 16:10b), as a prediction of our Lord's resurrection (Acts 13:35). But, while David was thus presented as uttering a predictive prophecy, it is uncertain if he actually knew that to be the case. On the surface he seems to have been grasping after a fruitful future earthly life for himself as he continued to walk with the Lord.

What we can say is that, as he thought of his own future, David was at the same time inspired by the Holy Spirit to speak more than he knew. His words thus had a double meaning, the second of which related to our Lord's resurrection. But for our present purpose a life of quality on earth rather than survival after death was probably the dominant issue in his mind.

2) Psalm 17:15

In this psalm David was praying to be delivered from the machinations of wicked men who were assailing him. Then he said:

> And I— in righteousness I shall see your face;
>> when I awake I shall be satisfied with seeing your likeness.

These words are sometimes taken as teaching conscious survival after death. However David's burden in the psalm was that he might avoid a premature death – "keep me from the wicked, who assail me, from my mortal enemies who surround me" (vv. 13, 14). He was expecting to awake each morning and find himself still under God's protection. His concern was not so much about the after-life as about being able to live in the enjoyment of God's presence here on earth.

That said, it is possible, perhaps even probable, that here again the words he used had a double meaning and pointed beyond his immediate knowledge to the truths that would be revealed in Christ and his gospel. While the text is not quoted in the New Testament, its words clearly fit in with and epitomise the hope of the Christian.

In the first place by beholding and contemplating the Lord's glory – seeing his face metaphorically but clearly through the written word and the Holy Spirit's activity – believers are transformed into his likeness with ever increasing glory (2 Cor. 3:17, 18). Secondly, believers expect to awake in heaven in the presence of their Lord and to be at home with him for ever. When that happens, "they will see his face, and his name will be on their foreheads" (Rev. 22:4). Not only so but, seeing him, they will, like Moses coming down from Mount Sinai, reflect his glory—"they (Christian believers) shall be like him because we shall see him as he is" (1 John 3:2).

3) Psalm 49:15

This verse, which has been discussed already in this chapter, is in a psalm from the "Sons of Korah" that has a strong ethos of ancient Hebrew "wisdom." It is basically a teaching, exposing the folly of trusting in wealth. It insists that riches are never sufficient to redeem a human soul and gain unending existence for it—"no payment is ever enough—that he (a rich man) should live on for ever and not see decay" (vv. 8b, 9).

This psalm also distinguishes between the fate of the wise and the foolish —"all can see that wise men die; the foolish and the senseless alike perish and leave their wealth to others." They decay in the grave like animals (vv. 10-15). The implication is that the lives of the "foolish" are "cut off" and are at an end —"their tombs will remain their houses for ever."

But the writer is not without hope of something different and adds rather enigmatically, "the upright will rule over them in the morning" (v. 14c). What he meant by, "in the morning," is far from clear. Most scholars seem to think it is simply an assertion that the tables will be turned and that the rich will cease to be the kind of rulers they had once been. Instead the righteous will be elevated to positions of power.

Some have thought that these words look forward to what later became known as "the resurrection morning" (Dan. 12:2; cf. Ps. 17:15). However, Leupold says cautiously,

No particular deductions are to be made from this statement. It would seem to imply nothing more than a strange reversal of role has taken place. When "the morning" comes, that is to say, when the night that threatened disaster to the godly is past, they will still be found on the scene when their wealthy oppressors ... have passed off it and are no more.

—HC Leupold, *Exposition of the Psalms*, p. 385

But then the writer, as already noted above, interjects:

God will redeem my life from the hand of the grave
> for he will take [hold of] me.

—my rendering

This has often been taken to mean that the psalmist believed he would be taken up like Enoch or Elijah to an after-death life with the Lord in heaven. But, while the Hebrew verb, *laqach*, is the one used of God "taking" Enoch away from the earth (Gen. 5:24) and of Elijah being caught up to heaven (2 Kgs. 2:3, 5 and 9), we have no indication that such a thought was in the author's mind at this point.

The writer was clearly drawing a sharp contrast between the prospect awaiting those he saw to be foolish and wicked rich people and that facing the godly wise, like himself. He saw the wicked as destined for the grave, where "death will feed on them and their forms will decay" (v. 14). In contrast to that dismal prospect his assured hope was that God would spare him and save him – at least for the foreseeable future – from a similar fate. He would "take hold of him" (another possible meaning of *laqach*) and so protect him from the grip of death and the grave.

In Psalms 56:13; 68:20 and 86:13 David asserted that the Lord had done just that for him: "You have delivered me from death ... that I may walk before God in the light of life" (56:13). The anonymous writer of Psalm 118:17 was also sure that the Lord would do that for him—"I will not die but live and will proclaim what the LORD has done."

As was suggested above in relation to Psalm 16:9-11, this writer may also have spoken more than he knew at the time. His words could have had two levels of meaning – an immediate one relating to his own future on earth and a more ultimate one relating to the believer's hope in Christ – hope of rapture or resurrection at the Lord's return and of life after death, when, as Paul put it, he would be "away from the body and at home with the Lord" (2 Cor. 5:8).

4) Psalm 73:23-26

In this psalm the prosperity of the wicked rather than the deprivations of righteous godly people created a problem for Asaph, the psalmist. It made him envious (v. 3) and embittered because it seemed to him that, while he had kept his heart pure, this was of no benefit, bringing no return, to himself (v. 13). But then he realised that God was in control and was exercising justice by putting the wicked on a slippery slope that would lead to their sudden destruction (vv. 18-20, cf. Ps. 92:7). In contrast, assured of God's presence with him (vv. 23, 24a), Asaph was able to say that, directed by God's counsel, he would be taken to or guided towards glory[6] (v. 24b).

But what did he mean? Again commentators differ:

Some see the psalmist as expressing a belief that he would enjoy life after death in the glory of God's presence in his heavenly dwelling. Leupold,[7] for example, says that such an interpretation is demanded by the fact that the Hebrew verb, *laqach*, usually translated as "take" is the same as is used in the story of God having "taken" Enoch away from the earth (Gen. 5:24) and in that of Elijah being caught up to heaven (2 Kgs. 2:3, 5 and 9).

Others regard Asaph as over-optimistically believing that he would emerge from the gloom of grief, bitterness and senseless ignorance, which he had expressed in verses 21 and 22 into honour and glory and a new future here on earth. The Hebrew word, *kabod*, that occurs here, is used in other psalms of the honour given to men in the earthly rather than the heavenly sphere. This, surely, was the case when the Sons of Korah sang:

> For the LORD God is a sun and shield;
>> the LORD bestows favour and *honour*;
> no good thing does he withhold

---

[6]The Hebrew, *tancheni we'char kabod*, translates literally as, "you will guide me. And afterwards honour/glory."

[7]HC Leupold, *Exposition of the Psalms*, EP, p. 532.

> from those whose walk is blameless.
>
> —Ps. 84:11

The Hebrew word, *kabod*, (honour) is similarly used of honour being given on earth in the books of Job and Proverbs with which this psalm has close affinities. Job spoke of God as wronging him by stripping him of his honour (his *kabod*, AV, his "glory" (Job 19:9). Later (29:20) he reflected on how he had hoped that his honour or glory (his *kabod*) would remain in him, even though now he was being given no honour. In Proverbs 3:16 we read that wisdom "has honour in her hand" meaning that wisdom can bestow honour on those who act wisely or, as verse 35 of the same chapter puts it, "The wise inherit honour."

What then do we make of this passage? The best answer seems to be that Asaph thought the Lord would bring him out of his gloom and into a place of honour as he enjoyed God's own presence with him in this life. But again it may be that he spoke more than he knew and that his expectation of glory and honour in this world is a picture or a prediction of the glory that is to be the lot of the believer, when he will be "at home with the Lord" (2 Cor. 5:8).

Conclusion

The psalmists do not seem then to have had a strong or even a clear belief in a conscious and active existence of the human soul after death. They seem to have thought mainly of wickedness being punished and righteousness being rewarded either within a person's lifetime or in the lives of his offspring as indicated in the expansion attached to the second commandment (Ex. 20:4-7).

Unlike the prophets, Isaiah (Isa. 26:19), Ezekiel (Ezek. 37:1-14) and Daniel (Dan. 12:1b-13), the psalmists do not in any sense proclaim the hope of resurrection. Indeed, the rhetorical questions of Psalm 88:10 seem to say that resurrection did not and would not happen: "Do you show your wonders to the dead? Do those who are dead rise up and praise you?"

However, it is likely that the psalmists, being borne along by the Holy Spirit (1 Pet. 1:21), spoke or wrote things that not only expressed their own beliefs at the time but pointed to realities that God would yet reveal.

This means that the psalmists, in effect, if not in name, became prophets. In inspiring their writings the Lord made them his spokesmen and included in their role words and ideas that had more than one meaning. That this is so triggers a further chapter in our study, namely an examination of the role of the psalmists as prophets. That role is highlighted by the many quotations from the psalms that we find embedded in the teachings of Jesus and his apostles. It is to these quotations and to their function in the New Testament revelation that we must now turn our attention.

CHAPTER 24

THE PSALMISTS AS PROPHETS

In Old Testament times a prophet was a person who spoke or called out a message on behalf of someone else. Thus Aaron was called to be a spokesperson for Moses (Ex. 4:16) and, *as such*, was called Moses' prophet (Ex. 7:1). Similarly "the prophets" were those whom God called to speak to men on his behalf. Moses, who is often thought of as a lawgiver, was, in fact, the supreme prophet of the Old Testament (Deut. 18 18).

In the Old Testament there are two Hebrew words for prophet (1 Sam. 9:9). The older word, *ro'eh*, meant a "seer," a man with insight, while the later and more common word, *nabhi*, was derived from a verb meaning to call, and meant either, "a person called to perform a task" or "one who called out," an announcer. A prophet was, then, a person to whom the Lord had given insight into his purposes (Amos 3:7) and who served him by proclaiming his word.

The prophets were enabled to reveal deep truths about God and his purposes for men. They therefore spoke critically of the behaviour, past and present, of those to whom or about whom they spoke. But they also looked forward and, in association with threats or promises, predicted events and happenings that were yet future. In what way, we ask, can psalmists be designated prophets?

The Psalmists were able to reveal God by proclaiming facts about his nature (cf. Chapter 19 above). They also emphasised God's moral requirements by stressing man's obligations and by lamenting over his failure to keep God's laws. In the wisdom psalms, particularly, they gave considerable attention to the law and to its worth in human life – the man who is blessed and on the right path of life is the one who delights in the law of the Lord and meditates on it by day and by night (Ps. 1:2; cf. Ps. 119:1-176).

At the same time the psalmists were privileged to say things, which, as we have seen, not only had a primary reference to their own times, but a second significance in relation to the incarnate life of Jesus, the Son of God, and to the lives of his followers. We have already encountered some of this in Chapter 23, "Prospects of life after death." In our present study we will examine this particular aspect of the Psalter from the perspective of its use in the New Testament.[1]

1. In the Gospels

Our Lord cited a number of passages from the Psalms and indicated that they pointed to and found fulfilment in his person and in his ministry:

1) Statements relating to Jesus' person

(1) John 2:17 citing Psalm 69:9

John tells us that our Lord's cleansing of the temple fulfilled the words of the psalmist—"Zeal for your house consumes me." Jesus, like the psalmist, who was possibly David, was zealous for the honour of the Lord, which should have been maintained by those privileged to enjoy his presence:

(2) Matthew 13:35, citing Psalm 78:2

When Jesus was asked why he spoke in parables, he quoted words of Asaph, first recorded in Psalm 78:

> I will open my mouth in parables ...
>
> —Ps 78:2

Jesus referred to these words as words of "the prophet," thus categorising one particular psalmist, Asaph, as a prophet, a spokesman for the Lord, whose prediction was being fulfilled in himself and in his ministry.

---

[1]Since the NT has many quotations from the Psalms, it is only possible to consider a selection of those quotations.

(3) Matthew 21:9, 16 citing Psalm 118:26

Matthew and each of the other three Gospel writers tell us that the actions of the crowds who welcomed Jesus to Jerusalem on Palm Sunday fulfilled Psalm 118:26: "Blessed is he who comes in the name of the LORD" (cf. Mark 11:9, 10; Luke 19:38; John 12:13).

(4) Matthew 21:42 citing Psalm 118:22–23

Jesus had just delivered his "Parable of the Tenants" and was about to tell those who had questioned his authority that "the kingdom of God" would be taken away from them. The tenants represented the Jews of the day, whose favoured position would be given to a new people, our Lord's followers, who would produce its fruit in a lifestyle of faith and obedience (v. 43). To introduce this to his Jewish listeners Jesus asked:

Have you never read in the Scriptures:
  The stone the builders rejected
    has become the capstone
  the Lord has done this,
    and it is marvellous in our eyes?

Jesus was using the words of Psalm 118:22–23 to assert that he, the one the Jews were rejecting, was the key person for the future kingdom, which would not be Jewish but would, in fact, be made up of his disciples. Thus the words of an anonymous psalmist, which will have had real meaning in his own day, had a second meaning that centred in our Lord's ministry. They illustrated what was about to happen as through his death, resurrection, ascension and the sending of the Holy Spirit, he would initiate a new kingdom in which he, the capstone, would always be the king.

In Psalm 118 it seems that the nation of Israel (or someone speaking as its representative) was giving thanks to God because he had made it "capstone," or key player among the nations of the day (v. 22). That Jesus used the same words of his own ministry indicates that he was claiming to be what Israel was meant to be in the purposes of God. The nation had been rejected and Christ had gathered up in his own person its various roles. The future was not with biological Israel but with Christ and those who by faith are joined with him as the New Israel, the true Israel of God (Matt. 21:42, cf. Mark 12:11; Luke 20:17; 1 Pet. 2:7).

(5) Matthew 22:44, citing Psalm 110:1
Jesus asked the Pharisees what they thought about the Christ – "Whose son is he?" They replied, "The son of David." Then he asked them a further question:

> How is it then that David speaking by the Spirit, calls him Lord? For he says,
> The LORD said to my Lord:
> > Sit at my right hand
> > until I put your enemies under your feet.
> If then David calls him Lord, how can he be his son?
> —Matt. 22:43-45

In posing this question Jesus was using the first verse of Psalm 110, which bears the heading, "a psalm *to* or *for* (Hebrew, *le*) David." This doesn't say that David was or was not the author – it could mean that the psalm was written to honour him in some way.

The opening words translated literally, read, "a solemn declaration of Yahweh (the LORD) to my lord (my *'adoni*, my master)." In delivering what was clearly a message from God, the author was acting as the Lord's prophet-spokesman. David, or a successor, is likely to have been the person addressed as "my Lord" (*'adoni*, my master). As king he was promised victories, and an empire (vv. 2, 3; 5-7) and a role unique for a Hebrew king, a priesthood in the order of Melchizedek (v. 4, cf. Heb. 5:6, 7:17 etc).

It seems unlikely that David himself would have been both the prophet through whom the Lord spoke and the king he addressed as, "my Lord" (*'adoni*). Leupold suggests that the prophet might have been Nathan, who expressed similar thoughts in 2 Samuel 7. Others think an unknown prophet brought the message to David or to one of his successors.

Jesus, however, declared that David spoke the words of verse 1. "How is it," he asked, "that David speaking by the Spirit calls him Lord. For he says, The

Lord said to my Lord ... ?" (Matt. 22:43-44). It is possible that Jesus was using the common Jewish belief that the psalms mainly came from David and were known as the Psalms of David, without attributing personal authorship to him. It may therefore be wise to leave the authorship question open and focus on the fact that, while the psalmist clearly had a Hebrew king in view, his words had a second and deeper meaning in relation to Christ.

Since the psalmist was delivering a solemn statement from the Lord, he was cast in the role of a prophet. He was the Lord's spokesman pointing to a priest-king of David's line, in the first place probably David himself, then to some of his successors and finally to Christ. (cf. Mark 12:36; Luke 20:41-44 and the citation of Ps. 110:4 in Heb. 7:24).

2) Statements pointing to our Lord's sufferings

Jesus cited several verses from the psalms to highlight his sufferings being the fulfilment of Scripture. In doing so he cast the psalmists concerned in the role of prophets:

(1) John 13:18, citing Psalm 41:9, which he related to his impending betrayal by Judas:

> He who shares my bread has lifted up his heel against me.

(2) John 15:25 citing Psalms 35:19 and 69:4:

> This is to fulfil what is written in their Law: they hated me without reason.

(3) Matthew 27:26 and Mark 15:34 citing Psalm 22:1

> My God, My God, why have you forsaken me?

(4) John 19:24 citing Psalm 22:18, which asserts that the experience of the psalmist had found its prophetic fulfilment in how our Lord's garments were treated at Calvary:

> They divide my garments among them

and cast lots for my clothing.

(5) John 19:36 citing Psalm 34:20. In this instance John asserts that the fact that none of our Lord's bones were broken, when he was crucified, was a fulfilment of the words of the psalmist:

> He protects all of his bones,
>> not one of them will be broken.

2. In the Acts

1) Concerning Judas' suicide

In Acts 1:20 we find two quotations from the psalms cited in relation to the suicide of Judas—"For it is written in the Book of Psalms, May his place be deserted; let there be no-one to dwell in it" (Ps. 69:25) – "May another take his place of leadership" (Ps. 109:8). A further quotation, from Psalm 2:1-2, is used to give a biblical basis for the opposition the early apostles faced in Jerusalem:

> Why do the nations rage
>> and the people plot in vain?
> The kings of the earth take their stand
>> and the rulers gather together against the Lord
>> and against his Anointed One.
>
> —Acts 4:25, 26

2) Concerning Jesus' resurrection

The main citations of the Psalms in Acts relate to our Lord's resurrection and ascension. Three passages are important:

(1) Peter's sermon at Pentecost

In his sermon on the Day of Pentecost Peter is recorded as having backed up his thesis about the resurrection by quoting twice from the Psalms. In the first (Acts 2:25-28), he used Psalm 16:8-11 as a prophetic prediction by David:

> David said about him. ...

> You will not abandon me to the grave,
>> nor will you let your Holy One see decay.

Peter went on to affirm that, since David had died, he was not speaking in the psalm about himself, but about Christ. David was, Peter said, "a prophet," who knew, because of what God had promised him, that one of his descendants would sit on his throne and knowing what was ahead could speak of the resurrection of Christ. (Acts 2:30).

Peter's second quotation (Acts 2:34, 35) is from Psalm 110:1 and relates to our Lord's ascension. He said that, though David did not himself ascend to heaven, he had said,

> The Lord said to my Lord: Sit at my right hand until I make your enemies
> a footstool for your feet.

Applying the implications of this statement, Peter could say, that all Israel should be assured "that God has made this Jesus, whom they had crucified, both Lord and Christ" (Acts 2:34-36). Peter was saying that the predictions of David, the poet-prophet of a millennium earlier, had been fulfilled, in our Lord's ascension.

Clearly Peter thought that David, the author of so many great psalms, was a spokesman for the Lord, a prophet. He was not merely saying that David's words had a double meaning, the first relating to his own life and the second relating to our Lord's resurrection.[2] He was dogmatically asserting that David was a prophet, who had predicted that the Christ would rise from the dead. Whatever was in David's mind as he wrote the psalm, Peter, who on the Day of Pentecost was clearly under the control of God's Spirit, regarded his words as predictive prophecy.

(2) The Jerusalem Church at prayer

The early Jerusalem Christians celebrated the Sanhedrin's release of Peter and John, by telling the Lord in prayer that he had spoken through the Holy Spirit

---

[2]Viewing the psalms from an Old Testament perspective, as we did in our earlier discussion about the prospects for life after death, the idea of a second meaning is in order. Peter, by virtue of the inspiration given to him had a new understanding of its meaning.

and through David in the words of Psalm 2:1-2 (Acts 4:25, 26). Again David is presented as God's prophet, whose words were fulfilled in the opposition of Jewish leaders to our Lord's disciples.

(3) Paul's sermon in Pisidian Antioch

In the synagogue at Antioch in Pisidia, Paul quoted the words of Psalm 16:10: "You will not let your Holy One see decay." He did so in order to prove to his Jewish listeners that the resurrection of Jesus fully harmonised with the Messianic expectations of the Old Testament and was, therefore, something it was completely proper for Jews to believe (Acts 13:35; cf. use of Ps. 2:7 in v. 34). In the previous verse Paul had cited the words of Isaiah 55:3 (referring to the blessings God had promised to David) as affirming and being fulfilled in our Lord's resurrection. Thus the psalmists' words are presented as prophetic in the same as those of Isaiah.

3. In the New Testament Epistles

1) Paul's letters

While Paul quite often quoted from the psalms in support of his exhortations about Christian living, he rarely used them as pointers to the person and work of Christ. One instance is the brief citation of Psalm 8:6: "he [God] has put everything under his feet" (1 Cor. 15:27). Paul's purpose was to affirm that the Christ would bring about the destruction of death and the restoration of all things at the end of time.

Writing about the gifts God apportions to each of his servants (Eph. 4:1-13), Paul cites Psalm 68:18 as a prediction both of Christ's ascension and of the bestowal of gifts that flowed from it:

> When he ascended on high,
>> he led captives in his train and gave gifts to men.

In the Epistle to the Romans (15:8-11), the apostle cites passages from two psalms, Pss. 18:49 and 117:1, in support of his assertion that Christ had fulfilled God's promises to Abraham that a time would come when all the peoples of the earth would be blessed through his descendants. In the fulfilment Gentiles were called upon to join in the praise of the Lord:

> For I tell you that Christ has become a servant of the Jews on behalf of God's truth, to confirm the promises made to the patriarchs, so that the Gentiles may glorify God for his mercy, as it is written:
>> Therefore I will praise you among the Gentiles;
>> I will sing hymns to your name.
>
> —v. 8f, cf. Ps. 18:49

And again,

> Praise the Lord, all you Gentiles,
>> and sing praises to him all you peoples.
>
> —v. 12b, cf. Ps. 117:1

2) Peter's first letter

Peter used two lines of Psalm 118:22 as part of his demonstration from the Old Testament that our Lord was the capstone, the apex of the spiritual temple of the church that God was building (1 Pet. 2:7). To those believers – the living stones being built into this temple – the capstone, i.e., the Lord Christ is precious, and, indeed, of infinite value. Again the words of the psalmist are treated as prophetic, as a divine announcement of Christ.

3) The Epistle to the Hebrews

This letter was addressed to Jewish believers and has some 15 definite quotations from the psalms. About half of them are used with reference to the Lord Jesus Christ.

The basic thesis of the Epistle is that Christ is better than everything in the Israelite/Jewish background of the readers. He is better than the prophets through whom God had spoken in the past. He is even better than the angels that inhabit the heavenly realm and who serve God there. To which of the angels, asks the writer, did God ever say:

> You are my Son;

today I have become your Father?
                                                —Heb. 1:5, citing Ps. 2:7; cf. Heb. 5:5

The writer's point is that Christ is in a unique relationship with God, as a Son to his Father. That uniqueness is supported by further quotations from the psalms.

In *verses* 7-9 of Hebrews 1 the writer uses Psalm 104 verse 4 and Psalm 45:6-7 to emphasise the contrast between the angels and Christ. The angels were but "winds" and "flames of fire," while the Son, God's Son indeed, has been specially anointed and set above his companions.

Then in *verses* 10-12 he uses Psalm 102:45-47, which is basically a record of a suffering man crying out to the Lord for help and ending his cry with an affirmation of the greatness of the God to whom he was appealing: "In the beginning you laid the foundations of the earth. ... your years will never end" (Ps. 102:25-27). Though there is no direct reference to the Son, it seems that the writer is assuming our Lord's deity and asserting that what is true of God, namely the attribute of eternity, is true of him. Thus the psalmist is presented as having spoken prophetically as an announcer for God.

Building on the identification of our Lord as the Divine Son this author again highlighted the stark contrast between the angels and the Son by asking:

> To which of the angels did God ever say,
> Sit at my right hand
>   until I make your enemies a footstool for your feet?

The rhetorical question expects the answer, "None!" It leads the writer to affirm that, at most, angels are ministering spirits serving those who inherit salvation. In contrast the Son is the Saviour, who provided salvation, who is now crowned with glory and honour and sovereign over everything. He is far above and far superior to the angels (Heb. 1:14-2:9, citing Ps. 8:4-6 in vv. 6-8).

The writer to the Hebrews also emphasises our Lord's eternal priesthood. He belongs, not to the Levitical order of Aaron, but to the order of Melchizedek. Melchizedek was king of Salem, which is probably the early name of Jeru-salem. The comparison between Melchizedek and Christ reminds us that Jesus was king as well as priest, and that he united both roles, as well as that of prophet, in his person. Appropriately, then, the writer on three occasions cites a verse from a royal/messianic psalm in support of this thesis:

> You are a priest for ever, in the order of Melchizedek.
> —Heb. 5:6: cf. 7:17; 7:21, cf. Ps. 110:4

The implication seems to be that Jesus fulfilled the full significance of the Old Testament roles of priest and king, roles that were, of course, of great significance to Jews and, therefore, to the Hebrew Christians to whom the Epistle to the Hebrews was written.

Whether David, the author of Psalm 110, was speaking of an Israelite king or prophesying predictively of Christ is, as we saw in our discussion of another Royal Psalm (Ps. 45 in Chapter 14 above) debatable. Probably his focus was on an earthly king, but, as is often the case, his words had a second and more ultimate meaning in relation to Christ. In that way David's words were prophetic – he was a prophet.

Conclusion

It is clear that our Lord regarded the psalmists, or, at least, some of them on some occasions, as prophet-spokesmen for God. He knew that many of their utterances either spoke directly of himself or had an application to him that arose as a level of meaning beyond the writer's original intention.

The writers of the Gospels and the New Testament Epistles clearly shared these convictions, and gave expression to them in the quotations they used from the psalms.

CHAPTER 25

IMPRECATION IN THE PSALMS

Imprecation[1] is asking God to visit others with adversity. Many of the psalms, including some that we have examined, have passages that pray for God's judgment to fall on the wicked and in particular on the enemies of Israel. These prayers often pose a moral problem for Christians, who find them out of harmony with the teachings and, indeed, with the spirit of Jesus.

However we view them, we have to acknowledge that, though they were written or sung by mere men, these passages were inspired by the Holy Spirit and were included in the Psalter by divine will and purpose.

1. The main imprecatory passages

Personal and community lament psalms are the most common setting for such passages. Most examples are in psalms attributed to David – Pss 35:1-25; 54:5; 58:6-8; 69:22-28; 109:6-20; 26-29; 137:5-9 and 139:19-22. For our study we will look at four examples of imprecation.

1) Psalm 69:22-28

This psalm is addressed to someone acting as a leader or director of music. This suggests that it was written for choral use in the worship of the temple. Its heading also relates it to David – "of David." This could mean that is was by David or more probably, as we have seen in other cases, that it was written "for" or "about" David.

---

[1]To imprecate, from the Latin *precari*, meaning to pray, is to pray (something) into someone.

Many scholars think that the psalm originated after David's time and was included in a Davidic hymn-book by later compilers. The references in verses 33 to the Lord's "captive people" (NRSV, "his own that are in bonds") and to Judah in verse 35 could suggest a date after the demise of Israel (721 BC) or possibly in the time of the exile (597/587 to 539/8 BC) rather than to that of David.

Kirkpatrick[2] thinks the author may have been Jeremiah, who ministered in Jerusalem before and during the first phase of the exile (597-c.580 BC) and whose experiences of opposition and suffering seem to harmonise quite closely with the contents of the psalmist's lament. He sees a harmony between our psalm and a number of passages in Jeremiah's prophecies, for example, Jeremiah 12:1-4; 15:10-11 and 17:14-18.

This passage (vv. 22-28) follows a passionate prayer asking God to deliver the psalmist from a crisis situation, in which he maintained he was being hated without reason. At the same time he admitted that he was in some way to blame for his problem: "many are my enemies without cause, those who seek to destroy me ... You know *my* folly, O God; *my* guilt is not hidden from you" (vv. 4, 5).

Its specific imprecations

After intense prayer (vv. 1-21) that God would rescue him from those who were troubling him – "Rescue me from the mire, do not let me sink; deliver me from those who hate me" (v. 14) – the psalmist turned to imprecation (vv. 22-28).

> May the table set before them become a snare;
>   may it become retribution and a trap.
> May their eyes be darkened so that they cannot see,
>   and their backs be bent for ever.
> Pour out your wrath on them;
>   let your fierce anger overtake them.
> May their place be deserted;

---

[2]A. F. Kirkpatrick, *The Book of Psalms*, The Cambridge Bible, 1951 ed. (Cambridge: Cambridge University Press, 1902), 397.

let there be no-one to dwell in their tents.
For they persecute those you wound
    and talk about the pain of those you hurt.
Charge them with crime upon crime;
    do not let them share in your salvation.
May they be blotted out of the book of life
    and not listed with the righteous.

These petitions largely speak for themselves. The psalmist was hurt by and was deeply angry because of the persecution he was suffering (cf. v. 29). He, therefore, wanted his persecutors to experience God's fierce anger (vv. 22-25) in a series of adversities that would affect their supply of food, their faculties of sight, their strength of body indicated by their straight and pain-free spines. Such divine punishment would entail exile from their comfortable places of residence – their place and their tents.

The psalmist wished these persecutors excluded from God's salvation, i.e., from the kind of deliverance that the psalmist sought from Yahweh. He also wanted them blotted out from "the book of life" and not listed with the righteous (vv. 27, 28). What he meant by this and how it relates to New Testament thought is not clear (cf., Luke 10:20; Rev. 20:12). He certainly saw them suffering the fate of the wicked, as it is described in Psalm 1:4, 5: "the wicked will not stand in the judgment, nor sinners in the assembly of the righteous."

The psalmist felt that God had brought him into his crisis experience and that his enemies were persecuting him, when he was already wounded—"they persecute those you wound and talk about the pain of those you hurt" (v. 26). His words remind us of similar complaints recorded of Job and Jeremiah (cf. Job 9:1-10:22; Jer. 15:17, 18).

Having delivered his soul of its burden to be saved from his enemies (vv. 13-18, 29) and for retribution to fall on his opponents (vv. 22-28), the psalmist turns to praising the Lord (vv. 30-36). He has accepted in his heart that the Lord would answer his prayers and would, at one and the same time, deliver him and deal with his enemies. He doesn't even wait for this to happen but in faith bursts into praise—"I will praise God's name in song and glorify him with thanksgiving. ... The LORD hears the needy and does not despise his captive people" (vv. 30, 33). On the basis of this faith he calls on heaven and earth to join in praise of the Lord, whom he knows will save Zion and restore Judah and its cities.

2) Psalm 54:5

> Let evil recoil on those who slander me;
>> in your faithfulness destroy them

This psalm derives from a time when David was running away from Saul. He first took refuge at Keilah to the south of Hebron and then among the Ziphites, who proceeded to disclose his whereabouts to Saul (1 Sam. 23:19). He was, no doubt, feeling angry at being betrayed and so prayed that the Lord would deliver him and vindicate him in the eyes of those whose actions had threatened his life. In fact, he believed that the Lord would do just that:

> Surely God is my help;
>> the LORD is the one who sustains me.

—v. 4

In the context of that faith in the Lord, he asked that the evils his enemies were imposing on him should be returned on them and that they should be destroyed. We don't know if such judgment fell on the Ziphites, but we do know that the Lord delivered David by sending the Philistines on a raid into Israel. Saul then had to stop his pursuit of David in order to defend his land against the Philistine invaders.

Looking back on this deliverance, David turned from imprecation to praise:

> I will sacrifice a freewill offering to you;
>> I will praise your name, O LORD, for it is good.
> For he has delivered me from all my troubles
>> and my eyes have looked in triumph on my foes'.

—vv. 6, 7; cf. 69:30-36

3) *Psalm 137:5-9*

Psalm 137 is another lament reflecting on the experience of the Jews and, in particular, of the writer, during their period of enforced exile in Babylon. Its well-known opening lines define the situation it describes:

> By the rivers of Babylon we sat and wept
>> when we remembered Zion ...

The psalmist was so attached to Jerusalem that he invited retribution on himself, if he should forget Zion, by singing its songs in a foreign land. He would rather lose the skills of his hands and the ability of his tongue to speak and sing for his Lord:

> If I forget you, O Jerusalem,
>> may my right hand forget its skill.
> May my tongue cling to the roof of my mouth
>> if I do not remember you ...

—vv. 5, 6

Then he invoked punishment on those who had conspired to bring about the exile. He called on the Lord to remember the actions of the Edomites, who had helped the Babylonians pillage and destroy Jerusalem (cf. Ezek. 25:12; Obadiah v.10ff.). The implication is that they should be punished for their actions more or less in the way Jeremiah had predicted (Jer. 49:7-22; cf. Amos 1:11 etc.). In effect, he prayed that Edom and Babylon should both suffer the same fate:

> Remember, O LORD, what the Edomites did
>> on the day Jerusalem fell.
> Tear it down, they cried,
>> tear it down to its foundations!
> O Daughter of Babylon, doomed to destruction,
>> happy is he who repays you
>> for what you have done to us—
> he who seizes your infants
>> and dashes them against the rocks.

—vv. 8-9

In the ancient world such cruel treatment of infants seems to have been commonly applied to vanquished enemies.[3] Isaiah had actually predicted that such a fate would overtake the infants of Babylon (Isa. 13:16). While it seems utterly abhorrent to us, it was part of the common cruelty of war in the ancient Near East and in this context seems to be simply a wish that a cruel enemy might, as a matter of justice, receive what it had inflicted on others.

4) Psalm 104:35

This psalm is different in tone from those we have examined. It is a not a lament or an urgent plea for divine deliverance from some adversity. It is a psalm of praise to the Lord for his works of creation and providence and a prayer that his glory may endure for ever. The anonymous psalmist actually wanted to spend his life singing God's praise and rejoicing in him, who had created such a wonderful universe (v. 33). He prayed that in doing so his thoughts would be pleasing to the Lord (v. 34).

This is not, then, the type of psalm in which we would expect to find imprecation. Yet words at the end (v. 35) appear to ask the Lord to consume and eradicate those he called "sinners" and "the wicked"—"May sinners vanish from the earth and the wicked be no more."

Are these words imprecatory? Possibly or even probably they are simply a request for the eradication not of sinful persons as such but of the sinfulness that damages God's handiwork in the created world. In that event verse 35 is not imprecation but prayer for "good order" to be maintained in the world.

2. Passages celebrating the demise of enemies

Imprecatory passages, like the laments in which they occur, tend to be followed by expressions of praise to the Lord (e.g., Pss. 69:30-36; 54:6-7). The praise indicates a sense of relief in the psalmists' minds as they looked forward in anticipation to the outpouring of God's wrath on their persecutors and enemies. In some passages there seems to be an element, not just of celebration, but of gloating.

---

[3]We get a picture of this cruel practice in 2 Kings 8:12.

1) Psalm 54:6, 7

> I will sacrifice a freewill offering to you;
>> I will praise your name, O LORD, for it is good.
> For he has delivered me from all my troubles,
>> And *my eyes have looked in triumph on my foes.*

We find similar passages in psalms, in which the writer relishes and may, indeed, to some degree gloat over the fate of the wicked or of his personal or national enemies.

2) Psalm 52:5-7

In this psalm Doeg, an Edomite, who like the Ziphites betrayed David to Saul, is in focus. David asserts that God will bring him down to everlasting ruin, but does not pray for that to happen. Addressing Doeg, he says:

> He will snatch you up and tear you from your tent;
> He will uproot you from the land of the living.

Addressing a wider audience, he seems to rejoice in, or, perhaps, gloat over, the end he envisaged for his enemy:

> The righteous will see and fear;
>> They will laugh at him, saying,
> Here now is the man
>> who did not make God his stronghold
> but trusted in his great wealth
>> and grew strong by destroying others!

3) Psalm 92:9-11

In these verses the anonymous writer addressed the Lord in praise: "You, O LORD, are exalted for ever" (v. 8). In support of his call that the Lord be praised (vv. 1-3), he says:

> For surely your enemies, O LORD,
>> surely your enemies will perish;
> all evildoers will be scattered.

You have exalted my horn like that of a wild ox;
    fine oils have been poured upon me.
My eyes have seen the defeat of my adversaries;
    my ears have heard the rout of my wicked foes.

It is thought by many scholars that the psalmist is speaking nationally rather than as an individual. His and his people's enemies were also the Lord's enemies and he is rejoicing in the Lord's triumph over them. Whether his rejoicing passes over into gloating is difficult to determine, but verse 11 can certainly be understood as suggesting that it does—"My eyes have seen the defeat of my adversaries; my ears have heard the rout of my wicked foes" (v. 11).

Such then are the imprecations and the near imprecations of the Psalter. How we, as Christians, understand them and how we respond to the criticisms that are made of them call for our attention before we move to another topic.

3. Handling imprecation in the Psalms

The imprecations of the psalms cause problems for some scholars, who see them as out of harmony with the demand of Leviticus 18:18: "Do not seek revenge or bear a grudge against one of your people, but love your neighbour as yourself." It is said that, if the writers had lived by that rule, they would never have wished the death of another human being, much less called on God to bring it about.

It is also maintained by many that these passages are totally at odds with the teaching of Jesus, who demands that we love not just our friends but also our enemies (Matt. 5:43-48). They are also regarded as being in sharp contrast with our Lord's own example. Whereas the psalmists, suffering what they regarded as undeserved antagonism, called down divine wrath on their persecutors, he prayed that God would forgive them—"Father, forgive them, for they do not know what they are doing" (Luke 23:34).

In response to these criticisms, we can say:

1.   Imprecation was and still is a natural reaction in those, who are victims of injustice and hurt. For the psalmists they were cries to God asking that he would vindicate his name by the exercise of justice. Jeremiah has a number

of similar prayers asking God to act against his accusers and persecutors, whom he wanted to be destroyed 'with double destruction' (Jer. 17:18; cf. 11:20; 18:21-23; 20:12b).

2.   The imprecatory prayers of the psalms and of Jeremiah belong to the era of the Old Covenant. In that era the Law of Moses required that crime be rewarded with punishment equal to its seriousness – an eye for an eye and a life for a life etc. Imprecations are essentially prayers that, in establishing a just order of national and international life, the Lord would eliminate sinful people and their sins.

3.   In their imprecations, those who were deeply disturbed by what had happened to them, may have used hyperbolic and allegorical language that is not meant to be understood in an absolutely literal way. In the heat of a desperate situation it was easy and perhaps natural to use picturesque exaggeration!

4.   The law of love in Leviticus 19:18 had to be balanced with other laws that demanded the punishment of offenders. The two complement rather than contradict each other and it could be that the psalmists, as fallible and fallen human beings, didn't get the balance quite right and so gave too much place to retaliation.

5.   Just as the Holy Spirit included in Scripture stories of the sins of its worthies – sins like David's adultery – so he has included a record of the verbal excesses of the psalmists and, indeed, of others like Job and Jeremiah. In doing so the Spirit was neither commending those excesses nor the sins of David.

6.   Scripture often includes a faithful record of human words without endorsing the sentiments expressed in them. Thus we have the example of righteous Job, who spoke "without knowledge" words that obscured Divine counsel. The Lord held him accountable for those words, which he had to repudiate as he repented in dust and ashes (Job. 38:2 and 42:1-6). While we have no record of David or other psalmists repenting in that way, it is surely possible that they too suffered from a lack of knowledge as a result of which they produced imprecations that somehow also obscured divine counsel.

It is sometimes said that in the new order established under the Law of Christ, imprecations, like those in the psalms, have no place at all. But, in fact, we find Jesus pronouncing woe (Greek, *ouai*, a denunciation) on the towns of Korazin and Bethsaida and on the Pharisees (Matt. 11:21; 18:7; 23:13-29 etc.). He and the apostles often spoke of a final destruction in which God's judgment will fall on the ungodly (e.g., Acts 17:31; Rom. 1:18f; 2:12f. 2. Thes. 1:9; Rev. 20:11-15).

Paul actually concluded his first letter to the Corinthians by pronouncing a "curse"[4] on anyone who does not love the Lord (1 Cor. 16:22). For Paul the effect of such a curse or woe was a matter of missing out on the benefits of the redemption Christ had effected by being made "a curse" for us (Gal. 3:10-14).

These pronouncements can, like the imprecations of the psalms, be understood as evidence of a fervent zeal for the honour of God, for his gospel and for his justice. Whatever is meant by loving enemies (Matt. 5:43-48; Rom. 12:9-21), Jesus and the apostles didn't allow it to eliminate zeal for God's honour either from their own lives or from the teachings they passed on to their followers.

In our reactions to evils in our world and to people who malign us, we Christians must also balance love for others with zeal for justice and for God's honour.

---

[4]Greek, an *anathema*, means "a thing imposed" and so a "sentence," whether of blessing or of its opposite, a destructive judgment or curse.

CHAPTER 26

PSALMS SUPPORTING CHRISTIAN LIVING

Just as the New Testament uses the psalms to give weight to the meaning of our Lord's life, death and resurrection, it uses them to support its principles for Christian living. Quotations from the psalms in relation to Christian devotion and behaviour are not found in the Gospels or the Acts, but do, as we shall see, occur in the writings of Paul and Peter and in the Epistle to the Hebrews.

The apostles regarded the Old Testament Scriptures, including the Psalms as inspired by God. Thus Paul told Timothy, "All Scripture is God-breathed and is useful for teaching, rebuking, correcting and training in righteousness so that the man of God may be thoroughly equipped for every good work" (2 Tim. 3:16, 17). Understanding the Old Testament in that way, they had no hesitation in using passages from it to support their instruction of the followers of Christ. Indeed they delighted to do so.

1. Warnings for lethargic Jewish believers

The writer of the letter to the Hebrews must have known that his readers were under some pressure to return to traditional Jewish beliefs and practices and in the process to abandon Christ. At best their Christianity seems to have been of such an elementary nature that they needed to grow and become mature in Christ (Heb. 6:1-3). The Epistle therefore brought them a number of warnings against being lethargic or becoming apostate.

In Hebrews 3 and 4 there are five distinct citations of Psalm 95:7-11 (Heb. 3:7-11, 15; 4:3, 5 and 7). The first is introduced by the words, "So, as the Holy Spirit says," indicating the writer's belief that the psalm, was a divinely inspired writing of continuing relevance.

The first quotation is of verses 7-11 in their entirety:

> Today, if you hear his voice,
>> do not harden your hearts
> as you did in the rebellion[1]
>> during the time of testing[2] in the desert,
> where your fathers tested and tried me
>> and for forty years saw what I did.
> That is why I was angry with that generation,
>> and I said, Their hearts are always going astray,
>> and they have not known my ways.
> So I declared on oath in my anger,
>> They shall never enter my rest.

By reminding his readers that rebellion kept the Israelites out of the Promised Land for forty years, the author was warning them against testing God as their forefathers had done. They must ensure that they did not fail, as the Israelites had done in the time of Moses, by allowing unbelief to turn them away from the living God. As Paul put it, quoting Psalm 19:4, The Israelites had heard but did not all accept the "good news," the announcement of which "had gone out to the ends of the world" (Rom. 10:16-18):

> Their voice has gone out into all the earth,
> Their words to the ends of the world.

The Hebrew Christians are told that they must hold firmly to the confidence they had when they first trusted Christ (Heb. 3:14), an exhortation that inspired a repeat quotation of Psalm 95:7c-9: "Today, if you will hear his voice, do not harden your hearts as you did in the rebellion" (Heb. 3:15).

---

[1] The Hebrew, *meribah*, means strife, contention, or rebellion.
[2] The Hebrew, *massah*, means trial or temptation (See Ex. 17:7 etc.).

The remaining three quotations of this psalm are in chapter 4 verses 3, 5 and 7, where the emphasis is on the "rest" of the people of God. For forty years the Israelites had missed that rest, which for them was to have been a settled life in the Promised Land – the land of milk and honey. They missed it because, while God had sent his "good news," his gospel, promising them freedom and blessing, it was of no use to them because they did not respond to it in, or combine it with, faith (Heb. 4:2).

The writer acknowledges that his believing readers were different and "were entering" into the rest that was promised to them in the gospel of Christ (4:3a), a rest prefigured by the land promised to ancient Israel. He was, therefore, desperately concerned that they should not dally or delay as did the Israelites, but would rather press on to enter fully into the blessings God had promised them. They should make every effort immediately – today – to enter and enjoy the rest God had provided for them and to avoid the folly of their ancestors. In support of his plea the writer twice quotes the verdict God had pronounced on the Israelites in Psalm 95:11—"they shall never enter my rest" (Heb. 4:3, 5).

The warning of the psalmist, based on the experiences of Israel during the wilderness wanderings in the time of Moses, was intended to reinforce the writer's call for a proper worship of the Lord. His call was to the people of his own day:

> Come let us bow down and worship
> > Let us kneel before the LORD our Maker,
> for he is our God
> > and we are the people of his pasture,
> > the flock under his care.
>
> —Ps. 95:6

What had been required of the people of the psalmist's day was equally important in the lives of the fledgling Jewish Christians to whom the epistle was written. They too must avoid any prevarication that would put the Lord to the test. Surely his words also warn all Christians, Gentile as well as Jewish, against lethargy in the Christian life. We must all, as Paul put it, press on to take hold of that, for which Christ has taken hold of us (Phil. 3:12).

2. Supporting worship and service

It is somewhat surprising that the apostles only rarely appealed to the psalms to support their demands that Christians worship and serve the Lord.

1) In relation to worship

As Paul concluded the doctrinal section of his letter to the church in Rome (Rom. 1-8), he became lyrical about the love of Christ. He asserted that no-one and no thing, no trouble or suffering could separate believers from that love. And to show that trouble and, indeed, suffering are part of the lot of God's children, he cited Psalm 44:22:

> For your (i.e., God's) sake we face death all day long;
>> we are considered as sheep to be slaughtered

—Rom. 8:36

But while trials and testings are part of our lot, we are "more than conquerors through him (Christ) who loved us." It is in the assurance that nothing "in all creation will be able to separate us from the love of God that is in Christ Jesus, our Lord" (Rom. 8:31-39), that we, like Paul, worship God, our Father and the Lord Jesus Christ

In similar vein Paul used Psalm 116:10: "I believed; therefore have I spoken," to affirm his own faith in the fact that, even though he and his colleagues were constantly being threatened with death, he had a sure hope that the God, who raised up Jesus, would ultimately raise up him and his fellow-workers. As he neared the end of the same epistle, Paul wrote of the Gentiles glorifying, that is, worshipping God for his mercy. Supporting this he quoted two passages from the Psalms:

(1) Romans 15:9, which cites Psalm 18:49

> Therefore I will praise you among the Gentiles;
>> I will sing hymns to your name.

(2) Romans 15:11, which cites Psalm 117:1

> Praise the Lord, all you Gentiles,
>> and sing praises to him all you peoples.

2) In relation to Christian service

We note two important passages:

(1) Second Corinthians 9:6-15

This is concerned with the apostle's call for generous "giving" to help the poor. Citing Psalm 112:9, he says that God has given us an example in this regard:

> He has scattered abroad his gifts to the poor;
> > his righteousness endures for ever.

The point is that, as God everlastingly expresses righteousness and justice in his care for dispossessed and underprivileged people, so his people should always be ready to share the riches he bestows on them with those who are in need. Indeed one of his methods of caring for the needy is to use the "giving" of those who are better off.

(2) Ephesians 4:8

This passage quotes and in the third line re-interprets the words of Psalm 68:18:

> When he ascended on high,
> > he led captives in his train and gave gifts to men.

The original Hebrew of the Psalm has, "You received gifts from men for the third line." It may be that Paul was remembering and using an early Aramaic paraphrase of the psalm, which read, "You (the LORD) gave gifts to men." Here Paul uses those words to affirm that the risen and ascended Christ bestows gifts for service on his people – "some apostles, some prophets, some evangelists, some pastors and teachers." One way in which those "gifts" would express themselves would surely be in the exercises of worship and in the leading of corporate acts of worship.

3. In support of proper Christian behaviour

1) Re eating meat that had been sacrificed to an idol

In First Corinthians 10 Paul had to treat a problem that must have been troubling some of his converts in Corinth. Meat from animals that had been offered in sacrifice in and idol-temple was being sold in the markets and could be offered to believers in the homes of non-Christian friends. The questions were, should believers buy or eat such meat.

Paul insisted that the idol was a mere material object, a non-entity without spiritual power. Meat was not changed by being offered to it and, when brought out and sold in a market, it could therefore be purchased and eaten by believers, because, says, Paul quoting Psalm 24:1, "the earth is the LORD's and everything in it." By this the apostle seems to mean that the animal providing the meat was and remained the Lord's property and could, therefore, be eaten without compromising one's faith.[3]

At the same time Paul was careful to introduce a complementary requirement, that of not to setting an example, which a weak believer with an idolatrous background might take to mean that it is in order for a Christian to engage in sacrifice to an idol. Hence his instruction:

> So whether you eat or drink or whatever you do, do it all for the glory of God. Do not cause anyone to stumble, whether Jews, Greeks or the church of God—even as I try to please everybody in e very way.
>
> —1 Cor. 10:31

2) Re the control of anger

In Ephesians 4:26, Psalm 4:4 seems to be the basis of the apostle's instruction, "In your anger do not sin. Do not let the sun go down while you are still angry." The verse of the Psalm reads:

> In your anger do not sin;
>> When you are on your beds
>> Search your hearts and be silent.

3) Re harmony among believers

The apostle Peter (1 Pet. 3:9-12) quotes Psalm 34:12-16 to support his admonition that Christians should live in loving and compassionate harmony with one another:

---

[3]Note Mark's comment that Jesus declared all food clean (Mark. 7:19).

> Whoever would love life and see good days
>> must keep his tongue from evil
>> and his lips from deceitful speech.
> He must turn from evil and do good;
>> he must seek peace and pursue it.
> For the eyes of the Lord are on the righteous
>> and his ears are attentive to their prayer,
> but the face of the LORD is against those who do evil.

Our duty before God is to turn from evil and give ourselves to doing good. That means controlling the words we speak and not allowing our tongues and our lips to be agents of antagonism or dishonesty. It means seeking and pursuing "peace," which in the mind of a Jew, like Peter, would have been enshrined in the word "*shalom*" and would have meant seeking the total well-being of others. Christian duty is then not merely a matter of aspiration for or of talk about caring for others, but the actual pursuit of that aim.

4) Re the challenge of justice

Justice is one of the great themes of the Old Testament prophets (cf. Amos 5:24) In the psalms justice is often presented as a fact both of God's nature and of his behaviour:

> The LORD is righteous, he loves justice.
>> —Ps. 11:7

> The LORD loves righteousness and justice.
>> —Ps. 33:5a

> Righteousness and justice are the foundation of your throne.
>> —Ps. 89:14, cf. 99:4 etc.

The expectation of the psalmists was that the Lord, their God, governed the peoples of the world with justice and would judge them in righteousness (Ps. 9:8). "A sceptre of justice would be the sceptre –the symbol – of his kingdom" (Ps. 46:6). In the light of this the psalmists consistently called upon their audiences to follow the Lord's example. Thus Psalm 72, which is headed, "of Solomon," begins with a prayer that the king might rule his people justly:

> Endow the king with your justice, O God,
>   the royal son with your righteousness.
> He will judge your people in righteousness,
>   your afflicted ones with justice.
>
> —Ps. 72:1, 2; cf. 99:4

It was in the context of a desire for justice that most of the imprecatory prayers we discussed earlier were uttered. The psalmists wanted their unjust tormentors to receive their due desert, their just reward. Thus we have David praying:

> Arise, O LORD, in your anger;
>   Rise up against the rage of my enemies.
> Awake, my God; decree *justice*.
>
> —Ps. 7:6

Often, as in Psalm 103:6, justice and righteousness are linked together: "The LORD works *righteousness and justice* for all the oppressed." In Psalm 89:14 Ethan the Ezrahite, addressing the Lord, says, "*Righteousness and justice* are the foundation of your throne." In Scripture justice and righteousness are two sides of the same coin – the same Hebrew and Greek words serve for both ideas.

When Scripture says that God is *righteous*, it means that all he does is right (cf. Gen. 18:25; Ps. 116:5; Jer. 9:24; 12:1; Hos. 14:9; Rom. 1:17; 3:5; 10:3; 2 Tim. 4:8 etc.). It also means that everything he does expresses and corresponds to his righteous character—He is "the righteous LORD."

God's justice is that righteous behaviour, by virtue of which he gives proper recognition and fair play to others. As an attribute, justice is his righteousness allocating to men and women the due and proper reward for their actions.

The psalmists affirm that those who maintain justice would be rewarded with blessing:

> Blessed are they who maintain justice,
>   who constantly do what is right.
>
> —Ps. 106:3

> Blessed is the man who fears the LORD,
>   the man whose righteousness endures

and who conducts his affairs with justice.

—Ps. 112:1-5

While we don't find in the New Testament a quotation from the psalms used to support the command that Christians should think and act in ways that are just, we can be sure that its writers with their intimate knowledge of the psalms, had their emphases strongly present in their minds.

There are, in fact, many references to justice in the New Testament. For example, Jesus indicated that it was part of his function on earth (Matt. 12:18-20). He deplored the fact that it was neglected by the Pharisees (Matt. 23:23; Luke 11:42). Paul similarly affirmed that God would judge the entire human race in justice (Acts 17:31; cf. Rev. 19:11). He also portrayed our Lord's death as a demonstration of God's justice—"He did this to demonstrate his justice ... so as to be just and the one who justifies those who have faith in Jesus" (Rom. 3:25, 26).

Who, we must ask, can meet the challenges to Christian living that are supported by the psalms? Who can reproduce the righteousness and the justice of God? Hebrews 13:5-6, citing Psalm 118:6-7 provides an answer. It is by living in a vital relationship with him that constantly enables his child to enjoy his help:

> God has said,
> Never will I leave you;
> never will I forsake you.
> So we say with confidence,
> The LORD is my helper; I will not be afraid.

Conclusion

From what we have been able to examine in this chapter, it should be evident that the Psalms of the Old Testament have a timelessness that makes them relevant in the Christian era. From the times of the apostles they have been prominent in Christian thinking and as the basis of much Christian devotion. The Christian, just as much as the Israelite of David's time, can revel in the fact that the LORD is his Shepherd (Ps. 23:1).

Words from the Psalms have been incorporated into the prayer and the songs of Christian people. Written liturgical prayers widely used in many denominations abound in words and phrases taken directly from the Psalms. And Christian hymns have followed the same pattern as we will seek to demonstrate in the Appendix that follows and which is entitled, "The Psalms in Christian Hymnody."

CHAPTER 27

THE PSALMS IN CHRISTIAN HYMNODY

We have seen that our Lord and the apostles used the psalms in their preaching and teaching. In this we note something of how the psalms have influenced the thought of English hymns, many of which are based on psalms.

In some cases these hymns are fairly close paraphrases of the text of either a complete psalm or a part of it. In others a single verse or even a line has been a trigger leading into an application of wider Christian truths – the theology of the psalm blends into that of the gospel. In this context it is only possible to cite a few examples.

Many of the older hymns that arise from the psalms were produced in the seventeenth and eighteenth centuries and are based on the Authorised (King James) Version of 1611. They are, therefore, written in the rather archaic language of that age – the singular second person pronouns, thee, thou and thine plus the verbal "st" and "edst" endings that went with them and the plural pronoun "ye." Such language tends to give modern readers the impression that they, and the religion they present, is out of date and irrelevant to the twenty-first century.

Much as modernisation of language is desirable, it is not always linguistically felicitous. It can damage or even lose the rhyme and the assonance that characterised the original poetry. Most of the older or original forms are therefore retained in recent hymnbooks and will be retained in the examples that are set out below. Mission Praise does, however, drop the initial capital letters for all but the first line of each verse. It also abandons the indentation of alternate lines that characterise traditional hymnbooks.

It will be wise to read these examples with an open Bible (whether the AV or a more recent version) at hand, so that the connections with the original texts can be appreciated.

1. Paraphrased psalms

The best-known example is surely the Scottish Metrical Version of Psalm 23, which is based on the AV of 1611:

> The Lord's my Shepherd, I'll not want,
>   He makes me down to lie
> In pastures green He leadeth me
>   The quiet waters by.
>
> My soul he doth restore again,
>   And me to walk doth make
> Within the paths of righteousness
>   E'en for his own name's sake.
>
> Yea, though I walk through death's dark vale
>   Yet will I fear none ill;
> For Thou art with me, and Thy rod
>   And staff me comfort still.
>
> My table Thou hast furnished
>   In presence of my foes;
> My head Thou dost with oil anoint
>   And my cup overflows.
>
> Goodness and mercy all my life
>   Shall surely follow me;
> And in God's house for ever more
>   My dwelling place shall be.

HW Baker's hymn, "The King of Love my Shepherd is," is also based on *Psalm 23*, but its third verse (in italics below) derives from our Lord's parable of the

Lost Sheep and his identification of himself as "The Good Shepherd" (Luke 15:3-7; John 10:1-18).

> The King of love my Shepherd is
>> Whose goodness faileth never
> I nothing lack, if I am His
>> and He is mine for ever.
>
> Where streams of living water flow
>> My ransomed soul he leadeth,
> And where the verdant pastures grow,
>> With food celestial feedeth.
>
> *Perverse and foolish oft I strayed;*
>> *But yet in love he sought me,*
> *And on his shoulder gently laid,*
>> *And home, rejoicing brought me.*
>
> In death's dark vale I fear no ill
>> With Thee, dear Lord, beside me:
> Thy rod and staff my comfort still,
>> Thy cross before to guide me.
>
> Thou spreadest a table in my sight;
>> Thy unction grace bestowerh
> And oh what transport of delight
>> From Thy pure chalice floweth.
>
> And so through all the length of days
>> Thy goodness faileth never;
> Good Shepherd, may I sing Thy praise
>> Within Thy house for ever.

Towards the end of the Puritan era (1600-1660), Francis Rous and William Barton paraphrased ***Psalm 24:7-10***:

> Ye gates, lift up your heads on high;
>> Ye doors that last for aye

Be lifted up that so the King
    Of glory enter may !
But who of glory is the King?
The mighty Lord is this,
E'en that same Lord that great in might
    And strong in battle is.

Ye gates, lift up your heads, ye doors,
    Doors that do last for aye,
Be lifted up that so the King
    Of glory enter may !
But who is He that is the King
    Of glory? Who is this?
The Lord of hosts and none but He,
    The King of glory is.

Psalm 40:1-5 was also paraphrased by Francis Rous and William Barton. Their hymn is:

I waited for the Lord my God,
    And patiently did bear;
At length to me he did incline
    My voice and cry to hear.

He took me from a fearful pit
    And from the miry clay
And on a rock he set my feet,
    Establishing my way.

He put a new song in my mouth,
    Our God to magnify:
Many shall see it and shall fear,
    And on the Lord rely.

Oh, blessed is the man whose trust
    Upon the Lord relies,
Respecting not the proud nor such

As turn aside to lies.

O Lord my God, full many are
    The wonders Thou hast done
Thy gracious thoughts to us-ward far
    Above all thoughts are gone.

In order none can reckon them
    To Thee; if them declare
And speak of them I would, they more
    Than can be numbered are.

The Old Hundredth, as it is known, is a paraphrase of **Psalm 100** and it, again, is found in the Scottish Metrical Psalter. It is attributed to William Kethe and dated 1560:

All people that on earth do dwell,
    Sing to the Lord with cheerful voice;
Him serve with mirth, his praise forth tell;
    Come ye before him and rejoice.

The Lord, ye know, is God indeed:
    Without our aid he did us make;
We are his flock, he doth us feed;
    And for his sheep he doth us take.

Oh, enter then his gates with praise,
    Approach with joy his courts unto
Praise, laud and bless his name always
    For it is seemly so to do.

For why? The Lord our God is good
    His mercy is for ever sure;
His truth at all times firmly stood,
    And shall from age to age endure.

Isaac Watts hymn, "Before Jehovah's awful throne" is more loosely based on the same psalm (***Psalm 100***). As we found to be the case with HW Baker's hymn, "The King of love my Shepherd is," elements of Christian thought have been added to those of the psalmist in order to make the hymn resonate with Christian experience.

> Before Jehovah's awful throne
> > Ye nations bow with sacred joy;
> Know that the Lord is God alone;
> > He can create, and he destroy.
>
> His sovereign power without our aid,
> > Made us of clay and formed us men;
> And when like wandering sheep we strayed,
> > He brought us back to his fold again.
>
> We are his people, we his care
> > Our souls and all our mortal frame;
> What lasting honours shall we rear
> > Almighty Maker, to thy name.
>
> We'll crowd thy gates with thankful songs,
> > High as the heavens our voices raise;
> And earth with her ten thousand tongues
> > Shall fill thy courts with sounding praise.
>
> Wide as the world is thy command;
> > Vast as eternity thy love;
> Firm as a rock thy truth shall stand,
> > When rolling years shall cease to move.

Henry Francis Lyte, who is probably best known for the hymn, "Abide with me," had a deep religious experience in 1818. This was brought on by the death of a much loved colleague in the ministry. Thereafter he began to present the Christian message and the Christian hope in poetry. Later (c. 1830), when Lyte was ministering in Brixton, Devon, he wrote a book called, "the Spirit of the

Psalms," in which was included a paraphrase of **Psalm 103**: the hymn, "Praise my soul the King of Heaven."

The hymn is still in wide use and was, in fact, chosen by Princess Elizabeth, now, of course, Queen Elizabeth II, to be sung at her marriage Prince Philip, Duke of Edinburgh in November 1947.

Praise my soul the King of Heaven,
 To his feet thy tribute bring,
Ransomed, healed, restored, forgiven,
 Who, like thee His praise should sing?
Praise Him! Praise Him! *
 Praise the everlasting King.

Praise him for his grace and favour
 To our fathers in distress.
Praise him still the same for ever,
 Slow to chide and swift to bless:
Praise Him! Praise Him! *
 Glorious in his faithfulness

Father-like he tends and spares us,
 Well our feeble frame he knows
In his hands he gently bears us,
 Rescues us from all our foes:
Praise Him! Praise Him! *
 Widely as his mercy flows.

Frail as summer's flowers we flourish;
 Blows the wind and it is gone;
But while mortals rise and perish
 God endures unchanging on.
Praise Him! Praise Him! *
 Praise the high eternal one.

Angels help us to adore him;
 Ye behold Him face to face;

Sun and moon bow down before Him,
    Dwellers all in time and space.
Praise Him! Praise Him! *
    Praise with us the God of grace.

* This line is sung twice to give 8 beats and a tune pattern of 8 7 8 7
8 7 8 7. Some American hymnals replace, "Praise Him! Praise Him!"
with "Al-le-lu-ia! Al-le-lu-ia!" meaning, of course, "Praise the Lord."*

The following paraphrase of **Psalm 121** is, like two already mentioned above, attributed to Francis Rous and William Barton. It has had a significant place in English-language Christian worship, but is relatively rarely used today.

I to the hills will lift mine eyes:
    From whence doth come mine aid?
My safety cometh from the Lord,
    Who heaven and earth hath made.

Thy foot He'll not let slide,
    nor will He slumber that thee keeps.
Behold, He that keeps Israel,
    He slumbers not, nor sleeps.

The Lord thee keeps; the Lord thy shade
    On thy right hand doth stay:
The moon by night thee shall not smite,
    Nor yet the sun by day.

The Lord shall keep thy soul; He shall
    Preserve thee from all ill;
Henceforth thy going out and in
    God keep for ever will.

The anonymous hymn, "Praise the Lord, ye heavens adore him," which appeared in the "Foundling Hospitals Collection of 1809," was clearly inspired by **Psalm 148:1-6**. Some books set out this hymn as two eight line verses, rather than as the 4 x 4 line verses below.

Praise the Lord, ye heavens adore him;
  Praise him, angels, in the height;
Sun and moon, rejoice before him;
  Praise him, all ye stars and light.

Praise the Lord, for he has spoken;
  Worlds his mighty voice obeyed:
Laws which never shall be broken,
  For their guidance he hath made.

Praise the Lord for he is glorious;
  Never shall his promise fail;
God hath made his saints victorious;
  Sin and death shall nor prevail.

Praise the God of our salvation;
  Hosts on high, his power proclaim;
Heaven and earth and all creation,
  Laud and magnify his Name.

Psalm 150 is the final doxology of the psalter and brings the whole book to an appropriate climax. Like the four psalms that precede it (146-149) it begins and ends with a call to give praise to the Lord – "Praise the Lord" (Hebrew, *Halleleujah*). It is the basis of HW Baker's hymn:

O praise ye the Lord!
  Praise him in the height!
Rejoice in his word,
  Ye angels of light:
Ye heavens adore him,
  By whom you were made,
And worship before him
  In brightness arrayed.

O praise ye the Lord!
  Praise him upon the earth,
In tuneful accord,

Ye sons of new birth;
Praise him who hath brought you
His grace from above
Praise Him who hath taught you
To sing of his love.

O praise ye the Lord!
Thanksgiving and song
To him be outpoured
All ages along
For love in creation
For heaven restored,
For grace of salvation
O praise ye the Lord!

Baker's hymn is not strictly a paraphrase, but a Christian expansion of the psalmist's call for unceasing praise of the Lord. Like the psalm that is the final doxology in the Book of the psalms, this hymn provides a fine culmination to our examination of the paraphrasing of the psalms in the hymnody of Christendom.

2. Psalms that influenced hymn-writers

Psalm 19 was obviously in the mind of Isaac Watts and was a trigger for his writing of a hymn that linked the wonders of the created universe with the power of God's word and of the Gospel. Verses 1, 3 and 5 will show the thrust of his thought and its links with the psalm:

1 The heavens declare Thy glory, Lord
In every star Thy wisdom shines;
But when our eyes behold Thy Word
we read Thy name in fairer lines.

3. Sun, moon and stars convey Thy praise
Round the whole earth and never stand:
So when Thy truth began its race,
It touched and glanced on every land.

5. Great Son of Righteousness arise,
    Bless the dark world with heavenly light:
The gospel makes the simple wise;
    Thy laws are pure, the judgments right.

Psalm 34:1-9 was clearly a strong influence on Nahum Tate and Nicholas Brady, who wrote the hymn, "Through all the changing scenes of life." The psalmist had been in great trouble and the Lord had heard and answered his prayer by delivering him. He saw this as giving him grounds for calling on others to taste and experience the goodness of the Lord. The psalm and the hymn that derives from it have often been a blessing to troubled Christians. Three verses below will illustrate the thought:

2. Of his deliverance I will boast;
    Till all that are distressed
From my example comfort take
    And charm their griefs to rest.

3. O magnify the Lord with me,
    With me exalt his name;
When in distress to him I called,
    He to my rescue came.

5. O make but trial of his love
    Experience will decide
How blessed are they, and only they
    Who in his truth abide.

Psalm 42:1-5 lies behind another seventeenth century hymn by Nahum Tate and Nicholas Brady, who paraphrased verses 1, 2 and 5 thus:

1. As pants the hart for living streams,
    When heated in the chase,
So longs my soul, O God, for Thee'
    And Thy refreshing grace.

4. When restless, why cast down, my soul?

> Hope still and thou shalt sing
> The praise of him who is thy God,
>> Thy health's eternal spring.

The first lines of this psalm *(42)* also provided the inspiration for Martin Nystrom's 1983 song (MP, 37):

> As the deer pants for water,
> so my soul longs after You.
> You alone are my heart's desire
> and I long to worship You.

The messianic implications of **Psalm 45:1-6** are developed in John Ryland's hymn, "Let us sing the King Messiah." The possibility of the psalmist thinking primarily of an Israelite king is not mentioned. We quote verses 1 and 3:

Let us sing the King Messiah,
  King of righteousness and peace;
Hail Him, all his happy subjects,
  Never let his praises cease;
    Ever hail him
  Never let his praises cease.
Gird Thy sword on, mighty Hero,
  Make the word of truth Thy car;
Prosper in Thy course majestic;
  All success attend Thy war
    Gracious Victor,
  Let mankind before Thee bow.

Psalm 72, a Royal and Messianic Psalm, seems to have been at least part of the inspiration behind two well-known hymns: "Hail to the Lord's Anointed" by James Montgomery, and "Jesus shall reign where'er the sun" by Isaac Watts.

The first lines of **Psalm 122**, "I rejoiced with those who said to me, Let us go to the house of the Lord," underlie the first verse of another hymn by Isaac Watts:

How pleased and blessed was I
    To hear the people cry,
Come let us seek our God today!
    Yes with a cheerful zeal
    We haste to Zion's hill,
And there our vows and homage pay.

Psalm 126 celebrates an occasion on which the Lord had restored the fortunes of his people after some unidentified adversity. It tells of exuberant joy and thankfulness on account of the great things the Lord had done for his people (vv. 1-3). It then asks the Lord to restore their fortunes so that those who had sown seed in a time of weeping might now bring in a harvest – sheaves of grain – with songs of joy (vv. 4-6).

The joyful hope of the last few lines is widely thought to have given inspiration to Henry Alford's well-known harvest hymn, verse 1 of which is:

Come ye thankful people, come,
Raise the song of harvest-home;
All is safely gathered in,
Ere the winter storms begin.
God, our Maker, doth provide
For our needs to be supplied:
Come to God's own temple, come
Raise the song of harvest home.

The modernised version of this hymn in Mission Praise is taken from Jubilate Hymns and involves a number of emendations,. For example, verse 1 (emendations shown in bold italic type) appears as:

Come you thankful people come,
raise the song of harvest home!
fruit and crops are gathered in
safe before the storms begin:
God, our *m*aker will provide
for our needs to be supplied;
come ***with all his people***, come
raise the song of harvest home!

The first verse of yet another hymn by Watts, "I'll praise my Maker while I've breath" is heavily reliant on ***Psalm 146:1-2***, which the AV rendered as:

> Praise ye the Lord.
> Praise the Lord, O my soul.
> While I live I will praise the Lord:
> I will song praises unto my God
> while I have any being.

Paraphrasing these lines, Watts wrote:

> I'll praise my Maker while I've breath;
> And when my voice is lost in death
>   Praise shall employ my nobler powers.
> My days of praise shall ne'er be past,
> While life and thought and being last,
>   Or immortality endures.

The fourth verse of this great hymn repeats the first verse with the exception of its first line, which reads, "I'll praise my maker while He *lends me* breath."

This hymn tends to be more widely used today than others of its age. It has even been accorded a place in Mission Praise (No. 320), where it is presented with a more modern layout than the one set out above.

Conclusion

The psalms enshrine the responses of the people of God in Old Testament times to his revelation of himself. Sometimes that response is marked by desperation, panic and frustration. More often, the emphasis is on praise to the Lord for what he is – a faithful and loving God – and for what he had done for his people by constantly providing for them and in frequently delivering them from their troubles. Together the psalms witness to the deep faith and the heartfelt religion of the psalmists – they were deeply concerned for truth, righteousness and godly living.

The psalmists often used the teaching methods of "the wise" to emphasise the place – the vital role – of faith and of obedience to God's law in the religious life.

As we noticed earlier, many psalms have a messianic dimension – they speak of the role of Davidic kings and then point beyond them to the ultimate King-Messiah. In doing so they link the faith of the Old Covenant with that of the New and so link in with the Christian revelation and with Christian worship.

It is this connection that has enabled so many Christian hymn writers to use, or, at least, to build on the words and thoughts of the psalmists and to produce psalm-based hymns, like those we have included in this chapter.

CHAPTER STUDY QUESTIONS

Prepared by Dwight Singer for
Faith in the Psalms: The Hymnal of the Old Testament
By Norman Shields

Preface

The study questions for each chapter require a careful reading with understanding of the Psalms material of each chapter. The questions will challenge the reader's understanding by encouraging a skilful use of the material in the further analysis and interpretation of the Psalms. The questions are designed for the upper level B.A. student, but many could challenge also the graduate student. A few of the questions intend to stimulate comprehensive study of the Psalms so do not get bogged down if you feel unable to answer a question completely. May the Spirit reward with spiritual fruit all your labours of meditating skilfully with knowledge on the Psalms day and night.

Study Questions

Chapter 1 Poetry in Scripture

1. Provide description or definition of the most important feature of biblical Hebrew poetry.
2. Read Psalms 38:4; 49:12; 73:20; 103:13; 119:162; 131:2. Describe the category of parallelism. (Hint: are there similes which you can identify?)
3. Read Psalms 20:7; 34:19; 96:5; 118:18; 119:67. Describe the category of parallelism. (Hint: the category is the same in each verse.)
4. What category of parallelism exhibits circularity of thought? Is circularity of thought embraced by African cultures? Explain.

5. Explain how the knowledge of Hebrew language helps in observing the poetic device of word play and acrostic. Give an illustration of word play in your mother tongue.

6. What is an alphabetic acrostic psalm? What does this poetic device reveal about the poetic skill of the author?

Chapter 2 The Songs of Scripture

1. In which of the major divisions of the Old Testament are hymns of thanksgiving found? (Hint: remember that the OT comprises the Law (or Moses), Prophets, and Writings (or sometimes designated Psalms.)

2. Consider that the reasons (or occasions) for laments are many and not just the attacks of enemies. What does the psalmist lament in Psalm 38?

3. What type of song (or psalm classification) is Micah 7:8-20?

4. What part of the OT are taunt songs found? Taunt songs often begin with a key word that marks their occurrence. What is that key word as found in Habbakuk 2:6-19?

5. 5. Can you find a song in 1 Timothy (or portion of a song)?

Chapter 3 The Book of Psalms

1. What features in the Psalms provide evidence of structure as a complete book?

2. Who are the sons of Korah, father of the family of worship leaders? (Hint: search 1Chronicles 9; and remember an incident from the Pentateuch.) Who is Asaph? (Hint: search 1 Chronicles 15 and 25 for clues.)

3. Can you suggest why an ancient poet would compose a poem with acrostic structure? (Hint: think of possible benefits of the acrostic device if the poem is spoken to hearers.)

4. What expression is repeated several times in the psalms which begin Book IV? (Hint: examine Psalms 90–100 but take note that the expression does not occur in every psalm.) Keep in mind that some Psalms scholars contend that these psalms present a climactic theme of the Psalms as a

book. How might a repeated expression support the idea that Psalms has a major theme?
5. Discuss the major contribution of Herman Gunkel to Psalms studies which benefit even evangelicals.

Chapter 4 In praise of God – Pss. 8 & 111

1. Observe the structure of Psalm 8 by comparing the beginning and ending sections of the psalm. What constitutes the middle of the psalm?
2. What does Psalm 8 suggest as the most effective weapon against God's enemies? Explain how Psalm 8 presents this idea.
3. Read another praise psalm, such as Psalm 113 (or the longer Psalm 139), and identify the reasons for praise.
4. Describe the relationships between Psalm 8 and Genesis 1. How does this link develop the message of the psalm?
5. How does the praise of Psalm 111 parallel the praise of Psalm 8? What additional grounds of praise are found in Psalm 111 beyond the praise of Psalm 8?
6. Explain how Psalm 111 ends differently than Psalm 8. (Hint: what is the unique subject matter of Psalm 111 and how does it relate to praise?)

Chapter 5 Individual thanksgivings – Pss. 30 & 32

1. What features/characteristics are distinct about individual thanksgiving psalms? (Hint: consider grammar and tone/mood.)
2. What was the occasion for David's thanks in Psalm 30? How does he expand his personal thanksgiving to include the community?
3. What features do you find in Psalm 138 which would identify the psalm as an individual thanksgiving psalm?
4. How does David seek to motivate God to answer his desperate prayer for deliverance in 30:8–10? Illustrate how another biblical character prays similarly?
5. What features/characteristics do you find in the individual thanksgiving Psalm 32 which is not found in the individual thanksgiving Psalm 30?

(Hint: read 32:1–2, 8–9.) What do you conclude about the structure of individual thanksgiving psalms as a result of this observation?

6.   What does Psalm 32, *based upon David's experience*, teach about sin, guilt, forgiveness, and thanksgiving in relationship to a vibrant spiritual life of a believer in Christ?

Chapter 6 Community thanksgivings – Pss. 107 & 124

1.   Describe the repeated patterns of Psalm 107. How do the patterns help you to understand the structure of the psalm and its message?

2.   Provide one Christ-centred reading for a stanza of Psalm 107 or for the psalm in its entirety. (Remember that a Christ-centred reading or interpretation must be related properly to the meaning of the ancient Old Testament context.)

3.   What was the occasion for the writing of Psalm 124? Does the title of the psalm provide certain background concerning the occasion?

4.   Since Psalm 124 begins with the exhortation specifically to Israel, "let Israel say now," does this imply that the psalm has no application for the church today? Explain the hermeneutics of your conclusions.

5.   The disparity in length between Psalms 107 and 124 may give the impression that they are very different. What parallels do you find between Psalms 107 and 124?

Chapter 7 Professions of trust in God – Pss. 4 & 23

1.   Compare and contrast the way that the profession of trust Psalms 4 and 23 begin. (In other words, what is similar about the structure of the psalms and what is different?)

2.   Examine the way in which two other profession of trust psalms, Psalms 16 and 62, begin in the initial verses. Compare and contrast the beginning of each of these two psalms with Psalms 4 and 23.

3. What are some repeated features and common themes that link Psalms 3 and 4? If these psalms are read together as closely associated, how is the message of each psalm deepened in view of the other?

4. What dominant metaphor of Psalm 23 directs the message of the entire psalm? Summarize how the metaphor illustrates what Psalm 23 intends to teach.

5. What New Testament passage uses the same metaphor as Psalm 23 yet in reference to Christ? In light of correlating this NT passage with Psalm 23, suggest how the psalm may be read with a Christological focus.

Chapter 8 In praise of the Lord's presence – Pss. 27 & 122

1. What do Psalms 27 and 122 (and any other songs of Zion psalms) indicate about the significance, especially spiritual significance, of Jerusalem (especially the holy hill there) for an ancient Israelite believer?

2. What is an obvious connection between Psalms 23 and 27, which is mentioned in this chapter? How would you argue that Psalm 27 has much to teach about trust in God (as does Psalm 23, the profession of trust psalm)?

3. What are your arguments for the unity of Psalm 27 against the contention of some OT scholars that the psalm should be viewed as two separate psalms? (Hint: consider thematic and verbal links between the two sections of the psalm.)

4. How do you understand the psalmist's desire to "dwell in the house of the LORD all the days of his life" (as expressed in Psalm 27)?

5. Explain fully the various aspects that David or the psalmist had in mind as he encouraged prayer for the peace of Jerusalem.

6. What would be a New Testament era application for the prayer for the peace of Jerusalem?

Chapter 9 Praising the Lord as King – Pss. 47 & 93

1. What is the unifying theme of Psalms 93–100, based upon the repeated expression (hint: found in Psalms 93, 96, 97, 99). Attempt to summarize in a brief paragraph the message of Psalms 93–100 as a unified grouping of psalms in view of this theme and expression.
2. What implications of God's Kingship does Psalm 47 reveal?
3. Suggest an eschatological (i.e. ultimate) fulfilment of Yahweh's Kingship in view of the message of Psalm 47.
4. What aspects of Yahweh's Kingship are developed in Psalm 93?
5. Summarize in one sentence the idea of 93:5. Relate this teaching with the message of the entire Psalm 93.
6. Suggest a contemporary application of the theme of Yahweh's Kingship in the Kingship Psalms to the contemporary African political situation.

Chapter 10 Personal Lament – David's desolation – Ps. 22

1. Identify the various complaints or causes for suffering in various typical lament psalms, such as Psalms 6, 7, 54, 57, 140, and 142.
2. The personal lament psalm (or prayers for help by the individual) have the following typical elements (but not all are always present): introductory cry to God, description of trouble and suffering, petition for God's help with reasons why God should hear the petition, confession of trust in God, and promise to praise God often with the appropriate sacrifice. Identify these elements in the personal lament Psalm 22.
3. How many verses of Psalm 22 are quoted in the gospels? (Hint: see Matthew 27 [or Mark 15] and John 19.) What are the implications concerning the message of Psalm 22 from the observation of its use in the New Testament?
4. What is the key word of the first section of Psalm 22, occurring in verses 1, 11, 19, which reveals the spiritual suffering of the psalmist?

5. Is this prayer of lament by the psalmist answered by God? (Hint: see the author's comments in this chapter on 22:19–21.) If this psalm speaks also of the experience of Christ on the cross, how would you suggest that his prayer is answered?

6. How does the second major section of Psalm 22 (verses 23–31) complement the first section of Psalm 22 (i.e. develop the unified message of the entire psalm from both parts)?

Chapter 11 Personal Lament – David's confession – Ps. 5

1. What historical occasion does the title of Psalm 51 attribute to the writing of this psalm? Why is this attribution sometimes debated by Old Testament scholars?

2. Assuming that the title does describe accurately the historical occasion for writing, what Levitical sacrifice(s) could David have offered to restore his broken relationship with Yahweh? According to especially 51:1–2, what is the only basis for David asking Yahweh for forgiveness?

3. In Psalm 51 the penitent psalmist seeks from God both forgiveness and renewal. Identify each of these elements in his petitions of 51:7–12. Also suggest implications for your spiritual life.

4. What does Psalm 51 teach about the nature of sin and concerning the attitude which makes confession acceptable?

5. How do the ideas of 51:15–19 complete the message of Psalm 51 in its entirety? (Hint: consider, in part, the effect of the sins of a leader upon the community.)

Chapter 12 Community Lament Psalms – Pss. 74 & 137

1. What is the proposed historical background for the writing of Psalm 74? What conditions of the community are described in the lament of 74:4–11? Identify parallels between the conditions lamented in Psalm 74 and Lamentations 2.

2. Is there evidence of penitence in the petitions of Psalm 74? What is the basis for the community's petitions? (Hint: consider, in part, the address of God in 74:12.)

3. Contrast the occasion for writing of Psalm 74 with the community lament Psalm 44 (Hint: read closely 44:17–26). Relate the teachings concerning prayer of these community lament psalms.

4. In Psalm 137:4–6 does the psalmist express merely sorrow over the loss of home or does he manifest a spiritual virtue? Provide a New Testament parallel to the psalmist's expression.

5. Is the psalmist's anger against Israel's enemies in Psalm 137 sinful and spiritually immature or a mark of spirituality? Is the prayer of the psalmist a New Testament prayer? Explain briefly.

Chapter 13 Wisdom Psalms – Pss. 1 & 78

1. What are the respective metaphors in Psalm 1 which describe the righteous person and the wicked person? What is the main characteristic of each metaphor associated with the respective person?

2. By virtue of the great disparity between lengths, Psalms 1 and 119 may seem unrelated, but read both and explain their thematic connection.

3. What is the basic message of Psalm 1 in light of the conclusion in 1:6? How does Psalm 73 complement this message of Psalm 1?

4. What events in Israel's history does Psalm 78 survey? Noting the themes of God's favor and Israel's repeated failures, discuss how 78:65–72 appropriately concludes the historical survey.

5. Does the conclusion of Psalm 78 have an eschatological look? Explain your answer.

6. What is similar between ancient Israel's wisdom writings and those of other cultures of the ancient Near East? What distinguishes Israel's inspired wisdom writings as unique?

Chapter 14 Wisdom and apparent injustice – Pss. 37, 49 & 73

1. According to Psalm 37 is the prosperity of the wicked real and permanent or only apparent and temporary? Explain your answer from the specific teachings of Psalm 37.
2. What is the repeated proverbial statement of Psalm 49 that summarizes the message of the psalm? Explain briefly the proverb in the context of the psalm.
3. Describe the climax of Psalm 73 when the psalmist had a sudden, yet also wholesome, change of mind about the matters which disturbed him. How did this godly change occur?
4. What do the wisdom Psalms 37, 49, and 73 teach about prosperity? Evaluate the views of prosperity preachers in West Africa against the teachings of these psalms.
5. Choose one verse from each of the three psalms that you would give to a university student who is planning his life goals. (Explain each verse briefly in light of their respective contexts in the psalm and in the context of the gospel.)

Chapter 15 Royal and Messianic Psalms (1) – Ps. 2

1. Describe the symmetrical structure of Psalm 2 by identifying the speaker and main idea in each of the four dramatic scenes.
2. Identify the New Testament passages which quote Psalm 2 and state briefly the application of this psalm in each NT passage.
3. Who is in view in a royal interpretation of Psalm 2? What is the messianic interpretation of Psalm 2?
4. Many contemporary Old Testament scholars argue that Psalms 1 and 2 form the introduction of the entire Book of Psalms and thus direct our reading of the Psalms. What are some key words and themes which link the two psalms and integrate their message? (Hint: examine the themes of torah [law] and kingship in Deuteronomy 17.)

5. James Luther Mays in his commentary on the Psalms in the Interpretation series (p. 50–51) suggests that the passage often cited as the Great Commission Matthew 28:18–20 represents the gospel-centred interpretation of Psalm 2:8. Can you offer an explanation?

Chapter 16 Royal and Messianic Psalms (2) – Ps. 45

1. Summarize the structure of Psalm 45 and note who is addressed in each section.
2. What is the "double meaning" of Psalm 45 according to the writer of this chapter? What is the "double meaning" of the marriage portrayed in Psalm 45?
3. What qualities of the king are praised in this psalm? In what way do such qualities apply to the Messiah?
4. What is the interpretation of verses 6 and 7 in the context of the psalm? What is their interpretation in the context of Hebrews 1:8–9?
5. What parallels (e.g. similar themes about Davidic kingship) do you discover between Psalm 45 and 2 Samuel 7:11–16? How do these parallels support a messianic interpretation of the psalm?

Chapter 17 Liturgical Psalms – Ps. 12

1. Explain what is meant by chiastic structure and how it is exhibited in Psalm 12. In view of the structure what is central to the psalm's message?
2. What are the circumstances which distress the psalmist (of Psalm 12)? Are such circumstances present in contemporary society? Explain. Can you suggest how such circumstances arise in society?
3. What fundamental contrast does the psalm present? (Hint: consider the contrast between the human and the divine.)
4. Psalm 12 may also be categorized as a community lament psalm. Review the characteristics of community lament psalms in chapter 12 and identify the elements of a community lament psalm in Psalm 12.
5. What does the psalmist pray? Are his prayers answered by the end of the psalm? Explain (hint: consider whether the psalmist's circumstances

changed while he prays.). What application regarding faith (and prayer) results from your observations?

Chapter 18 An instructional Liturgy – Ps. 15

1. What is the psalmist asking by the questions which open Psalm 15? How does the psalm conclude? Explain the significance of the conclusion.
2. Do the qualities of Psalm 15, which provide the answer to the opening question, focus upon inner character or outward behaviour? Explain. While each quality is crucial, which one would you suggest as the most relevant for your contemporary context? What is the psalmist asking by the questions which open Psalm 15? How does the psalm conclude? Explain the significance of the conclusion.
3. According to the psalm what is the relationship between ethics and worship?
4. Theological thought question: how does Christ fulfil the requirements of the psalm for the believer today? (Consider whether any person can fulfil all the requirements without fail at all times.)
5. Compare the qualities which disqualify a person from OT temple worship (i.e. the opposite of the ethical qualities given in Psalm 15) with the qualities of the wicked in 12:2–4. What conclusions and applications do you draw out from the comparison?
6. Commentators in the ancient church often read and interpreted Psalms 14 and 15 together. How does Psalm 15 answer Psalm 14?

Chapter 19 The theology of the Psalmists

1. How does Psalm 97 link the themes of creation and Kingship of the LORD?
2. How does Psalm 139 develop the theme of God's personalness (i.e. God has personality and so functions as a person in thinking, feeling, willing)?
3. The theme of God's sovereignty over human history could incorporate discussion about the psalmist's enemies, often referred to as the wicked.

While examining particularly the lament psalms, develop a theology of enemies, the wicked, including their character and machinations.

4.   What attributes of God are explicitly praised in Psalm 99? What does this psalm teach about God's holiness and its relationship with some of his other attributes?

5.   What psalm repeats, in every verse, praise of the LORD's steadfast (faithful) love (or mercy as translated by NKJ)? What does the psalm teach about the LORD's covenant love?

6.   A key word which is an important part of the theology of the Psalms is "refuge." The word appears as a noun or a verb in 27 psalms (e.g. 2:12; and well known verses 46:2; 91:4; also 5:12; 16:1; 18:30; 73:28; 118:8–9; 142:6). From these psalms and others which you find, summarize what the psalms teach about the LORD as a refuge.

Chapter 20 The Anthropology of the Psalmists

1.   If Psalm 8 implicitly tells of man created in the image of God, what aspects of the image of God in man are revealed in the psalm?

2.   What image is used in Psalm 95 (and implicitly in Psalm 23) to describe the people of God as a community? Suggest several implications of this image concerning the nature of man under God.

3.   What does Psalm 38 teach, from the psalmist's experience, about the relationship between sin and sickness? (Caution: do not draw a conclusion like those of Job's three false comforters.)

4.   Survey the penitential psalms (i.e. Psalms 6, 32, 102, 130, 143, in addition to 38 and 51 [see Chapter 11]) and summarize the teaching concerning man's sinfulness (hint: note, for one, the different words for sin) and the godly response to personal sin.

5.   Psalms gives attention to the "poor" (also described as afflicted, needy). Read Psalms 9–10 and 72, and identify their character and conflicts, also the LORD's care for them (hint: the LORD's care is expressed through the king).

Chapter 21 Covenant in the Psalms

1. Correlate the universal dimension of the Abrahamic promise (or covenant) in Genesis 12:1–3 (i.e. God's concern for all nations) with the message of Psalm 67.
2. What two covenant attributes of Yahweh are revealed in Psalm 117? State concisely the message of Psalm 117 with these two attributes in view.
3. Explain the movement of Psalm 89 from hymn in 89:1–37 to lament in 89:38–52 by considering Psalm 89 both a commentary on the Davidic covenant (2 Samuel 7:11–16) in light of the situation contemporary to the psalmist, the Babylonian exile.
4. Provide an interpretation of Psalm 89 which finds the solution to the lament of the psalm in the person of Christ.
5. Where does "covenant" occur in Psalm 132? Compare (and contrast) the message of Psalms 132 and 89, with the background of the Davidic covenant in mind.
6. What does Psalm 78 teach about God's faithfulness to his covenants throughout the history of Israel? In your answer identify which covenants are referred to (directly or indirectly) in the psalm.

Chapter 22 The Psalmists knowledge of God

1. How many times does the key word "know" appear in Psalm 139? Explain how the psalmist's final prayer in 139:23–24 flows from Yahweh's knowledge of him?
2. Develop an outline of the main points of a message addressing the topic "To know God (or his name)," using the psalm texts 9:10; 91:14; and 79:6; 83:18–19 (and any other relevant psalm texts which you find).
3. Develop an outline of a missions message from Psalm 87. Let 87:4 stand as a key verse, which speaks of the nations who "know" God. (Hint: consider the traits of each nation cited in the psalm and attempt to relate to the contemporary situation. Also relate the message of Psalm 87 to the gospel.)

4.   Read closely the confessions of trust in Psalms 16:2; 31:14; 142:5; 140:6
      (and in the context of each psalm), where the psalmist tells what he
      speaks to the LORD. Summarize what these confessions indicate about
      the psalmist's knowledge of God and his consequent relationship with
      him.

Chapter 23 Prospects of life after death

1.   List the various words and images related to "death" in Psalm 88, an
      individual lament psalm. Summarize the psalm's teaching on death.
2.   How does the NT (the Book of Acts) interpret the psalmist's hope of
      16:10? Is the NT's interpretation of Psalm 16 consistent with the OT
      meaning of the psalm? Explain the hermeneutics of your answer.
3.   B. K. Waltke, *An Old Testament Theology*, p. 229, 910, cites Psalm 49:15 (as
      one among several passages) to contend that "death is not God and death
      does not have the last word" in the OT, thus arguing that the OT does
      teach about the afterlife with the LORD. Do you agree? Why or why not?
4.   If the promise of "glory" for the believer (Psalm 73:24) contrasts with
      the destiny of the wicked (73:17), would this connection strengthen the
      argument that 73:23–26 does speak of the afterlife (i.e. life after death)?
      Explain.

Chapter 24 The Psalmists as prophets

1.   What evidence can be found in 2 Samuel 23:1–7 that the OT regarded
      David as a prophet? (Hint: compare the words/phrase of 2 Samuel 23 with
      Numbers 24:2–4.) How might this observation support the attribution of
      Psalms as prophecy? (Second hint: note that 2 Samuel 22, linked to David's
      last words of 2 Samuel 23 is the same as Psalm 18.)
2.   Cite the passages in the NT where David is regarded as a prophet.
3.   How does 1 Chronicles 25:1–6 contribute to the idea that Psalms is a
      prophetic book?
4.   If Psalm 110 is classified as a royal prophecy (i.e. as some OT scholars do),
      then the psalm has definite Messianic meaning. Explain.

5. Determine what psalms are cited in the first two chapters of Hebrews and summarize how these psalms support the message of Hebrews 1–2. What are the hermeneutical implications of how Psalms is used in Hebrews 1–2?

6. Kidner, in his TOTC Psalms commentary (I:23–24) writes that the Davidic king in the Psalter foreshadows the Messiah. What are the interpretative implications of his position? Illustrate his point from Psalm 22.

Chapter 25 Imprecation in the Psalms

1. In Psalm 69:22–28 the psalmist may appear to be vindictive because of his imprecation against his enemies. How does the testimony of the psalmist in 69:6–12 (and his prayer, 69:13–18) counter the charge of vindictiveness? (Hint: consider also the character of the psalmist's enemies, as voiced in Psalm 139:19–22.)

2. If a psalm is a holy prayer, as evidenced by praise to the LORD in Psalm 69:30–36, for example, would it be theologically sound to regard some parts of the psalm, such as the prayer against enemies, as derived from fallen human nature?

3. How does the psalmist's testimony in 109:2–5, which precedes the strong imprecation of 109:6–21, argue against attributing a spirit of vindictiveness to the psalmist?

4. If the imprecation of Psalm 137:9 is an expression of hyperbole (i.e. intended exaggeration more appropriate to warfare in the ancient Near East), how might the intention of the psalmist's prayer against the enemy nation be restated?

5. How does progressive revelation and the gospel of Christ alter the application of imprecatory prayers in our contemporary situation?

Chapter 26 The Psalms in support of Christian living

1. This chapter argues that Psalm 95 is used by Hebrews 3–4 to exhort NT believers in Christian living. Read Psalm 95 and determine what Exodus events the psalm uses in verses 7–11 to exhort the OT people of God to

obedient living. Are the exhortations of Psalm 95 and Hebrews 3–4 the same? Hint: consider the reference to "today" and to "rest" in both passages.

2.   Read Psalm 34 and summarize the message of the psalm, keeping in mind the historical situation attributed to Psalm 34 (the title) and its classification as an individual psalm of thanksgiving. Then describe how Psalm 34:12–16 in view of its placement in the entire psalm is appropriate to the message of 1 Peter 3:8–17 (i.e. holy living amidst suffering from hostility towards the gospel).

3.   Read royal Psalms 72 and 101 and summarize the king's responsibility for justice and righteousness according to these psalms. What application to the contemporary African (or global) context do you make?

4.   Outline the topics you would include in developing a theology of worship from the book of Psalms. Hints: Do the psalmists worship? What inspires their worship? How do they conduct themselves in worship?

Chapter 27 The Psalms in Christian hymnody

1.   Compose your own psalms, one a hymn or a thanksgiving and the other a lament, in accordance with the general patterns of the Psalms. However, write your psalm from the perspective of the cross of Christ. Extra: find a musician to compose instrumental accompaniment for your composition.

SUGGESTIONS FOR FURTHER READING

The principal books suggested here for further reading are largely limited to books often found in ACTS bookshops or other better stocked Christian bookshops. These are the books with full bibliographic information, which appear immediately under the respective subject titles.

Hebrew Poetry and Parallelism

Longman, Tremper III. *How to Read the Psalms*. IL: Downers Grove: InterVarsity, 1988.
and

Futato, Mark D. *Interpreting the Psalms: An Exegetical Handbook*. Handbooks for Old Testament Exegesis. Grand Rapids: Kregel Academic & Professional, 2007.
or

Futato, Mark D. *Transformed by Praise: The Purpose and Message of the Psalms*. Handbooks for Old Testament Exegesis. Phillipsburg: NJ: P&R Publishing, 2002.

Both Longman and Futato will supplement the approach to parallelism by Shields. Shields follows an approach closer to the traditional understanding of parallelism while Longman and Futato present the current approach to parallelism. Futato's *Transformed by Praise* is a shortened treatment of many of the topics in his *Interpreting the Psalms*, which does include some Biblical Hebrew fonts (though translation of Hebrew is provided).

Theology (with emphasis on Christ-centred Reading)

Grogan, Geoffrey W. *Prayer, Praise, and Prophecy: A Theology of the Book of Psalms*. Mentor. Fearn, United Kingdom: Christian Focus, 2001.

Belcher, Richard P. *The Messiah and the Psalms: Preaching Christ from All the Psalms.* Mentor. Fearn, Scotland: Christian Focus, 2006.

Lefebvre, Michael. *Singing the Songs of Jesus: Revisiting the Psalms.* Mentor. Fearn, Scotland: Christian Focus, 2010.
Grogan and Belcher put forward guidelines for a Christ-centred reading of the Psalter. Grogan considers the arrangement and agenda of the Psalms as a book with a messianic focus. Belcher provides messianic interpretation for individual psalms. Lefebvre's work advocates the use of the Psalter as a hymnal for the church today.

also

Mays, James L. *The Lord Reigns: A Theological Handbook to the Psalms.* Louisville: KY: Westminster John Knox, 1994.

McCann, J. Clinton, Jr. *A Theological Introduction to the Book of Psalms: Psalms as Torah.* Nashville: TN: Abingdon, 1993.

Kraus, Hans-Joachim. *Theology of the Psalms.* Translated by Keith Crim. Minneapolis: MN: Augsburg, 1986.

Chisholm, Robert. *A Biblical Theology of the Old Testament.* "A Theology of the Psalms." Pages 257–304 in. Chicago: Moody, 1991.

Waltke, Bruce K. "Psalms: Theology of." Pages 1100–15 in NIDOTTE (New International Dictionary of Old Testament Theology & Exegesis). Edited by Willem A. VanGemeren. Grand Rapids: Zondervan, 1997.
The sources above (Mays, McCann, Kraus, Chisholm's article, Waltke's article) should be found in theological libraries but not necessarily in ACTS bookshops. Mays and McCann are well respected Psalms scholars, whose works are particularly helpful in understanding the Psalms as a book with a coherent message. Kraus and Chisholm provide thorough treatments of key theological themes (and words) in the Psalms. Waltke supplies solid introductory material.

Imprecations

Day, John N. *Crying for Justice: What the Psalms Teach Us About Mercy and Vengeance in an Age of Terrorism.* Grand Rapids: Kregel, 2005.
Day comments upon Psalms 58, 109, and 137 in particular, also making compelling biblical theological connections in addressing the issue of imprecation for the OT believer and for the church today. Willem VanGemeren in his Psalms commentary in the Expositor's Bible Commentary series (listed below) also offers several useful articles relating to imprecations under "Appendix" sections.

Introduction

Bullock, C. Hassell. *Encountering the Book of Psalms: A Literary and Theological Introduction.* Grand Rapids: Baker Academic, 2001.
Bullock's work is a comprehensive introduction with much material to assimilate. His work includes a major section on the types of psalms and can be consulted for every topic of introduction to the Psalter. Longman, *How to Read the Psalms* (noted above) also concisely covers the types (i.e. genres) of individual psalms.

and

Miller, Patrick D. *Interpreting the Psalms.* Philadelphia: Fortress, 1986.

DeClassié-Walford, Nancy L. *Introduction to the Psalms: A Song from Ancient Israel.* St. Louis: MO: Chalice, 2004.

Anderson, Bernard and Steven Bishop. *Out of the Depths: The Psalms Speak for Us Today.* Louisville: KY: Westminster John Knox, 2000.

Seybold, Klaus D. *Introducing the Psalms.* Translated by Graeme Dunphy. Edinburgh: T&T Clark, 1990.
Search for these concise books of introduction in theological libraries (rather than bookshops). Miller writes insightful chapters on Hebrew poetry and the

major psalm types and provides expositions on several psalms. DeClassié-Walford is strong on psalm types and understanding the arrangement of the Psalms as a whole book. Some Hebrew appears but is translated. Anderson and Bishop maintain the same strengths in their introduction (i.e. psalm types and reading the Psalms as a whole book). Seybold's useful introduction is well acquainted with critical scholarship.

Commentaries

Mays, James Luther. *Psalms.* Interpretation: A Bible Commentary for Teaching and Preaching. Louisville: KY: John Knox, 1994.

Kidner, Derek. *Psalms 1–72 and Psalms 73–150.* Tyndale Old Testament Commentary. Downers Grove: IL: InterVarsity, 1973, 1975.

Grogan, Geoffrey W. *Psalms.* Two Horizons OT Commentary. Grand Rapids: Eerdmans, 2008.

VanGemeren, Willem A. *Expositor's Bible Commentary.* "Psalms." Pages 1–880 in vol. 5 . Edited by Frank E. Gæbelein. Grand Rapids: Zondervan Academic and Professional Books, 1991.

For the pastor who is preaching the Psalms, Mays will never disappoint. His homiletical insights derive from careful exposition and sound theology. Kidner's commentary, as characteristic of the Tyndale series, is brief, yet his comments speak much with few words. Grogan's lengthy commentary is theologically rich, including short expositions of each psalm and extensive sections of robust and reliable biblical theology. VanGemeren's expositions comment completely on each verse of every psalm. In addition, as mentioned above, he provides several helpful articles on important theological topics relevant to the Psalms and to the Old Testament.

Some valuable commentaries will go unmentioned in this section. This is because their enormous length, their heavy use of biblical Hebrew, and/or a publishing house not well known in Africa makes them less accessible to the average degree level student. Others are cited only in passing, since they may also be regarded as more scholarly works. J. Clinton McCann compiles a valuable commentary in volume 4 of *The Interpreter's Bible* (Abingdon). The

3 volume commentary of Allen P. Ross has been recently published (except for the third volume by Kregel Exegetical Library), and it will be regarded as one of the most thorough expositions on the Psalms. The three volumes of the Word Biblical Commentary series (Thomas Nelson) are exceptionally helpful, particularly the revised edition of volume 3 (Psalms 101–150) by Leslie C. Allen. The NIV Application Commentary series holds great promise, though only volume 1 by Gerald H. Wilson has been published (by Zondervan). Though it is dated, exegetical gems can be mined still from Franz Delitzsch's comments on the Psalms in volume 5 of the Keil and Delitzsch OT Commentaries. The two volumes co-authored by Bruce K. Waltke and James M. Houston (Eerdmans) afford immaculate exegesis on selected psalms under the categories of psalms as Christian worship and psalms as Christian lament. The authors also survey the history of the interpretation of the various psalms. Konrad Schaefer's commentary in the Berit Olam series (Liturgical Press, Lutheran) expounds with eloquence the literary features of individual psalms (with generous use of transliterated biblical Hebrew).

Finally, for the disciplined student and well informed pastor a rich collection of articles, representing current Psalms scholarship and addressing topics of poetry, psalm types, theology, practical ministry use of the Psalms, is found in:

Firth, David and Phillip S. Johnston, editors. *Interpreting the Psalms: Issues and Approaches*. IL: Downers Grove: IVP Academic, 2005.

www.ingramcontent.com/pod-product-compliance
Lightning Source LLC
Chambersburg PA
CBHW051941090426
42741CB00008B/1226